Mersey Ferries

Volume 1

Woodside to Eastham

Mersey Ferries

Volume 1

Woodside to Eastham

by

T. B. MAUND, FCIT

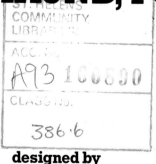

designed by
Alan Townsin

Transport Publishing Co Ltd : Glossop : Derbyshire : England

© T. B. Maund
November 1991

ISBN 086317 166 4

Other historical works by the same author:-
With J. B. Horne

Liverpool Transport, Vol 1, 1830-1900
Light Railway Transport League, 1976
Liverpool Transport, Vol 2, 1900-30
Light Rail Transit Association and Transport Publishing Co. 1982.
Liverpool Transport, Vol 3, 1931-39
Light Rail Transit Association and Transport Publishing Co 1987
Liverpool Transport, Vol 4, 1939-57
Transport Publishing Co Ltd 1989
Liverpool Transport, Vol 5, 1957-86
Transport Publishing Co Ltd 1991

With M. Jenkins

The Tramways of Birkenhead and Wallasey Light Rail Transit Association 1987

Typeset and produced for the Publishers by
Mopok Graphics, 128 Pikes Lane, Glossop, Derbyshire
Printed and bound in Great Britain

CONTENTS

INTRODUCTION

While brief reference is made to the medieval origins of the Mersey ferries, the object of this work is to chronicle the development of the ferry services and the vessels employed from the time of the adoption of steam in the years immediately following the end of the Napoleonic wars to the present day. In the preceding 50 years, some ferries had developed in conjunction with stage coach services in an age when the roads on the Cheshire side of the river were in some measure superior to those radiating from Liverpool itself.

The coming of steam was the first of a series of major events which revolutionised cross-river travel and enabled Merseyside to develop into one socio-economic unit. The other factors were municipal ownership of the principal ferries which brought about reliability and cheap fares thus creating labour mobility; huge capital investment in safe landing facilities usable at all states of the tide and, finally, in the twentieth century, the construction of road tunnels after many years of frustration in commercial circles because of the cost and difficulty of getting vehicular traffic from one side of the river to the other.

The privately owned ferries, often operating with second-hand vessels on shoe-string budgets in highly competitive conditions, are less well-documented than the municipal enterprises but nevertheless, enough evidence has survived to enable reasonably coherent stories to be put together. However there are some enigmatic details which have not come to light such as the reasons for the Lord of the Manor, hereditary owner of the Woodside ferry rights, allowing a rival ferry to be established at Birkenhead in 1820 and full details of the rights of ferry at Eastham. The author will be grateful for any information on these or any other topic.

Railway companies, too, became involved in ferry matters from an early age but after years of controversy and a decade when railway-owned steamers crossed the Mersey, they realised the wisdom of using the superior facilities of Woodside and built a new railway station on the ferry approach.

The purpose-built vehicular ferries, now but a dim memory of the past, made an enormous contribution to the commercial well-being of the port and so stimulated cross-river traffic that they became a victim of their own success, being overwhelmed when motor vehicles took over from horses.

This book traces the history of the seven ferries which existed between Woodside and Eastham in some detail. The three Wallasey ferries to the north—Seacombe, Egremont and New Brighton—will be the subject of Volume 2.

The heyday of the ferries has long passed, but it is gratifying that some investment has been made in new landing stages to enable sailings, now considered to be leisure services, to continue.

The author is aware that as his previous works on Merseyside transport history have been concerned with land transport, he must be considered to be essentially a landlubber. He excuses this aquatic deviation because he believes that the Mersey ferries were essentially part of the urban transport network, staffed by men who, despite their navigational skills, demonstrated daily to thousands of Merseysiders, were considered by the nautical community to be unqualified. However, he has done his best to use the correct nautical terms whenever appropriate and has submitted his work for perusal by seafaring men. Nevertheless, he apologises in advance for any terminological solecisms which may have crept into this work. There is undoubtedly scope for a definitive work on the technical development and evolution of the Mersey ferry fleets by someone better qualified than the present author.

1 HIGHWAY ACROSS THE WATER

At the time of the Norman Conquest, Chester was the centre of such political and economic activity that existed in North Cheshire. To the north of the city, the Forest of Wirral occupied a desolate, sparsely populated tongue of land, flanked on the east by the River Mersey and on the west by the River Dee. The latter was important as a barrier against the warlike Welsh and over the centuries, Chester and certain of the coastal fishing villages along the Wirral bank attained some importance as ports engaged in coastal and Irish trade.

In 1207 the Liver Pool on the Mersey came to the notice of King John who fortified what had hitherto been an obscure hamlet unworthy of any mention in the Domesday survey. Doubtless John had political reasons for undermining the supremacy of Chester and, whilst there was little progress for 500 years, the decline of Chester and the rise of Liverpool in maritime matters can be measured from that point. The characteristics of the Dee and the Mersey were quite different. The former, tidal to the weir at Chester, was a wide sluggish river flanked in many parts by treacherous sandbanks; the Mersey, after flowing swiftly through the Runcorn Gap, followed a wide shallow bend but narrowed at its mouth. This estuarial constriction created swift running tides of six knots and an unusually high tidal range exceeding 30 feet.

Its Cheshire bank was deeply indented by tidal creeks, fed by the minor streams which drained the sandstone uplands of the peninsula. The northernmost inlet, the Wallasey Pool, penetrating two miles inland, provided sheltered anchorage in the jagged fringes of water reaching out northwards and groups of cottages grew into the villages of Poulton and Seacombe. The Tranmere (or Birket) Pool, a little further south, was less extensive. It was fed by a stream which followed the course of present day Borough Road, widening out into a shallow estuary where Birkenhead Central station now stands. At low water it was easily forded but high tides brought deep, treacherous surges of water resulting in many drownings over the centuries.

Between the two was a picturesque, wooded tongue of land to which has been attributed the name 'Birchen Head'. This is a convenient way to account for the name Birkenhead but others say that it is derived from Byrkehaved, the last part of which comes from the Norse word for harbour. The tip of this peninsula acquired the name Woodside and the southern indentation of Wallasey Pool became known as Woodside Bay. The accompanying map shows the extent to which the Cheshire bank of the Mersey differed from its present day regular configuration in the days before land reclamation added many acres to the Wirral shore.

The passage from Woodside to the Liver Pool was less than a mile and, although the tide flowed strongly, it was the most suitable place for a river crossing. The foreshore was rocky and accessible at most states of the tide whereas at Tranmere the water receded 500 feet or so at low water. A Benedictine Priory was endowed by a local nobleman, Hamo de Masey, in 1150. There were 16 monks who, by virtue of the tenets of the Order, were obliged to provide shelter to travellers unable to cross the river because of bad weather.

The Right of Passage

The principle of the right of passage was derived from the right of a landlord to control the movement of persons across his land. The Norman invaders confiscated lands and, with them, entrenched 'rights' and in the course of time a great many such rights became vested in the Crown. From this state of affairs flows the concept that the right to pursue any activity which is potentially monopolistic or otherwise advantageous must be authorised in some way by the state. Ancient ferry rights were claimed by men of Liverpool. In 1266 Robert de Ferrers lost these and other rights over Liverpool to the Crown who awarded them to Edmund, Earl of Lancaster. His son, Thomas, rebelled against Edward II and the right of ferry reverted to the Crown in 1323. Meanwhile in 1318, Edward II granted the Prior of Birkenhead the right to build lodging houses and to 'buy and sell provisions for the support of the men thereabout to cross the said arm of the sea .... on account of great contrariety of weather and frequent storms.' In 1330 Edward III confirmed the earlier Charter granting the legal rights of ferry between Birkenhead and Liverpool to the Prior and his successors for ever. The ferry thus became part of the King's Highway and in modern times this is symbolised by crowns mounted on the gangway posts.

The title to some subsidiary rights of passage across and between Wallasey and Tranmere Pools was disputed by a local landowner, William Lascelles but the courts upheld the Prior's right to these as well as to the main passage. The monks developed a ferry across the Wallasey Pool at 'The Hooks' close to the position of the present Duke Street Bridge, in order to reach their lands in Wallasey. This resulted in a further dispute with the Lascelles family and the 'men of Seacombe' who claimed a share in the right of passage across the Pool at Tokesford, believed to have been on or near the site of Poulton Bridge. It is of interest to note that this right was claimed as including the right of passage from the north bank of Wallasey Pool to Liverpool and some historians believe that the right of passage of

The deeply indented coast line of the Wirral shore between Seacombe and Tranmere is clearly visible in this map published in 1768.

Seacombe may derive from Tokesford. The Lascelles family failed to convince the court of the legitimacy of their claim and the Tokesford passage was vested in the Earls of Chester from whom it passed in course of time to the Stanleys of Hooton and then to the Vyners of Bidston. The grant of ferry rights to men on both sides of the river was a potential source of conflict which continued until the last vestiges of feudal rights were extinguished in the nineteenth century. In the fourteenth century the monks had the best of both worlds as they established a storehouse in Liverpool and thus, as burgesses of that town, enjoyed ferry rights there in addition to those at Woodside derived from the 1330 Charter.

In early times the numbers crossing the Mersey were very small. In 1282 the annual takings were £2.0.0d and in 1324 the 'King's Boat in Mersea' took £2.16.4d. In 1357 the tolls were as follows:-

For a foot passenger on a market day	¼d
For a foot passenger on other days	½d
For a footman with a pack	1d
For a man with an unladen horse	1d
For a man and a laden horse	2d

At the time of Dissolution in 1536, the ferry tolls were said to be worth £5.0.0d per year, indicating that the traffic had about doubled from a very low base in the course of two centuries.

The conflicting rights of Birkenhead and Liverpool were to surface from time to time for the next 300 years. Doubtless the Liverpool rights were bestowed on various individuals over the centuries. It is known that in 1528 they were 'granted, delivered and let to farm' by Henry VIII, on the advice of the Duchy of Lancaster, to Henry Akers for 21 years. The grant included 'the farm of the town and lordship of Liverpool with its appurtenances and the farm of a boat and of the passage over the water of the Mersey ....'. There were also rights of markets, fairs and the use of certain mills.

Upon the Dissolution of the monasteries, the Woodside ferry rights reverted to the Crown and, on 17th May 1544 the manorial privileges and Priory property, including ferry rights, were purchased by Ralph Worsley of Worsley, Lancashire for £586.11.6d. The ferry house, 'ferry bote' and the profit are all specifically mentioned in the deed of conveyance.

The ferry was let out to individual boatmen whose commercial scruples did not measure up to those of the monks. Many travellers complained of over-charging or being charged the return fare only to find that the boatman could not be found when the time came to make the return trip. An edict of the Town Council of Liverpool in 1581 to the effect that Cheshire boats were not to load goods originating on the Lancashire coast was largely ignored and there was continual friction between the Cheshire and Lancashire ferry men. At a public enquiry held in 1626, Lancashire boatmen demanded a common tariff to prevent undercutting and proposed that the 'home' boat should always be the first to load. In somewhat contradictory evidence, there is a suggestion that the franchise holders of Eastham, Tranmere, 'Birkett' and Wallasey paid levies to the owners of the King's Ferry

(Woodside) right of passage on goods and passengers carried. This evidence of competition certainly indicates a great increase in the cross-river traffic, a reflection of the expansion of commercial activity and the slow growth in the population. But even by the early eighteenth century, the total of all the traffic carried in a month was but a fraction of one boat-load two centuries later, as few cared to undertake the hazardous river crossing 'except under pressure of business or necessity'. The majority of locally born people never crossed the river in a whole lifetime.

The Liverpool ferry rights had been acquired by the Molyneux family in the late sixteenth century and Liverpool Town Council purchased the right of passage in 1777. As the Cheshire boats were beyond control, the Corporation made its quays and wharves open to all and, in doing so, virtually surrendered their ferry rights. During the enquiry preceding the formation of the Mersey Docks and Harbour Board, the Council was accused of squandering their traditional rights. Liverpool Corporation operated a ferry for a short time in the 1840s and theoretically retains its rights but Birkenhead and Wallasey secured statutory authority to levy tolls in both directions though money was never collected on the Liverpool side of the river until recent times.

The origins of the Mersey ferries further upstream are less well documented. In calm weather it was advantageous to travel as far as possible by water to avoid the dreadful road conditions which generally prevailed and this encouraged the establishment of ferries closer to Chester, which remained the commercial centre of the region despite the gradual decay of its port. The monks of the Abbey of St. Werburgh in Chester provided a ferry between Eastham and Liverpool. There are references to this passage as early as 1509. In the 19th century (and perhaps earlier) it was known as Job's Ferry and, whilst occasional passengers were doubtless carried, the conveyance of agricultural produce to Liverpool was the main activity.

John Poole of Sutton was granted ferry rights at Tranmere in 1586 on the grounds that the ferry at Seacombe was decayed, though the logic of this is hard to follow. Poole offered to pay the 9s 8d rent previously paid for the Seacombe passage and an additional one shilling for the passage of Tranmere 'for which hithertofore there hath been no rent paid to my knowledge'. This suggests the pre-existence of the Tranmere ferry. Rock House ferry is believed to have existed by 1660 and is specifically mentioned in Nicholas Blundell's diary in 1709.

Woodside ferry remained in the same family for about 170 years. In 1579 it is recorded that freemen and their families were exempted from paying ferriage at Birkenhead; there were similar provisions at Liverpool. At the end of the seventeenth century the owner was Sir Thomas Powell, a descendant of Worsley and about 1712 the Powell estates and ferry rights were acquired by Alderman John Clieveland. Born at Hinckley on 3rd August 1661, he became Mayor of Liverpool in 1703 and M.P. for the town in 1710. He died on 1st August 1716, his remains being laid to rest in St. Nicholas' churchyard. In the course of time he gave his name (by now simplified) to Cleveland Square, Liverpool and Cleveland Street,

Woodside in 1818, before the introduction of steam boats led to urbanisation and the rapid growth of traffic. The original hotel is almost the only building visible.

Birkenhead.

Woodside ferry house was built in 1715-16 and a quay in 1717. In 1716-17 there were four ferrymen employed and three boats were in use; six men besides the Master worked on Saturdays. Their wages were 5/- per week and the passenger toll throughout most of the eighteenth century was 1d. The ancient rivalry between Liverpool and Birkenhead-based ferries surfaced once more and it is on record that Clieveland caused Thomas Barton's Liverpool ferry to be driven away from Woodside quay.

The Chester Coaches

As the Dee silted up and ships increased in size, maritime activity moved downstream from Chester; the port was in decline by the early sixteenth century and mail packets plied regularly between Neston and Ireland by about 1540. For many years, Neston was the largest township in Wirral and was not overtaken in population until well into the nineteenth century. Early in the eighteenth century, Neston's harbour, the New Quay, was abandoned because of silting up and the traffic moved a little further down river to Parkgate, which for almost a century became a thriving port with twelve coaching inns. Ferries were established across the Dee to Flint and Bagillt so as to avoid the long road journey through Chester.

It is reasonably certain that stage waggons were travelling regularly between London and Chester by the early seventeenth century and the journey would have occupied ten or eleven days according to the time of year. These were heavy cumbersome covered vehicles capable of carrying twenty passengers as well as merchandise. They had broad wheels, suitable for deeply rutted roads, and were drawn at walking pace by up to eight horses in tandem. There is no definite record of their use in the Wirral Peninsula.

Queen Elizabeth I was presented with a coach of Dutch design which started a vogue among the aristocracy and by the year 1600, coaches which were little more than ornate, roofed carts, were in common use. Coaches for public hire within London appeared about 1605 and the

stage coach for longer journeys followed in 1640. The old coaches had leather curtains instead of glass windows, which were not fitted to stage coaches until 1680. One of the first stage coach routes of which precise records exist, ran between London and Chester in 1657. An advertisement in the *Mercurius Politicus* for 4th August 1657 states :-

'For the convenient accommodation of passengers from and betwixt the Cities of London and Westchester, there is provided several stage coaches which go from the George Inn without Aldersgate upon every Monday, Wednesday and Friday, to Coventry in two days for 25/-, to Stone in three days for 30/- and to Chester in four days for 35/- and thence to return upon the same days, which is performed with much safety to the passengers, having fresh horses once a day.'

It was unusual to have changes of horses at this time as there were so few coaches running that the necessary organisation did not exist, and the normal practice was for the same team of horses to accompany the coach throughout its journey. This coach, like all the other pioneers, was strictly a fair-weather service and operated from Spring to Michaelmas only. In 1661 a contemporary report stated that there were only six stage coaches in operation in the country and, presumably, the Chester coach was one of these. By 1670 it was again running twice a week but now took six days for its journey, carrying its six passengers at about four miles an hour. There is evidence of Liverpool people using these coaches and presumably they travelled on horseback between a ferry and Chester. Until the middle of the eighteenth century Liverpool had no road in or out of the town suitable for wheeled traffic and it was necessary, therefore, for travellers to make for Chester or travel by river boat to Warrington to catch a conveyance to the South. Chester developed as a coaching centre of considerable importance and the desire of Liverpool people to travel southwards via Chester stimulated the growth of the Mersey ferries.

A regular coach service between Chester and Woodside

Ferry by the direct route was advertised on 4th June 1762, when it was announced that a new 'machine with six able horses' would set out from the Golden Talbot, in Chester, for the Woodside Ferry Boat-house every Tuesday, Thursday, and Saturday morning at eight o'clock, taking passengers for 4/- each and returning at four o'clock on the same day to Chester. The same 'machine' went every Monday, Wednesday and Friday from Chester to Parkgate for a fare of 2/6d. Boats would attend at the Woodside Ferry on the above days to carry passengers to Liverpool.

The early coaches followed the line of the present Chester Road from Chester to Bromborough then by Spital Road, Lower Bebington and Dacre Hill to Tranmere, along what is now Church Road, down Whetstone Lane to Grange Lane and down Chester Street to Woodside. About 1790, the Chester Road was improved and the coaches, after passing Lower Bebington, turned to the right at Dacre Hill, along the Old Chester Road, crossing the Tranmere Pool by a recently completed embankment, then roughly along the line of the later railway to Grange Lane and by Chester Street to Woodside.

The Chester-Woodside, Chester-Parkgate and Great Neston-Woodside roads were turnpiked in 1787 along with a number of branches i.e. Hooton-Willaston, Eastham-Carlett Ferry, Lower Bebington-New Ferry and Dacre Hill-Rock Ferry (Rock Lane). There were toll bars at Tranmere Ferry, Well Lane and Howley Lane (Bebington Station). The New Chester Road, connecting Bromborough Village with Birkenhead and avoiding the steep gradients by Lower Bebington, is quite a modern road, having been made in 1833 by Thomas Brassey, the well-known contractor. This long straight stretch of road was then turnpiked and New Ferry Toll Bar, a name still used today, was established.

New Ferry had been established by 1774 and for almost half a century the various ferries survived mainly on coach traffic and local farm goods. The growth of Liverpool as a port, following the construction of the first enclosed dock in 1715, stimulated travel and created new markets for the agricultural produce of Cheshire and North Wales. The improvement of inland navigation enlarged the hinterland of Liverpool and new all-water routes, including passenger services to Chester, Northwich and Manchester were created. These were slow but usually more comfortable than coach travel over the dreadful roads of the late eighteenth century.

In 1801 the two largest settlements in Wirral were Neston (population 1,486) and Tranmere (353) but the next twenty years were to see the foundation of industries which accelerated rapidly after the victorious end of the Napoleonic Wars in 1815. The inflationary consequences of the war had increased the ferry toll to 3d for common people and 6d for the more well-to-do. However competition and greater volumes brought the fare down to 2d quite soon.

In the first three decades of the nineteenth century, coaching reached the zenith of its development and throughout the land, 30,000 people were said to have been employed as coachmen, guards, ostlers, horse-keepers, etc. Coaching went hand-in-hand with

innkeeping and, in Wirral, both were closely associated with the ferries. As the mail contracts were changed over from time to time, the various hotels assumed the 'Royal' prefix. Thus at different times there were the 'Royal Woodside', the 'Royal Tranmere' and the 'Royal Rock' hotels. As most of the business came from Liverpool, there was a close contact with coach booking offices there and many contemporary advertisements ignored the existence of the ferries and quoted times for the arrival and departure of the passengers in Liverpool.

The various ferry proprietors were soon forced to improve the amenities of their businesses. Substantial stone slipways were built using local sandstone from the quarry at Tranmere and vessels tended to increase in size and operate more reliably. But there could be no major progress while the boats were at the mercy of the weather. They were frequently becalmed and connections with coaches were missed, sometimes by as much as an hour. The innkeepers doubtless welcomed the extra trade and

This coach bill advertises departures from Chester of coaches which have come through from Birkenhead. Note the practice of referring to departures 'from Liverpool'.

GENERAL

COACHING OFFICE

R. SMITH & CO.

GRATEFUL for the numerous favors conferred on them, embrace the opportunity of informing their long tried and valued friends, also the public generally, that their exertions and aim in establishing conveyances to every part of the kingdom, have (in face of opposition the most determined) ultimately proved successful; and that now they confidently pledge themselves to accommodate their friends with first-rate Coaches and horses, also the most steady and experienced drivers; and every attention will be paid to Passengers and to the punctual delivery of every article committed to their care. They beg, leave respectfully to inform the public that the following

PATENT SAFETY COACHES,

LEAVE THE

WHITE LION HOTEL, NORTHGATE-STREET,

AND

KING'S HEAD, GROSVENOR-STREET,

Royal Mail and Universal Coach Offices,

CHESTER,

AND

THE ANGEL HOTEL, COACH OFFICE, DALE STREET,

AND

MRS. DODD'S, GENERAL COACH OFFICE, JAMES-STREET,

LIVERPOOL

AS UNDER:

CHELTENHAM.—L'HIRONDELLE, every Morning, (Sunday excepted) at Half-past Eight, on its arrival from Liverpool, through Wrexham, Overton, Ellesmere, Shrewsbury, Ironbridge, Bridgnorth, Kidderminster, Worcester, to the Plough Hotel, Cheltenham, at six o'clock.

CARNARVON.—GENERAL CHASSE, the Original Queen of Trumps, at Nine o'clock every day (Sunday excepted) on its arrival from Liverpool, through Holywell, St. Asaph, Abergele, Conway, Aber, and Bangor, arriving at the Sportsman's Hotel, Carnarvon, at Four o'clock each Evening.

ABERYSTWYTH.—THE PRINCE OF WALES leaves Liverpool on Mondays, Wednesdays, and Fridays, at Eight o'clock in the Morning, arrives at Chester at Ten, and proceeds through Wrexham, Oswestry, Welshpool, Newtown, Machynlleth, and arrives at the Belle Vue Hotel, Aberystwyth, at Eight in the same Evening.

perhaps the passengers' wrath was soothed by good ale. When the first steam-powered vessel was put into service on the Tranmere ferry in 1817, a revolution started not only on the Mersey ferries but in the economic development of the whole Merseyside region. Three years later, as described in Chapter 4, George La French, who had been operating Tranmere Ferry, obtained the consent of the Lord of the Manor and owner of the Woodside ferry rights, F. R. Price, to the opening of a new steam ferry (the Birkenhead Ferry) between Liverpool and Mears' Birkenhead Hotel which had been newly built on the river bank near the foot of Abbey Street. At the time the whole of Birkenhead township lay between the Birkenhead and Woodside ferries and the latter rapidly lost traffic to the steam ferries.

In November 1808, the prestigious mail contract had been taken from Tranmere by Woodside. By 1818 the lease of Woodside ferry was in the hands of William Woods and the following advertisement appeared in Gore's *Liverpool Directory* for that year:-

'WOODSIDE ROYAL MAIL FERRY, Royal Chester and Holyhead Mail Coach 4 p.m. Chester and Shrewsbury Commercial Coach, 8.45 a.m., to Chester, via Sutton, through Wrexham, Overton, Ellesmere, to Shrewsbury, at which place it is met by coaches to Oswestry, Welshpool, &c., and all parts of South Wales. Returns every day at 4 o'clock.

WILLIAM WOODS,
WOODSIDE ROYAL MAIL FERRY'

In 1822 Woods disposed of the lease of the ferry to Hugh Williams, keeper of the Woodside Hotel who introduced a steamer, *Countess of Bridgewater* which had seen service on the Ellesmere Port service. He undertook to provide a boat punctually every hour 'provided enough passengers offered'. On the instructions of F. R. Price, a new slipway 30ft. wide was built in front of a new, larger hotel and Williams replaced *Countess* by *Royal Mail*, launched on

A reproduction of a press notice advertising the facilities at the Birkenhead Hotel by James Ball, who took it over in 1827.

13th March 1822. The importance of the ferry can be judged by the size of his rent — £1,000 per annum, increasing by £250 every five years.

Coaching stables of the Royal Rock Hotel, photographed before demolition in quite modern times. The cobbled yard and hay lofts were still clearly visible.

2 MUNICIPAL OWNERSHIP AND THE RAILWAY FERRY

At the time of the mechanisation of the Mersey ferries, Birkenhead was on the verge of a population explosion. The 1821 census records 310 residents; 10 years later there were 2,790 and at the end of the period spanned by this chapter, (1861), the population numbered 36,000, excluding residents of the outlying districts of Tranmere, Oxton and Claughton-cum-Grange which remained separate townships until 1877. There were already several small factories on both sides of the Wallasey Pool. John Laird's boiler works was built near Livingstone Street in 1824 followed a year later by his first ship-building yard nearby. Laird was a pioneer of iron ships and was to become the most important man in Birkenhead, his family retaining considerable influence throughout the nineteenth century. In 1827 Laird, in conjunction with Sir John Tobin, sometime Mayor of Liverpool and John Askew, the harbourmaster, purchased land on the banks of the Pool and planned a system of docks to rival those of Liverpool. The following year the eminent engineers, Thomas Telford, Robert Stevenson and Alexander Nimmo, were commissioned to make a survey and published a report entitled 'The Intended Ship Canal between the Rivers Dee and Mersey'. The idea was to extend the Pool across North Wirral to the Dee estuary so that Liverpool, where the port dues were considered to be excessive, could be avoided altogether. The proposed cost of £1.5 million discouraged the promoters but the plan, which was one of several designed to revitalise navigation on the Dee, evoked considerable alarm in Liverpool, and the Corporation bought several tracts of land on the Pool for considerably more than the original purchase price, ensuring that the scheme was stillborn.

The Birkenhead Improvement Act 1833 authorised the appointment of Improvement Commissioners for the town and the newly constituted body met for the first time on 25th June 1833. The Commissioners, by definition, were concerned with improvements, particularly to public health services and roads and their functions evolved into those of the later local authorities but lacked the dignity and ceremonial. These belonged to those feudal relics, the Lords of the Manor to whom the Commissioners were obliged to show proper respect. The roll of founding Commissioners contained many well-known names — John Laird, the Hetheringtons (father and son), Thomas Brassey, William Ravenscroft, Michael Humble and Hugh Williams. Joseph Mallaby was appointed Clerk. The Act entitled Liverpool Corporation to appoint three of the Commissioners; doubtless at the time it was considered desirable to have watchdogs both for guidance in handling civic affairs and to protect Liverpool's interests against the ambitions of a rival authority across the river.

Tranmere and Oxton achieved the somewhat lesser status of Local Board of Health in 1860 and 1863 respectively.

With industrial expansion and population growth, the role of the ferries as a link between highways on each side of the river, mainly catering for travellers into and out of the area, was changing and in a very short time they were carrying mainly local passengers. The stage coaches reached their peak in the 1830s and the ultimate extent of the facilities offered can be judged by reference to Appendix 1 which lists the Woodside coaches running in 1834. The opening of the railway between Chester and Birkenhead in 1840 sealed their fate. Mail coaches were withdrawn immediately a railway route opened but some of the coaches tried in vain to compete. A race was arranged between a train and a coach from Birkenhead to Chester and, even though the coach was given half an hour's start, the train reached Chester first.

The private owners of the various ferries had limited capital resources and found it impossible to adjust their services to the new circumstances. In November 1834 the Commissioners resolved to send a 'memorial' to the Clerk to Mr. F. R. Price, Lord of the Manor and the owner of the ferry rights, requesting greater regularity in the Woodside Ferry sailings. There is no doubt that, despite the existence of several competing ferries, there was considerable dissatisfaction at the lack of regularity, reliability and safety. Hugh Williams, lessee of Woodside, who was himself a Commissioner, must have realised his limitations and it seems likely that he was a fully consenting party to the events of 1835. On 13th July of that year, 18 prominent Birkonians attended a public meeting in the Commissioners' Rooms, New Market and appointed a Committee to consider establishing a new ferry or improving the existing one. One of the members was William Jackson, sometime MP for Newcastle-under-Lyme, who lived at the Manor House, Claughton and was reputedly the biggest landowner in Birkenhead. Five days later, at a further meeting, it was agreed to form a company, the North Birkenhead, Woodside and Liverpool Steam Ferry Company with a capital of £25,000 in £5 shares. John Laird now joined the Committee with Joseph Mallaby as solicitor and it was empowered to treat with F. R. Price, Hugh Williams and Michael Humble, a ship-builder who owned land adjacent to Woodside. The Committee was also authorised to negotiate for the purchase of Birkenhead ferry but this was not followed up. Williams' lease ran until 30th April 1841 and the company desired to obtain a 21-year lease thereafter. The terms proposed and those ultimately agreed were as follows:-

	Annual lease	
	Proposed	Agreed
	£	£
1st May 1841 — 30th April 1846	1,300	1,250
1st May 1846 — 30th April 1851	1,600	1,500
1st May 1851 — 30th April 1856	2,000	1,750
1st May 1856 — 30th April 1862	2,500	2,000

An artist's impression of the Mersey at Woodside in the 1840s. On the right is the end of the stone ferry pier with its lighthouse, of which parts remain on the river wall today. A wooden paddle steamer is leaving for Liverpool where the Albert Dock warehouses, Custom House and the spire of St. George's Church can be identified. The print shows how ships anchored in mid-river in the ferry track, creating a hazard to steamers for over a century.

Alternatively, the company could pay £6,000 on 1st May 1836 and then £1,000 per annum. Williams' price for goodwill and two of his steamboats was £9,500. With the remarkable rapidity at which events moved in those uncomplicated days, a sub-committee was appointed on 20th July 1835 to negotiate with Hugh Williams; this included in its membership Laird and Jackson, the latter being, by all accounts, a formidable negotiator. Bargaining started immediately at Mr Poole's hotel where no doubt the hunger and thirst of the parties could be more adequately assuaged than at the Commissioners' Rooms. Hugh Williams made the following proposal in writing:-

'I offer to the Committee of the Ferry Company to sell my interest in the residue of my lease in

15

Woodside ferry and three steamboats and their appurtenances and small boat to each and landing boats as now worked for the sum of £12,000, subject to the contract with Mr. Rigby for Boilers for the 'Kingfisher' if that steamboat be purchased and to the contract for the iron landing boat now making by Vernon and Co. and to the contracts made by me with subscribers, the company to receive their proportion for the unexpired term of those subscribers. I am to give a correct list to the Committee of all my subscribers when possession of the ferry is delivered up.

But I agree to allow and deduct from the said sum of £2,500 for any one of the said steamboats the company choose to give up to me. I am ready to send the 'Kingfisher' immediately to get the boilers put in if the Committee requires it. Or, I am ready to lend to the Company the steamboat which may be given up to me if the Company take the 'Kingfisher' until the Company can get the new boilers put into her, the Company paying damage and cost of working.

I am to have three months to remove my articles which are now on the wharf. Payment to be made as follows. One third on taking possession deducting four months' interest at 5%; one third six months adding two months' interest; one third in twelve months adding eight months' interest. The Company may pay before those periods and be allowed interest accordingly.

I will sell my land adjoining Mr. Humble at 15/- per yard and this offer I allow to remain open one month. I engage whether the Company take the land or not that I will not erect or engage with others to erect or ply any ferry in this township.'

Signed Hugh Williams.

There are some interesting terms used in the letter. In the days before floating landing stages were employed, ferries could not get close inshore at low tide without running aground and it was common practice for the vessel to stand off and to transfer passengers to and from landing boats which were often old lifeboats or rowing boats. Doubtless the 'landing boats as now worked' were of this type. However, the 'iron landing boat now making' could scarcely be a rowing boat and it seems to have been an early form of pontoon to bridge the gap between vessel and shore. Old ships or barges had been used before pontoons of iron plate were specifically built for this purpose.

The 'subscribers' referred to were, in Merseyside parlance, 'contractors' or season ticket holders who, in effect, subscribed their fares for a year in advance, albeit at a greatly reduced rate.

The company agreed to accept, subject to Price's confirmation and the speed of events and the acceptance of the terms without haggling suggests that the real negotiating had already taken place. The company took possession on Wednesday 5th August 1835 with the steamboats *Ribble* and *Kingfisher*, £3,000 being paid as a first instalment. Williams' third boat, which was not acquired, was *Ann* a wooden paddler launched in June 1834 of which little is known except that its 34nhp engine was supplied by Fawcett. Its subsequent fate is unknown.

At a General Meeting on 17th August 1835, 15 directors were appointed including John Laird, William Jackson, J. Aspinall, Thos. Harrison and Hugh Williams. A Superintendent was engaged at £3 per week. A third boat, *Alexandra* was purchased at cost from Thomas Morecroft of Rock Ferry, 'engines to be put in perfect order without expence to the company'. Mr Laird was requested to prepare a specification for an iron steamboat not exceeding 90ft. long by 18ft. beam, with engines of 50hp and 4ft. stroke. Laird tendered £4,850 and, not surprisingly, got the order. This boat took to the water as *Eliza Price*. Other tenderers were Horsley Iron Co. and Page and Grantham. A second order was awarded to the latter for £4,600 a month later. This vessel was named *Cleveland*. A sub-committee went to Glasgow and purchased another boat, *Helensburgh* second hand from Stevenson and others for £1,175. This was a wooden paddler built by William Denny of Dumbarton in 1825.

In September annual contracts were fixed at £2, or £3 for two members of the same family. It is not clear if the ordinary fare was 1d or 2d at this time but coach proprietors were to be supplied with ferry tickets at 3d per passenger thus perpetuating the class system which applied in earlier centuries. It was resolved that any person may, weather permitting, have a steamboat from Woodside to Liverpool after the regular hours at £1 before midnight or £2 after midnight, the proceeds being divided equally between the company and the crew. A contract was concluded with the Postmaster General for the conveyance of mails.

On 7th December 1835 a sub-committee was appointed to purchase the Rock Ferry rights for 21 or more years and to take the Rock Ferry Inn on rent but a month later it reported that Rock Ferry had ceased to run. Negotiations were in hand with Brethertons, the coach proprietors, about terms for passengers of their coaches 'Hibernia' and 'Bang-Up'. Rock Ferry had charged 3d and free stabling, lame horses occasionally being conveyed free but the Woodside company agreed on 3d and no free stabling.

Monks Ferry

The route between Chester and Birkenhead was seen by railway promoters as a route to Liverpool and its says much for the optimism of the times that a small matter like the crossing of three quarters of a mile of swift flowing, tidal water should have been seen as presenting no long term obstacle. Two schemes were placed before Parliament in the 1836-37 Session both with Woodside, the shortest passage, as their objective. The respective promoters formed the Chester Junction Railway (otherwise referred to as the Birkenhead and Chester Railway Co.) and the Chester and Birkenhead Railway Co. and both Bills passed their second readings whereupon Parliament appointed arbitrators to examine the merits of the two schemes. In the face of opposition from all the other ferries, the arbitrators

These Birkenhead pioneers, the Lairds, Jacksons and the great contractor, Thomas Brassey, are all immortalised in the names of what are today rather shabby streets.

recommended a neutral solution as a result of which a clause was put in the Chester and Birkenhead Railway Act, passed on 12th July 1837, terminating the line at Grange Lane and forbidding any extension to Woodside until branches had been built to serve Tranmere and Birkenhead ferries. Booking offices were to be situated only at Grange Lane and within the town of Liverpool and the strict interpretation of this restriction made it necessary to seek further powers to have booking offices at Chester and intermediate stations along the line.

The Company's proprietors included many names well-known in Birkenhead, among them F. R. Price, who was elected Chairman (but did not hold the office for very long), William Jackson and his brother, J. S. Jackson, William Ravenscroft and Richard and James Bryans.

Obviously building and running train services on branches to every ferry would have been expensive and inconvenient and an alternative arrangement had to be found. In 1837 members of the Bryans family formed the Monks Ferry Company and quickly built a stone slip and hotel at Ivy Rock about 400 yards south of Woodside. Attractive gardens faced the river and the promoters claimed that their ferry was on the site of the former priory ferry and was its true successor.

The involvement of members of the same family in both the railway and ferry projects in the same year is scarcely likely to have been coincidental and it is reasonable to assume that the Monks Ferry scheme was hastily put together when the restrictions in the Railway Company's Act became known. Price, as owner of the Woodside ferry rights and a railway shareholder, was in an ambivalent position and later events suggest that he was not a party to the scheme.

Railways take longer to build than ferry slipways and sailings at Monks Ferry commenced in April 1838 using two wooden paddlers, *Monk* (71GT) built in 1837 by W. Seddon of Birkenhead and engined by Johnson and Co. and *Abbey* (53GT) built in 1838 by Humble and Milcrest. Both vessels were about 88ft. long. An iron paddle steamer *Dolphin* (62.56GT) was added to the fleet in January 1840. She was built at Dumbarton in 1834 by J. Lang and had been re-engined by Johnson and Co. Both the Woodside company as lessees and F. R. Price as hereditary owner of the right of ferry at Woodside, brought a successful action at Chester Summer Sessions. A new trial was ordered on a technicality but the decision in 1839 was the same; Monks Ferry was *ultra vires* and must close.

The Monks Ferry case relied to some extent on events in the 13th and 14th centuries. It was argued that as there was a pre-existing ferry from Liverpool to Birkenhead, the 1330 Charter was null and void or, alternatively, it authorised a ferry from Birkenhead to Liverpool and not both ways. The lease from Price clearly stated 'both ways'. It was further argued that Price, by agreeing to the establishment of Birkenhead ferry had, in any case, forfeited his exclusive rights.

The Railway Company was acutely aware that they needed to control the whole route between Chester and Liverpool and in July 1838 they authorised William Jackson and Christopher Bentham to negotiate with the Woodside company resulting in an agreement to exchange 1,000 £25 ferry company shares for 500 £50 railway shares. Most of the ferry shareholders accepted, the railway acquiring 997 shares, and the date of takeover was agreed as 1st December 1838. The deal had been subject to Price extending the lease for 12 years to 30th April 1853, the rent to be the subject of arbitration at the time the current lease expired in 1841. However, the ultimate objective was acquisition of the ferry rights and Price was sounded out at a meeting in Chester on Christmas Eve 1839 which had been arranged to advise him that a further attempt to get Parliamentary powers to extend the line to Woodside and delete the branch line clause was precluded by Standing Orders. This meeting was apparently encouraging but inconclusive.

The Monks Ferry Company continued to operate in competition with Woodside while litigation (Pym v Curell) about their right to do so continued. In May 1839, the fare at Monks Ferry was reduced from 3d to 2d so Woodside was obliged to do the same. In February 1840, the Monks Ferry Company offered to cease operations and drop any further legal proceedings, if Price would forego his costs and the lessees would abandon their claim for 'mesne profits'. Sailings ceased at the end of the month and the railway company stepped in and purchased the property and three boats for £25,000 on 7th March.

There is no firm evidence that the railway company obtained legal opinion to the effect that a private ferry for railway passengers only would not contravene the statutory rights of Woodside provided that separate ferry tolls were not charged. The purchase of Monks Ferry seems to have been influenced by the fact that it was not mentioned in the 1837 Act and was therefore 'neutral' in relation to the rights of the other ferries to have rail connections.

The next problem was the establishment of a link between the railway station and the waterfront. A scheme for a tramroad along Ivy Street was discussed with the Commissioners on 7th April 1840 but, following public opposition, it was abandoned in August when a contract to supply omnibuses was made with Mr Henry Hilliar. The railway was opened to the public on 23rd September 1840, following a trip to Chester and back in a special train for invited guests and a dinner at the Monks Ferry Hotel on the previous day. The directors had already decided that Monks Ferry would reopen when the railway opened and that a boat would be engaged from Woodside ferry to leave George's Pier Head, Liverpool 20 minutes before train departures from Grange Lane, carrying railway passengers free of charge. Three days before the official opening, the times were announced—there were at first only five trains a day—and it was also decided to make the boats available to the general public. This provoked an official demand from Price to the railway company to discontinue running Monks Ferry in contravention of his established rights. However, as the railway company was the lessee of Woodside, this was but a precautionary legal gesture.

In June 1840 plans were considered for a new vessel. Duckworth and Langmuir in *West Coast Steamers* record the withdrawal of *Monk* on 21st July 1843 and *Abbey* and *Dolphin* in 1845 but their subsequent fate is unknown. They also attribute a further wooden paddler, *James Dennistoun* (about 80GT), built 1836 by Hunter & Dow, Glasgow with engines by R. Napier, to Monks Ferry. The accuracy of these reports has not been confirmed and it seems likely that some of these vessels were used for goods only as one boat would have been adequate for the passenger traffic. Specifications and models were received from Page and Grantham, Devonport; Grindrod and Patrick and Lairds and the latter's tender of £5,485 for an iron paddle steamer with 60hp engines on the upright principle by Forrester and Co. of Liverpool was recommended for acceptance. This vessel, which entered service at the end of the year, was named *Nun* (187GT).

The wholly-owned Woodside company managed the service between Liverpool and Monks Ferry on behalf of the railway from the beginning. In March 1841 the sale of *Nun* by the railway company to the Woodside company was agreed at cost price, interest being payable on the purchase money until the debt was discharged. The ferry company also agreed 'to sail a boat for the accommodation of railway passengers to the Monks Ferry at the rate before charged'. This seems to have been a ploy to improve the railway company's accounts as many of the shareholders were critical of the directors' performance. At a Shareholders' Meeting on 10th April 1841 a committee was appointed to enquire into the purchase and present position of Woodside and Monks Ferries and certain land not in use. At an adjourned meeting in May, the directors were criticised for spending £32,000 on buying Woodside and incurring rent for unproductive land of about £1,500 per annum when they knew that they

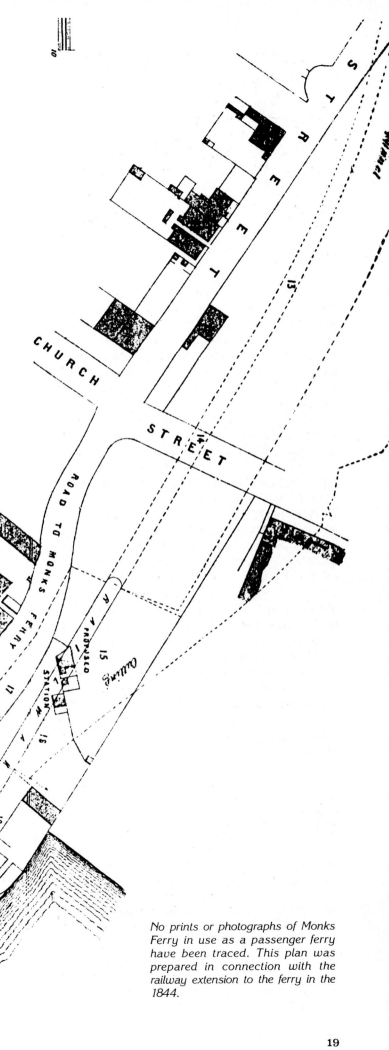

No prints or photographs of Monks Ferry in use as a passenger ferry have been traced. This plan was prepared in connection with the railway extension to the ferry in the 1844.

could not extend the line to Woodside. The gross profit for the most recent eight months was £1,040. The report 'expressed disapprobation of this purchase as being highly improvident and not calculated to aid either effectively or permanently the well-being of the railway'. It was also reported that the receipts at Monks Ferry from casual passengers from 23rd September 1840 to 1st May 1841 totalled less than £97. Omnibus hire cost £1,456 per annum.

The directors were then instructed to reopen negotiations with Price for the sale of the reversionary ferry rights the cost of which would be about £51,000. A new Board was elected, only William Jackson being reappointed.

Having established the cross-river link, the railway company turned its attention to securing a permanent land connection between Grange Lane and Monks Ferry. It was proposed to build a pier of sufficient length for the Irish Mail to berth at low water and the Conservator of the Mersey was approached for his views on the extension of Monks Ferry pier. There were second thoughts, no doubt on economy grounds, about the purchase of the ferry rights and plans were drawn up for a tunnel beneath Ivy Street between Grange Lane station and Monks Ferry. In September 1841 the company wrote to the Commissioners requesting permission to construct it and as a *quid pro quo* offered to sell them Woodside ferry including all boats and appurtenances provided the railway company was conceded the right of ferry for railway passengers and goods between Monks Ferry and Liverpool. There followed some difficult negotiations and at the half-year meeting on 7th October 1841, the railway shareholders were told:

'..to their great surprise and regret their propositions which were fair and liberal in the extreme and calculated to have proved beneficial to all parties, were met on the part of the Commissioners by demands of so irrelevant and extraordinary a nature as compelled the directors to abandon their negotiations and with it their hopes to be able to construct a tunnel until a time should arrive when a more rational view of the matter should be taken by the Birkenhead Commissioners and when the funds of the company would be in a state more equal to so great an undertaking....'

On 27th September 1840, the directors of the Woodside company, who were all railway nominees, had considered a proposal by Willoughbys, the lessees of Tranmere ferry, that from 1st October the ordinary fare should be 3d, single contracts should be £3-10-0d and contracts for two persons should be £5-10-0d per annum. An amendment that, because of fraud, no further contracts be issued was carried by the Chairman's casting vote and then a further proposal was adopted fixing the fare at 2d but abolishing both contracts and workmen's tickets. Willoughbys would not go along with the abolition of contracts and it seems likely that these proposals and the suspension of some late sailings, which evoked considerable public criticism, were calculated to influence the Birkenhead Commissioners' attitude.

After some preliminary haggling, the Commissioners agreed, subject to a formal agreement with the railway company 'to oblige them to work Woodside ferry with boats at least equal in power and capacity to those now employed, to run as frequently and as early and late as at present'. The charge per passenger was not to exceed 2d and contracts were to be continued at £3 p.a. (plus £2 for the second member of a family and £1 for third and subsequent members). This suggests that the Commissioners were thinking about buying the ferry rights but leasing them back to the railway company which was not the latter's intention. Negotiations to purchase which started almost immediately, were conducted by William Jackson who had a foot in both camps. On 15th October 1841 agreement was reached and Jackson offered his contract to the Commissioners. On 18th the books of the ferry company were examined, the revenue found to be satisfactory and a Public Meeting at the Town Hall approved of the purchase the same day. The Public Meeting also requested the resumption of contracts and reinstatement of the last boat from Woodside at 10.00pm. All this was agreed. The Commissioners were invited to attend ferry company board meetings pending a formal transfer, but with no voting rights, and the railway company decided to charge its passengers for ferriage from 20th November.

Public Ownership

The Commissioners now applied to Parliament for the necessary powers and commenced negotiations with Mr Price for the purchase of the ferry rights. The Woodside company was formally notified of their intention to purchase on 14th December 1841.

Acquisition of the hereditary rights for £44,000 was agreed in April 1842, the Act received the Royal Assent in May and the Commissioners met to finalise the ferry purchase on 15th June 1842. The Commissioners had no money and mortgaged the ferry to the Chester and Birkenhead Railway Co. for £28,257-4s-0d in exchange for nine transfers of shares in the ferry company. They took possession on or about 1st July 1842, made byelaws and regulations and decided to borrow £30,000 on the security of the tolls and the rates and property of the township that same month. An agreement was made to run Monks Ferry on behalf of the railway for five years. The hours of operation at Woodside were extended to midnight and contract tickets reintroduced.

Despite the lack of funds, the Birkenhead Commissioners now had the bit between their teeth and decided that they should own all the ferries in the township including Monks Ferry. However, Birkenhead Ferry, by then owned by Liverpool Corporation, was not for sale. A draft agreement was drawn up in September 1843 for the sale by the railway company of the Monks Ferry property, with the ferry rights and slip for £20,000 with

An engraving of Woodside ferry pier before the addition of the two slips. Gough's Hotel, which forms part of the present day Woodside Hotel is recognisable at the pier head, whilst Gleave's Adelphi Hotel is on the left.

Woodside ferry pier viewed from the river about 1849. Two steamers lie at one of the two slipways which were added in 1844.

options to purchase other adjoining land. The making of the railway tunnel was to be an essential part of the arrangement and conclusion of the deal was to depend solely on the railway company being able to carry out that objective. The Commissioners on their part were to continue to carry the railway passengers and goods traffic efficiently on the basis of the existing traffic but the railway company was to have sole control of the times of sailings from both sides of the river. The railway could engage other boats if there was any unreasonable delay in providing boats and charge the Commissioners for the expense incurred though there was provision for arbitration. The Birkenhead Improvement Act, 1844 extended the powers in other Acts to permit the purchase of Monks Ferry. Woodside mortgages were to have priority and the tolls were to be the same as at Woodside. The formal contract was not signed until 31st May 1847.

The train service to Monks Ferry commenced on 23rd October 1844, the same day that Sir Philip Egerton laid the foundation stone of Birkenhead Docks. The Commissioners experimented with a regular half-hourly ferry service quite independently of the railway boats. This started about 1st June 1846 but was discontinued on 13th August as passengers were few and some disruption was caused to the railway services. The railway company complained that, whilst awaiting arrival of trains at the station, the railway boat was moored outside the half-hourly boats and the Ferry Manager was instructed by the Committee to see that the railway boat had the privilege of lying alongside the slip. New destination boards were fitted to the steamers in July reading 'Birkenhead by Woodside Ferry' or 'Birkenhead by Monks Ferry' and Woodside contractors (season ticket holders) were permitted to use Monks Ferry. On discontinuation of the half-hourly service, extra boats were put on at Woodside between 8.30 and 10.00am and 4.00 and 6.00pm and the contractors were allowed to use the railway boats.

Monks Ferry was managed by a Committee of four, comprising two Commissioners and two railway directors who met at 9.30am each Tuesday in the Railway Offices, Argyle Street. One of the conditions of the 1847 agreement was a drawback of 20% of the tolls in favour of the railway company.

The failure of Monks Ferry as a regular ferry for Birkenhead people made the Commissioners realise that their empire building had been misguided. It seems that the General Board of Commissioners had been more enthusiastic than the Ferry Committee who endeavoured to dissociate themselves from responsibility for the losses. Matters were made worse when, on 9th June 1848, Liverpool Corporation decided to reduce the passenger fare on their Birkenhead Ferry from 2d to 1d. The fare on Woodside and Tranmere (but not Monks) Ferries was reduced on 14th June and the Commissioners found themselves in serious financial difficulties. Retrenchments and wage reductions followed immediately and a proposal to introduce a weekly contract was deferred, though as a concession to working men, the 5.00 and 5.30am boats from Woodside were run free of charge from 6th September. This was discontinued from 1st May 1849.

The prosperity of Birkenhead seemed to be assured by the passing of the Birkenhead Dock Act, 1844, which authorised the first stage of the conversion of the Wallasey Pool into a system of enclosed docks. In the same year, Liverpool Corporation sold their land in Birkenhead. The first two docks, appropriately named Morpeth and Egerton, were opened on 5th April 1847. This was, in fact, a triple celebration for Birkenhead as, on the same day, Birkenhead Park, laid out by Sir Joseph Paxton, was opened to the public. This was the first public park established by a local authority in Britain. Also opened with some ceremony was the railway extension in tunnel and cutting beneath the town from Grange Lane to Egerton Dock. The railway company built a warehouse right on the water's edge.

Financial Crisis

However the financial crisis which followed the Railway Mania prevented the planned further expansion of the docks and a serious depression struck the town. Labourers who had been engaged on these many works left the town and houses stood empty. The debts which had been incurred with confidence by the Commissioners became a severe burden and this was to affect the ferry undertaking very seriously. To complete the story, trustees for the docks were appointed in 1850 and whilst some work was done, the whole estate was sold to Liverpool Corporation in 1855, the outcome being the vesting of the docks on both sides of the river in the Mersey Docks and Harbour Board on 1st January 1858.

In 1848 the ferry was, in effect, bankrupt. In November, working capital was raised by 'selling' the newest steamer, *Wirral*, to J. H and W. Hind, prominent local businessmen, for £3,150 and hiring it back for two years at £3 per day (except for three days a month allowed for repairs) with an option to repurchase after six months. When it was realised that the rent was equivalent to interest of 31%, the option was exercised, *Wirral* being transferred into the name of William Rudd, the ferry manager, in January 1850 to prevent attachment for debt; mortgages were taken out with the Hinds on *Wirral* and *Queen*. These were paid off later that year following agreement with the trustees of F. R. Price. The unusual practice of having two boats registered in the name of the manager seems to have become accepted to the extent that it was altogether forgotten. Rudd left the Commissioners' service about July 1855 by which time both *Wirral* and *Queen* were registered in his name and remained so until August 1856 when they were hastily 'sold' to Samuel Reed, the new manager. The oversight was apparently brought to the Committee's attention because of a claim by Rudd for compensation for the risk taken by having the steamers in his name. The Committee said that they could not believe that he was serious.

In January 1849 the Ferry Committee was unable to pay its bills and instructed the manager to prepare a statement of the cost of working Monks Ferry so that the

By 1850 the town had expanded considerably. This low tide view shows the stone jetty with the lighthouse at the river end. The Woodside Hotel, houses in Bridge Street and the twin inclines of Chester Street and Hamilton Street are easily discerned.

Improvement Commissioners could be debited with the loss. In February the Committee was advised that the funds of Woodside could not legally be used for supporting Monks Ferry and they resolved that after settling wages and accounts up to the present time, they would incur no further responsibility for conducting Monks Ferry as at present. This was so much hot air as the Ferry Committee was itself no more than a part of the General Board of Commissioners and responsible to it. On 21st July 1849 the Committee agreed to pay an instalment of 10/- in the £ to creditors with accounts due in June 1848.

Price was owed not just £44,000 for the ferry rights but £59,372-12s-0d for several tracts of land in the town including the Park, a total of £103,372-12s-0d. Mortgages totalling £31,595-13s-6d were given to Price over properties in Conway Street, the Town Hall site and 'Forest Land'. Price's security was to extend over the tolls, boats and plant of Woodside Ferry. In consideration of this agreement, Price was to complete transfer of the various lands and lease the ferry to the Commissioners for 21 years at £4,574-18s-0d per year, giving them the option to purchase the ferry rights at any time during that period for the sum of £103,372-12s-0d. The cost of purchase of the Park, the Town Hall site and other lands were thereby to be borne by Woodside Ferry.

Despite these early difficulties, the first decade of public ownership saw many improvements and the reduction of the fare to 1d had long term benefits as it led to a considerable increase in traffic. In the violent and licentious days of the late twentieth century, it is of interest to see what precautions were necessary against criminal acts in the mid-nineteenth century. It was customary to carry a policeman on board many boats in the 1840s; in June 1848 their number was reduced and seamen were sworn in as Special Constables instead but, when all-night boats were introduced at the end of 1849, a policeman was engaged at 18/- per week plus cost of clothing, to travel on the night boat from 8.00pm to 5.00am. No doubt the most common nuisance was caused by drunks but, in December 1850, there were complaints of a great number of prostitutes coming from Liverpool between 7.00pm and midnight, their disgraceful conduct on board causing annoyance to respectable passengers. An extra policeman was suggested.

The 1840s were momentous years for the ferries. Traffic increased dramatically and despite the lack of funds, the Birkenhead Commissioners did everything possible to develop the ferries undertaking as a public service for the benefit of the town's inhabitants. One of their first acts was to reintroduce annual contracts and also to make contracts available for six and three months, a boon for those who found it impossible to lay out a year's travel expenditure at one time. The practice of allowing subsequent members of the same family to purchase contracts at reduced rates became established and was to survive for more than a century on all the Mersey ferries. Unlimited travel for one person cost £2-10s-0d for a year in 1842; for two persons it was £3-10s-0d and 15/- for each additional member of the same family. The definition of 'family' was flexible, though lodgers and female servants were specifically excluded. The basic annual charge was halved to £1-5s-0d on 1st July 1844.

At the end of 1848, despite the desperate financial plight of the undertaking, the Ferries Committee refused to increase the annual contract to £2-2s-0d but the General Board prudently reversed this decision. The prevailing rate averaged less than ½d on the basis of twelve trips per week for 50 weeks a year. Many contractors crossed the river to their homes for lunch and so travelled for little more than a farthing.

The greatest achievement of the Commissioners' ferries, however, was the establishment of reliability. No longer were boats arbitrarily withdrawn at quiet times to tow becalmed sailing ships and this was the principal factor in establishing the later prosperity of Woodside. Another cherished ambition was the provision of an all night service. Birkenhead approached Liverpool Corporation in January 1846 for landing facilities at night and when this was refused, imprudently requested to be allowed to purchase the stage. This understandably was also refused. In support of their submission, Birkenhead wrote 'there are now seven steam packets regularly plying the ferry and

two flats for goods and two additional packets building'. The daily passenger traffic was estimated at over 9,000 people. The commissioning of a floating landing stage at George's Pier Head in 1847 improved facilities greatly and in September 1849, following a change of heart by Liverpool Corporation, it was resolved to run a night boat hourly from Woodside between 12.30 and 4.30am and half an hour later from Liverpool. This replaced the arrangement whereby a special boat could be hired for £1-10-0d, reduced to 10/- from July 1847. From 12th November 1849, a 6d fare was charged but in January 1863 a passenger refused to pay more than 1d and the prosecution brought against him subsequently failed as the maximum fare authorised by Parliament was 2d. From 11th February to 29th August 1863, night passengers travelled for 1d until statutory powers could be obtained to charge a higher fare. Other innovations were improved wages and uniforms for staff (See Appendix 2). Turnstiles, or 'cheque gates' as they were sometimes called, then a new invention, were purchased. Ten were ordered in October 1846 for Woodside and Monks Ferries; later another two were added and the full installation was opened on 13th March 1848. They could register up to 20,000 passengers and were supplied by Stevens and Son, of Southwark Bridge Road, London S.E. for £50 each. In 1865 the same firm supplied another, 'equally as good' for only £30.

To cope with increased traffic and competition from the privately owned ferries, boats were run 'regardless of time', between 8.00am and 6.00pm from 10th January 1848. This gave, in effect, a 7 to 15 minute service using three or four boats and, despite complaints from contractors, this way of working was continued because revenue increased. This 'on demand' service may have provoked Liverpool Corporation into reducing the fare on their Birkenhead Ferry to 1d.

Relations with the Railway

Clearly the purchase of Monks Ferry by the Commissioners had been a blunder of major proportions. While the expenses of operating it were, per passenger, much greater than Woodside, the passenger traffic was much less. The goods traffic, on the other hand, was expensive to handle and unpredictable in quantity. Late running trains created operational problems and the railway company complained if a boat was not immediately available. The steamer *Kingfisher* was usually allocated to Monks Ferry and the railway constantly complained about it. In 1851 it was described as a 'luggage boat'. In 1852 the Ferries Committee told the railway company that if they could arrange the trains so that one boat would suffice, they would buy a new boat specially equipped for railway service and cross the river in 10 minutes. The railway company, wisely, would not positively bind themselves to one boat but would use their 'best endeavours'.

One of the severest tests of railway-ferry co-ordination was Chester Races, held annually early in May. As the railway network developed, there were demands for acceptance of through tickets from other railways such as the Lancashire and Yorkshire and East Lancashire lines. The Commissioners, fearful of losing their tolls, were reluctant to agree to through tickets which included ferriage. In July 1850, the railway proposed to place a booking hut on board the Monks Ferry steamers and gradually, as mutual trust developed, the Commissioners' attitude became less rigid. By 1855 they were prepared to allow the manager to negotiate reduced tolls for excursion passengers. However, a scheme for including ferriage in railway tickets ran into difficulties. It had been foolishly timed to come into effect from 1st May 1853, just prior to Chester Races and if it had been arranged to commence at quiet time, all would probably have gone well. The

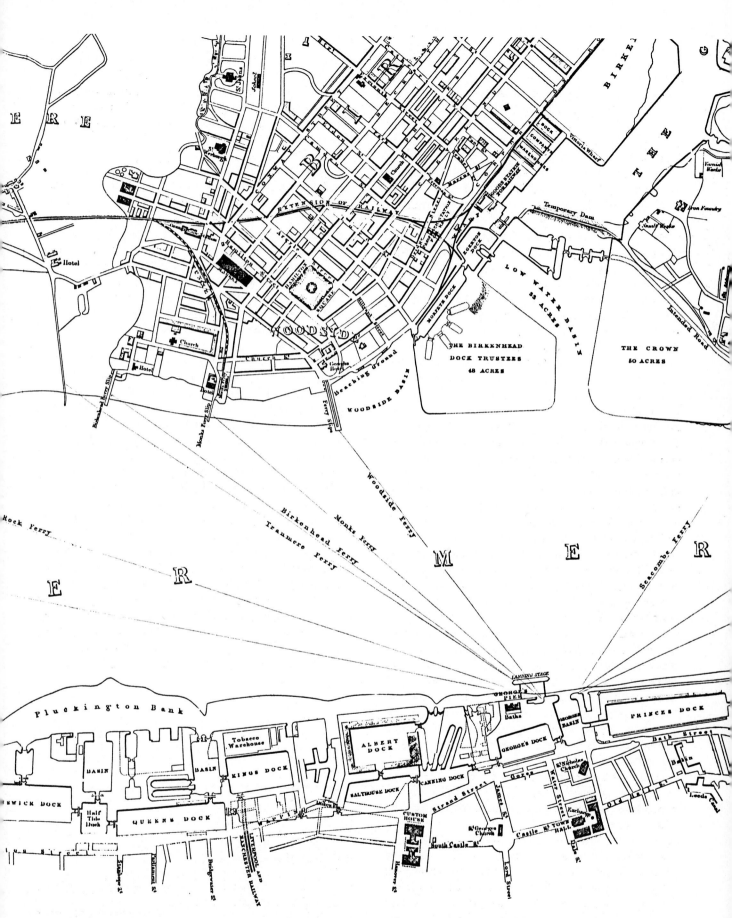

This map was prepared for use in connection with one of Rendel's schemes for developing the Birkenhead docks. It shows the position as it was in the early 1850s. The solid lines adjacent to the land reclamation areas represented work already completed and the dotted lines were work in hand. Note the four ferry slips at Birkenhead and Tranmere and the stream along the line of Borough Road, separating the two townships. At Liverpool, the disused ferry basin, is behind the 1847 landing stage.

principle of inclusive railway tickets was disapproved by the Committee and eventually a compromise was reached in that ferry tickets were sold in bulk to the railway company. The booking hut on board the steamer was the direct ancestor of the railway booking office which was situated on George's landing stage until the 1939-45 war. Conversely, many railway stations carried stocks of ferry tickets until quite modern times.

The co-ordination of train and boat was not always easy as was illustrated on the occasion of Chester Races in 1851. After a gap of 90 minutes with no trains, four or five trains arrived almost together. Some passengers, detained at Limekiln Lane (St. Paul's Road) for half an hour, jumped down on to the line and ran down to the rival Tranmere Ferry. On this occasion the Commissioners, usually on the receiving end of such complaints, told the railway that unless they co-operated in the sensible regulation of the traffic, no extra boats would be provided.

In an effort to improve the ferries' finances, the Ferry and Parliamentary Committees worked out a scheme in 1852 to lease the Monks Ferry for 3, 5 or 7 years and also the goods traffic at Woodside. The railway company was to pay all the expenses of the traffic, provide its own boats and hand over 25% of the net profit to the Commissioners. A letter written in February 1852 by T. H. Stevens, Manager of the Shrewsbury and Chester and Shrewsbury and Birmingham Railway Companies, originating from the 'Goods Manager's Office, Great Float Station' obviously confirmed previous discussions and read as follows:-

'On behalf of the Shrewsbury and Chester Railway and subject to the passing of Bills now before Parliament for amalgamation with the Great Western and Shrewsbury and Birmingham Railways and also subject to passing of an Act for leasing the Birkenhead, Lancashire and Cheshire Junction Railways, I beg to propose a lease of the Monks Ferry for seven years ....'

The Parliamentary and Ferries Committees met jointly on 5th March to consider the proposal but Price's trustees also had to be consulted and they objected to a lease but would consent to a licence (not exclusive) being allowed to any party. The Commissioners, therefore, resolved that the grant of any licence for the goods traffic at Woodside should be contingent upon the purchase by the same licensee of Monks Ferry at cost price and a sub-committee was authorised to continue negotiations on this basis. It was also agreed to reduce the 25% profit clause to one farthing per passenger which was 12½% and plans were to be made to remove the goods traffic from Woodside slip altogether.

The failure of the Great Western Railway's scheme to lease the Birkenhead line through its surrogate, the Shrewsbury and Chester, put an end to this scheme, but following objections to various Parliamentary Railway Bills by the Commissioners, an agreement was made with the BL & CJ Railway Co., successor to the original company, on 6th May 1852 whereby the Commissioners surrendered their right under an earlier agreement to have a new road built in substitution for the Old Township Road upon the site of which the railway goods station stood, in return for the railway company releasing and giving up the 20% drawback on the Monks Ferry tolls. The railway company also agreed to reduce the rate of interest on the Monks Ferry purchase money from 5% to 4% and to extend the time for payment until 31st May 1857, subject to the interest being paid punctually. The first payment was due on 31st May 1853. The Commissioners were still liable for the arrears.

Problems of rail and ferry co-ordination continued. An undated document of the 1850s complains that '...the convenience of the Railway Company is not now considered. Great annoyance is caused to railway passengers by the manner in which the goods traffic is conducted on Monks Ferry slip and personal damage caused to them. Great inconvenience is caused by the railway boat *Wirral* being continually without notice taken off the station to ply at Woodside causing irregularity to trains and the loss of the services of the booking clerk who is idle while the boat is not running to Monks Ferry.'

In March 1855 a further approach was made to the railway company to try to arrange the trains so that only one boat was required and, after a measure of agreement had been reached, a newer boat, *Woodside* of 1853, was allocated to Monks Ferry, but the Commissioners' attitude was generally unco-operative. A proposal by the railway company to charge for newspaper traffic on a mileage basis was haughtily rejected as was a request for a boat to meet a train from Chester due at 11.40pm. At this time the Commissioners were using a boat as a tender for the City of Dublin Steamship Co's Kingstown (Dun Laoghaire) sailings, embarking and disembarking passengers at Monks Ferry, but this was given up from 1st October 1855.

Despite the 1852 concessions, Monks Ferry could still not be worked profitably and it remained official policy to get rid of it if at all possible. In late 1856 or early 1857, by which time it was clear that the purchase money could not be raised by the due date, a new round of talks started, culminating in an Agreement dated 28th May 1857 and written into the Birkenhead, Lancashire and Cheshire

Mr McKelvie, who was ferry manager in the 1860s, kept a note book which has survived. These notes on Monks Ferry traffic are believed to have been written in his own hand.

Monks Ferry. Average receipts per year 1854 to 1861 £3295. 10. 0
average per month for that time 274. 12. 6
— n - increase in receipts for 10 years ending 1862. 20%
Increase in receipts 1861 over 1852. 36%

Total Number of Contractors at Woodside for the undermentioned years.

Year ending	Yearly 25/	10/	Half Yearly 17/6	7/6	Quarterly 12/6	5/	Total
1849	916	904	54	44	18	9	1945
1850	1394	642	121	24	51	11	2243
1851	1179	930	99	14	65	29	2316
1852	1088	914	93	17	47	13	2172
1853	1332	832	116	7	47	11	2345
1854	1423	895	91	20	51	12	2492
1855	1514	854	97	9	55	9	2538
1856 ✷	363	254	905	480	517	188	2707
1857	1485	826	193	32	122	46	2704
1858	1570	792	204	36	100	11	2653
1859	1417	740	172	43	69	19	2460
1860	1423	824	140	39	63	10	2499
1861	1474	867	144	23	66	5	2579
1862	1464	835	188	23	41	14	2565
1863	1480	865	116	11	49	8	2529
Average	1298	798	182	55	91	26	2450

✷ The contracts taken out in 1856 under the head of six months were for periods of from 6 to 11 Months. and those under the head of three months for periods of 3 to 5 Months — This arrangement was made in order to end the year together. Previous to issuing yearly Contracts from January only.

In 1860 the Residence of the Contractors by Woodside was (as near as can be ascertained) as under.

	For the Year 25/	10/	Short period		Total
Birkenhead	823	506	63	20	1412
Claughton	147	94	8	-	249
Oxton	143	83	2	-	258
Tranmere	175	61	5	2	243
Out Townships	57	8	-	-	59
Liverpool	35	7	2	2	46
					2267

In the early municipal days, the Contractors were treated with great deference as they provided useful working capital. The growth of their numbers was watched carefully but, after the ferry was improved, the casuals increased more rapidly. The 1860 survey of the geographical spread of contract holders is of interest, as it shows that the Tranmere contractors were almost as numerous as those from the prestigous suburb of Oxton.

Junction Railway Bill 1857. The railway company was to take back the Monks Ferry slip, hotel etc., and the contract of 1847 insofar as it remained uncompleted, was to be cancelled.

The railway company was to have a right of ferry but only for passengers, cattle, goods and other railway traffic conveyed by the company from outside the Township of Birkenhead (and vice versa), an acknowledgement payment being fixed at £50 p.a. until passengers reached one million, £75 p.a. up to 1.5 million and so on in proportion. The Commissioners were to transfer the steamer *Woodside* to the company in lieu of arrears of interest, a Township Bond of £2,000 being given up to the Commissioners and cancelled.

The Agreement was, of course, subject to the Bill becoming an Act, and as the Lords rejected a clause relating to the stopping up of part of Canning Street, the Bill was not read a third time. The Agreement was, therefore, null and void.

Growth at Woodside

For Woodside Ferry the 1850s were years of expansion and consolidation. The increase in traffic demanded new boats the size of which was restricted by the poor landing facilities. *Woodside*, built by Jordan Getty and engined by Fawcett Preston, entered service in 1853 and was the first ferry vessel to have a 'glass saloon' on deck. Like other vessels previously mentioned, she was registered in the name of the ferry manager, W. T. Rudd, having been launched by Mrs Rudd, but was transferred to F. R. Price in November 1853. In January 1857 she fouled the anchor of Coulbourns' steamer *Fairy* and sank in Prince's basin. After being raised, she was sold to Willoughbys for service on Tranmere ferry. In 1855, two new boats intended to be named *Liverpool* and *Empress Eugenie* were ordered from John Laird. The former was commissioned in October 1855, spending some time on the Monks Ferry service, but the second boat was sold to the Admiralty, serving as a

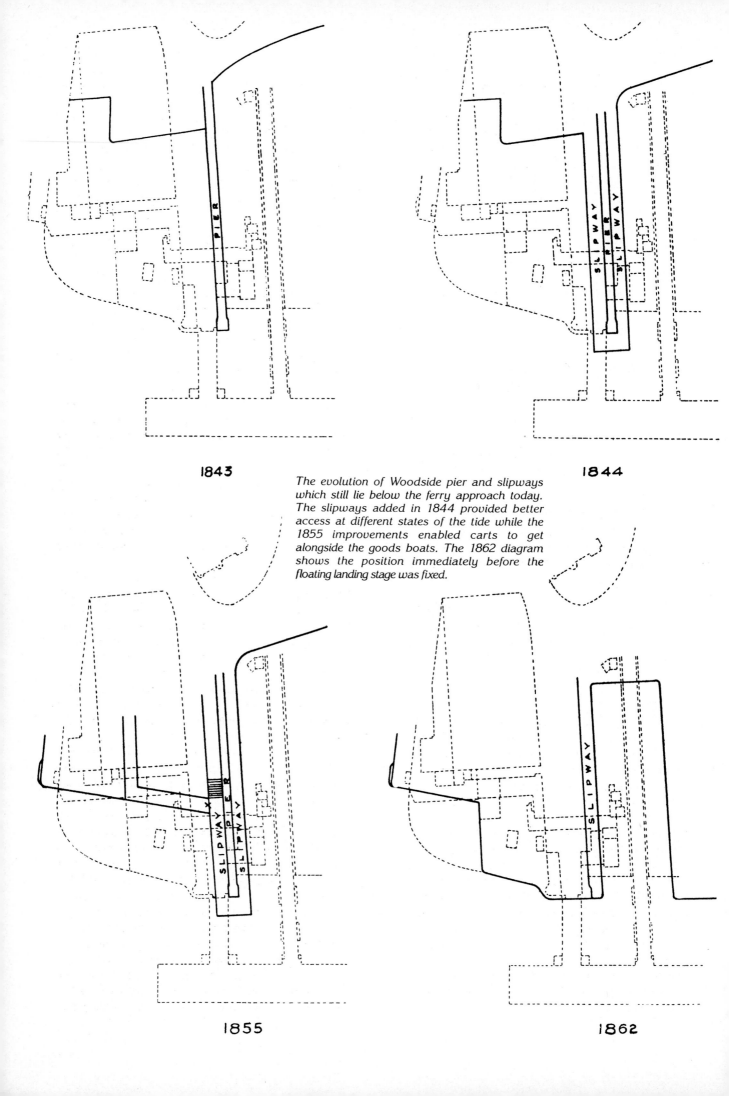

1843

1844

The evolution of Woodside pier and slipways which still lie below the ferry approach today. The slipways added in 1844 provided better access at different states of the tide while the 1855 improvements enabled carts to get alongside the goods boats. The 1862 diagram shows the position immediately before the floating landing stage was fixed.

1855

1862

tank boat under the name *Thais*. *Liverpool* was eventually sold to Samuel Davies of Tranmere in 1882.

With greater regularity, the flow of daily cross river business traffic increased. It became practicable for middle class Liverpool businessmen to forsake the overcrowded disease-ridden city for comfortable villas in the healthy upland districts of Wirral. Omnibus services were running to and from Woodside by 1849, most of them from the fashionable district of Oxton but some on a once daily basis from as far afield as Hoylake and West Kirby. These well-to-do gentlemen, the contractors, comprised the backbone of the regular ferry traffic and were treated with great respect by the Commissioners. They paid their fares in advance, often for a whole year and provided the working capital of the ferries undertaking. New rules issued in October 1855 made it clear that the Ferry Committee was reluctant to put them to the inconvenience of even showing their contract tickets when passing to and from the boats.

'Resolved that in future all contractors' tickets be signed by Mr. Nicholls and before being issued they be countersigned by the attendants at the Contractors' Gate and be delivered to the parties contracting in order that the attendants at the gate may identify the parties and render any further production of the tickets of such contractors unnecessary.

And this Committee will consider such counter-signature of the attendant at the Gate as evidence of their having seen those contractors and of them being able to identify them.'

Whilst the number of contractors was relatively small, the attendants needed to be very alert to prevent any well-dressed interloper from passing through the gate and, at the same time, avoiding incurring the wrath of a genuine contractor by challenging him to produce his ticket. It is clear that contracts were, in fact, card tickets at this time, metal tokens which could be worn on a watch chain being introduced from 1861. There is some evidence of fraud or perhaps forgery as a new design was introduced in March 1855, all existing tickets being called in and exchanged. Rates for 6- or 3-monthly contracts were fixed at £1-1s-0d and 18/- in October 1856; interavailability of Woodside and Monks Ferry tickets was abolished at the same time.

The ferry service was steadily improved during the 1850s, a 10-minute service being run throughout most of the day at five minutes past the hour etc. from November 1855, the late evening half-hourly service being run until 1.00am from 1st October 1857. Following complaints of smoking and spitting, smoking, which had hitherto been permitted only in certain parts of the vessels, was banned altogether, crews being exhorted to enforce the bye-laws strictly. Boats were obviously becoming crowded at peak hours as from about the same time, all large packages or luggage were banned from passenger boats between 7.30 and 10.30am from Woodside and 3.00 and 7.00pm from Liverpool.

A growing population generated more revenue from the rates and the improved finances of the ferry enabled the Commissioners to give serious consideration to the completion of the purchase of the ferry rights. F. R. Price had died on 21st December 1853 without an heir, his only child having died aged eight, in 1821 and his trustees were anxious to proceed with the sale. The Birkenhead Improvement (General Mortgages) Act, 1858 enabled the Commissioners to regain possession of *Wirral* and *Queen* and to raise the necessary money to purchase the ancient rights outright. After many months of negotiation, representatives of the Commissioners went to the trustees' offices in Chester on 31st August 1860 and formally took possession of the ferry property and rights for £103,372-12s-0d. Appendix 4 gives details of the transaction.

The Woodside Landing Stage

Meanwhile there remained the problem of the landing arrangements at Woodside. Many people, especially women and the elderly, were deterred from travelling by ferry because of the hazardous landing conditions. Stone slipways or steps were potentially dangerous in any conditions and the six knot tide and 30ft. tidal range on the Mersey estuary added to the problem. The depth of water at low tide often made landing difficult or impossible and it will be recalled that when Hugh Williams sold his assets to the newly formed Woodside Company he included 'landing boats'. At very low water the ferry boat stood off the slipway or quay and the passengers transferred first to the landing boat in which they were rowed ashore. Passengers were sometimes carried ashore by hefty seamen.

Traffic could not be carried in volume under these conditions and a scheme for erection of a 'landing jetty' to be added to the Woodside ferry pier had been prepared by Rendel in 1846 but rejected by the Commissioners. Whilst some ingenious devices were installed by the Wallasey ferries, it was clear that the answer lay in the floating landing stage, moored by chains and connected to the mainland by bridges pivoted at each end. The installation of the first landing stage at Liverpool Pier Head in 1847 improved conditions there enormously but, to a small local authority like Birkenhead, the cost of any kind of sophisticated landing facility for Woodside was prohibitive.

In the course of the minor improvements to Woodside jetty, its level had been raised to that of the South Reserve wall. In February 1855 it was decided to remove the engines and boiler from *Eliza Price*, the last remaining ex-company vessel, and use the hulk as a floating landing stage. It is not known if this was done but, if so, it was not a success, as *Eliza Price* was ordered to be sold that August. In September, the Surveyor was instructed to investigate the cost of blasting and excavating the rock at the end of the slip to enable boats to come in at all states of the tide, but this was apparently found to be impracticable. In April 1856, *Queen* grounded on the end of the slip but suffered little damage. John Jones, the master, was accused of stupidity or carelessness and reduced to a hand. The provision of another floating

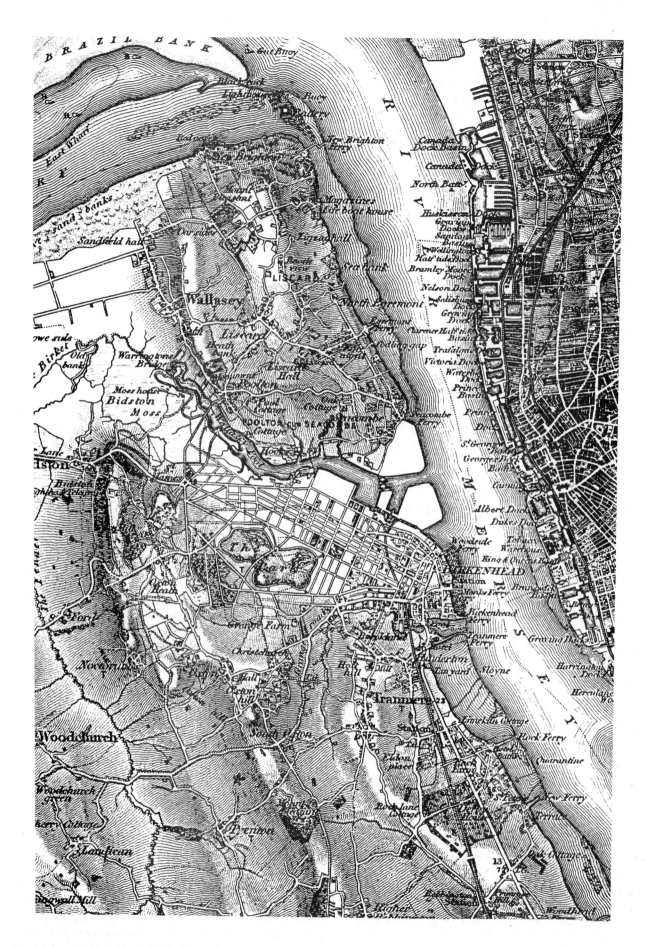

The Mersey estuary about 1860. The map clearly shows the original coastline between Woodside and Seacombe and the two extensive areas of reclaimed land contained behind the massive river walls, known as North Reserve and South Reserve. The Low Water Basin and Vittoria Wharf, also reclaimed, can be clearly discerned.

Oct. 23/1844 Laying Foundation stone of B'head Docks   Woodside 328

Monks 141 t 469   Fare 2

Opening of Docks   Woodside 352

Monks 41 t 393 — .. —

'50 May 20	147		'57 April 10	139		'60 May 28	164
'51 Oct 9	185		June 1	200		June 2	172
'52 May 31	160		" 2	132		March 29	165
'53 may 16	174		" 5	142		may 20	191
" 21	132		" 6	200		" 24	145
'54 may 25	137		'58 May 29	172		" 25	158
June 5	214		Aug 23	128		June 15	174
" 10	156		'59 April 22	157		Aug 19	144
'55 may 28	193		June 13	174		" 31	132
Oct 9	158		14	137		'62 April 18	137
'56 Mar 21	132		" 17	157		June 4	169
May 16	139		" 18	187		" 14	156
" 17	188		Aug 13	141		'63 April 3	176
" 29	195		'60 April 6	157		" 24	186

Year	Good Friday	Whit Sunday	Whit Monday
1857	103	11 1	89	..
2	120	..	84	..
3	94	..	87	..
4	137	..	117	..
5	91	..	193	..
6	132	..	113	..
7	139	..	117	..
8	102	..	112	..
9	157	..	107	..
1860	157	..	93	..
1	165	..	125	..
2	137	..	99	..
3	176	..	116	..
4	227		153	8 9
5	167	51		
6	206	177		
7	186	134		
8	210	148		

Mr McKelvie kept records of days on which there was exceptional traffic. The laying of Birkenhead Docks foundation stone on 23rd October 1844 (which was also the opening day of the railway line to Monks Ferry) and the opening of Morpeth and Egerton Docks (and of Birkenhead Park) on 5th April 1847, obviously attracted large crowds from Liverpool.

stage, (Prince's) at Liverpool in 1857, increased the clamour for better facilities at Woodside.

John Laird and George Harrison, chairman of the Ferry Committee, had made a strong case to Liverpool Corporation in 1856 and preparatory planning was started almost immediately. Statutory powers were granted to the Mersey Docks and Harbour Board (MDHB) within months of its formation in 1858. The Mersey Docks and Harbour (Works) Act 1858 authorised extensive dock works and the erection of a substantial river wall northwards from Woodside to Seacombe with dock entrances, lock gates and bridges. Part of the Woodside Basin was to be enclosed and the shape of the river bank drastically changed. Attached to the river wall at Woodside there was to be a floating landing stage of which 300ft. at the southern end was to be under the control and management and 'to be kept in good and substantial repair by the

Birkenhead Improvement Commissioners'. This portion was to be used exclusively for Woodside ferry without any charge being made by the Dock Board. The remainder of the stage was to be used only by steam vessels plying beyond the port of Liverpool. The works were to facilitate the later installation of floating bridges at Woodside and Prince's landing stages and a rectangular inlet was to be left behind the stage for this purpose. All the works authorised by the Act, including a few in Liverpool, were expected to cost £1.75 million.

The news was greeted with great satisfaction in Birkenhead, and work on the river wall started quite soon. By this time the quay and slipways were becoming dangerously overcrowded at certain times. In November 1859 the manager reported upon the great danger arising from the crush of passengers on both the slip and the boats during foggy weather and ferry staff were instructed to

*The first floating landing stage for Woodside ferry was built on the West Float and launched like a ship in 1861. This engraving first appeared in **Illustrated London News** on 12th October 1861.*

allow only one boat load of passengers on the slip at any one time.

Although details have escaped the record, the Woodside ferry service must have been seriously disrupted during the building of the river wall and it is on record that £143 was spent on 'fitting up temporary landing slips, waiting room, etc.' in 1861-62; these were probably in Woodside Basin. There is also mention of a temporary bridge secured to the end of the stone jetty, described at the time as 'very dangerous'.

The Woodside floating stage was built in two parts by Liverpool shipbuilders, Thomas Vernon and Sons, launched like a ship and towed into position. The first, or northern half, for the use of the MDHB, was placed in position in October 1861 and the second half, exclusive to the ferries, was secured to the wall with some difficulty on 5th December 1861. The stage was moored by chains originally made for the *Great Eastern*, then the world's largest ship, and was linked to the mainland by two double bridges. The northern one was owned by the Dock Board whilst the southern bridge, the property of the

Commissioners and used solely for ferry traffic, was brought into use on 10th February 1862. This bridge was originally open to the elements and it was covered by an arched glazed roof in 1863 at a cost of £915. The Commissioners' portion of the stage was supported by twenty floating pontoons, all 10ft. wide and 5ft. 6in. in depth, but of varying lengths as shown in the diagram on page 104.

The north-south line of the new river wall was almost level with the outer end of the stone pier, which disappeared under the material which was tipped behind the wall to create new land. All that remained in view was the lighthouse, which had stood on the end of the pier and which now found itself on a river wall.

Of no less importance to passengers was the provision of safe gangways to pass between vessel and stage. A permanent gangway was fitted to the new stage at Woodside early in 1862 and, in July of that year, the MDHB granted permission for a similar one to be fitted at Liverpool. These were the forerunners of the counter-weighted gangways with a swivelling capability which

were ultimately used by all municipal ferries on the Mersey. The *Birkenhead and Cheshire Advertiser* of 6th June 1863 made reference to a Mr Harkness, inventor of the passenger gangway and remarked that 'next to the landing stage, nothing had contributed more to the success of the ferries'.

3 WOODSIDE 1860-1899

1860-64 were momentous years in the history of the Birkenhead ferries and, indeed, of the town itself. The completion of the negotiations for the acquisition of the Woodside ferry rights on 31st August 1860 had been preceded on the previous day by the opening of the first purpose-built street tramway in Great Britain, between Woodside ferry approach and Birkenhead Park. The line originally terminated outside the Woodside Hotel and then followed Shore Road, Argyle Street and Conway Street but Shore Road was already earmarked as part of the Dock Estate and, in 1861, when the route was extended to Palm Grove, Oxton, the track was relaid along Bridge Street. The enterprise was led by an American, George Francis Train, the representative of his family's shipping line in Liverpool who had become well-known to William Laird and other public figures. The full story is told in *The Tramways of Birkenhead and Wallasey* (Maund & Jenkins) Light Rail Transit Association 1987.

A costing of the materials used in the construction of the first floating landing stage at Woodside in 1861-62. The cost was borne by the Mersey Docks and Harbour Board

The Birkenhead Street Railway Co, who ran the line until 1877, encountered great opposition, but the service endured; it provided a reliable feeder between the ferry and the better class residential districts, vastly superior to the service given by the cramped, uncomfortable omnibuses. Train, with characteristic foresight, wanted through ferry and tram tickets from the outset, but the Commissioners would have nothing to do with the idea. It took nearly half a century to achieve that goal.

Land reclamation to the south of the jetty enabled the Commissioners to lay out a spacious square, and work on the ferry terminal area was spread over three years, 1861-64, the final stage being the erection of a drinking fountain and ornamental lighting pillars. The booking hall, leading directly to the south bridge, was built in 1864 by Holme and Nichol and remained virtually unaltered for 120 years. The tramway was extended to the ferry entrance; the rails, which ended in two sidings, were the property of the Ferries Committee and this short section of about 150yds was the first length of municipally owned tramway in Britain. Rent of £100 per annum was demanded from the company but this was subsequently reduced.

	Including Interest	Exclusive of Interest
1850 - 51	84 3/4	64
51 - 52	81	58 1/4
52 - 53	81 1/4	60 1/2
53 - 54	85	68
54 - 55	85 1/2	70
55 - 56	97 1/4	81 1/2
56 - 57	70 1/4	56
57 - 58	71 3/8	57
58 - 59	78 3/4	63 3/4
59 - 60	77 3/8	63
60 - 61	70 1/4	61
61 - 62	68	54
62 - 63	61	48 1/2
63 - 64		
64		

Contractors.

Passed through the gate & counted
1862 Oct. 27. To Liverpool 2051
" " " From —"— 2138
" " 28 To —"— 2107
" " " From —"— 2286
Half of them go between 8.15 & 10.15 A.
— ditto —return —"— 4.30 & 6.30 P.

1 July 1844
Contracts reduced from 50/ to 25/-

Contract check № 1832 for 1863 was
transferred from one to another brother in June

Contractors Luggage. not exceeding
112 lbs free — minute 30 Dec.1857.
See 6 pages further on
for Continuation of Contracts

By speeding up passenger handling and encouraging patronage, the new landing stage reduced the percentage of revenue absorbed by operating expenditure, as shown by Mr McKelvie's notes.

A census was taken on 27th and 28th October 1862 to determine the travel habits of contractors. Mr McKelvie added a few more observations.

The Last Days of Monks Ferry

The final seal on the prosperity of the ferries was the resolution of the Monks Ferry question which had drained the undertaking financially for almost two decades. Early in 1859, the Commissioners had made further overtures to the railway company, members of the Parliamentary Committee being deputed to meet the railway board of directors. They proposed the same terms as in 1857 except that, the new river wall having been completed, they included reclaimed land in front of the coal wharf in the deal. However, at a meeting on 11th February 1859, the railway company peremptorily declined to take the ferry back and proposed new conditions. The company would cancel the Commissioners' bond for £2,000 and the Monks Ferry debt, fixed at £20,000, would be rescheduled to be payable at the end of fifteen years, bearing interest from the date of agreement at 3% for five years, 4% for the next five years and 5% for the third period. The Commissioners would have the right to pay the debt off at any time, in which case the rate of interest would be 4%.

The Commissioners, with some reluctance, provisionally accepted this arrangement, but events were overtaken by the London and North Western and Great Western Railways agreeing to purchase the Chester-Birkenhead line jointly. This ended a decade of wrangling between the two companies and the wily Commissioners, sensing that railway rivalry might be turned to good use, had a clause inserted in the Bill terminating the ferry agreement upon amalgamation and forcing the companies to negotiate rather than risk all-out opposition from what was now a forceful local authority. The Commissioners not only relieved themselves from working Monks Ferry but had their debt of £20,000 for its purchase cancelled.

The railway companies, for a nominal sum of £1 per year, were given the right to convey railway traffic of every description across the river between Liverpool and Monks Ferry. It was agreed that, in the event of Monks Ferry proving inadequate, alternative facilities would be made available at the South Reserve, the reclaimed land to the north of Woodside.

The date of transfer of Monks Ferry back to the railways was fixed as 1st January 1862 and this was duly done. However the railways, having no boats, were obliged to ask the Birkenhead Commissioners to hire boats to them and this was agreed, at £100 per week, on the understanding that the arrangement was to be temporary. This proved to be a lucrative arrangement for the Commissioners as, during the first full year of railway ownership (1862-63), receipts from hire of boats at Monks Ferry totalled £5,859 compared with revenue of £3,272 in 1860-61. The railway companies made no effort to order boats and, in May 1864, the Commissioners gave three months' notice of the withdrawal of their steamers. This resulted in a new agreement to continue the service for £112 per week, which was increased to £120 from 1st July 1867, following the service of yet another notice to terminate. However, this time the Commissioners really meant business, as the steamers *Nun* and *Wirral*, used on the Woodside service, were reaching the end of their useful lives and the two Monks Ferry boats were needed to replace them. Six months' notice was therefore given to the LNW/GW Joint Railways on 1st October 1867. The railways had insufficient statutory powers and clauses were inserted in the LNWR (Additional Powers) Act 1868, granting powers to 'buy, hire, use and maintain steam or other vessels'. A scale of maximum charges was laid down and the 1861 powers were broadened to facilitate sailing to and from points other than Monks Ferry.

Faced with the final ultimatum from the Birkenhead Commissioners, the LNW Railway Co. placed an order with Bowdler and Chaffer's Seacombe yard for three new steamers, *Thames*, *Mersey* and *Severn* of which two were launched on 9th April 1868. They were 105ft. long, 20ft. in beam and drew 8ft. 6in. with a gross tonnage of 125; their funnels were black with a yellow band and they were somewhat similar to the Woodside boat *Cheshire*, being double bowed and steerable from either end. The precise date when Birkenhead municipal steamers ceased operating Monks Ferry has not been recorded but all available evidence points to it having happened on or about 1st June 1868. *Nun* and *Wirral* were sold on 12th June. The three railway steamers continued to ply the station until Monks Ferry was closed to passenger traffic on 31st March 1878 when the new Woodside railway station was opened. They were then transferred to railway service elsewhere. *Mersey* and *Severn* remained with the LNWR for service between Warrenpoint and Greenore on Carlingford Lough in Northern Ireland whilst *Thames* was sold by the GWR in 1882 to the London, Tilbury and Southend Railway for the Tilbury-Gravesend service.

The Monks Ferry installations were adapted for use as a coal depot.

There is little doubt that, after it became clear that the Admiralty would not agree to a long pier, the Joint Railways had regarded Monks Ferry as a temporary expedient. Although trains could proceed virtually to the water's edge, the primitive slipway, without a pier or floating landing stage, contrasted unfavourably with the modern facilities at Woodside, a mere 400 yards to the north. The running powers on to the dock estate obtained by the erstwhile Shrewsbury and Chester Railway in 1851 had specified 'goods, cattle, minerals and general traffic **other** than passengers' and the need to cross a dock bridge

to reach the South Reserve made it unlikely that its use by passenger trains was seriously considered then. The original Low Water Basin scheme provided for a slipway in its south-eastern wall where railway steamers could have tied up, and an Act of 1856 had authorised the installation of a landing stage, 200ft. long and 25ft. wide, recessed into the wall of the south side of the Great Low Water Basin. Rendel himself gave evidence to the Select Committee and specifically mentioned the intention to handle railway and ferry traffic there.

In 1862, when the Commissioners succeeded in returning Monks Ferry to the railway, some satisfaction was expressed that any expansion of ferry facilities would take place at the South Reserve at no expense to the Town. However following the formal opening of the Great Float dock system from 1860 and the completion of the Low Water Basin in 1863, the latter silted up, and it was decided to convert it to a wet dock with access only at its western end. Entry was to be confined to the Morpeth and Alfred Dock channels.

The Cattle Stage

In April 1865, Wallasey Local Board informed the Dock Board that they wanted to run their boats to the Low Water Basin landing stage during bad weather and when Seacombe slip was under repair. Birkenhead objected strongly, claiming that it would be tantamount to an infringement of their ferry rights, but it seems likely that some ferry boats took refuge in the Basin during storms. On 13th March 1866, the LNW and GW Railways and the MDHB signed an Agreement whereby part of the Low Water Basin landing stage would be placed in the river outside the South Reserve just north of the Morpeth Channel. The draft for this Agreement provided for the erection of a shelter at Liverpool for the use of railway passengers, so passenger traffic was obviously contemplated. The Author believes that any enthusiasm for this course of action was confined to the Great Western as, following the bridging of the Mersey at Runcorn in 1869, the LNW opened a short line from Frodsham Junction to Halton Junction on 1st May 1873 and diverted its North Wales and Chester-Liverpool traffic direct to Lime Street.

Morpeth Dock goods station, which had been developed in stages between 1861 and 1869, was adjacent to the Low Water Basin landing stage. The railways agreed to pay £5,500 to the MDHB ie one moiety of the estimated cost of removal and construction of the stage. The Agreement was written into the Mersey Docks (Liverpool River Approaches) Act 1871 and, in the same Parliamentary session, the Great Western Railway (Additional Facilities) Act authorised extension of the railway from Grange Lane to Woodside, where a new passenger station was to be built on the south side of the ferry approach.

The MDHB secured the new stage to the South Reserve wall on 15th May 1876; it was 352ft. long and 72ft. wide and built on the West Float at Canada Works. The three bridges came from the Low Water Basin stage and, as they were too short to achieve the depth of water needed at low tide, three short piers were built out from the river wall; these were still in position in 1988.

It was officially named (quite erroneously) the Wallasey Landing Stage but was usually known as the cattle stage. The full extent of its use by the Great Western is not known but, in 1890, as part of the extension of Morpeth Dock goods station, the GW asked the MDHB to build a branch dock inside the depot; their Liverpool depot had been established at Manchester Dock, just south of the Pier Head, and they wanted to send goods across the river by lighter. The extent of the Manchester Dock premises was somewhat curtailed in 1914, after which goods were mainly carted to Birkenhead by the goods ferry from four receiving depots in Liverpool, though the branch dock saw limited use until it was filled in during the reconstruction of the goods station in 1928-29.

Financial Prosperity

The conversion of the Wallasey Pool into the Birkenhead Docks during the 1860s attracted many new industries to dockside sites and expansion of the port would have been faster but for the reduction of trade during the American Civil War. With the burden of Monks Ferry removed and modern facilities installed at Woodside, the ferry had never been so prosperous.

In May 1862, £5,000 of surplus ferry revenue was voted to be handed over to the Finance Committee towards paying interest on the bonded debt of the township. There had been some contributions towards the town's funds during the 1850s but henceforth the ferries made regular profits. The salary of the ferry manager, Mr. McKelvie, was increased from £350 to £400 and he was awarded a £50 gratuity for efficient service.

One sequel was a demand for boats to match the style and appointments of the ferry terminal. The rise in passenger traffic had created a need for larger, more powerful boats, as a 10-minute service at Woodside needed four boats. Early in 1862, George Harrison, Chairman of the Ferries Committee, drew up a report with suggested specifications for future vessels, which is summarised below:-

Passenger Boat
Length 150-160ft. Beam 27ft.
Draught with 50 tons on board—no more than 7ft.
Power—2 engines, not more than 100 hp each wheel
Construction—iron. Steerable from both ends
Watertight bulkheads. Deck level with new landing stage at Woodside. (6ft. above water level)
Separate accommodation for ladies and children if practicable.

Luggage Boats
Length 150-160ft. Beam 30-35ft.
Draught with 100 tons on board—8ft.
Power—120-180 hp
Construction—iron. Steerable from both ends.

The report described the below-deck cabins on the existing boats as 'most miserable places and no person will enter them unless obliged to do so'. The suggested cabin was 100ft. by 16ft. and rounded at each end with a 2ft. roof overhang. This design owed something to American practice and was turned into reality by *Cheshire*, completed in July 1863. This was the precursor in design of most ferry steamers placed in service on the Mersey during the next 100 years. It was not until 1879 however, that a purpose-built luggage boat was commissioned.

Cheshire, built at Liverpool by H. M. Laurence and Co, had two funnels athwartships. She cost £9,600, had a gross tonnage of 421 and a passenger certificate for 1,612 persons; she was quite the largest ferry steamer to have entered service on the Mersey, her main dimensions being 150ft. x 30ft. (main) x 12ft. with a breadth across the paddle boxes of 50ft. 3in. Her working draught was 6ft. Two further boats of similar dimensions but slightly less gross tonnage were ordered from C. J. Mare and Co. Northfleet, entering service in 1865 as *Lancashire* and *Woodside*, the 1853 boat of the latter name being sold. Their passenger capacity was 1,500.

Inevitably, there were demands for this prosperity to be passed on to the users. Weekly and monthly contracts were frequently demanded as it was held, correctly, that the poor man could never accumulate the sum required to buy an annual contract ticket. As the *Advertiser* commented in 1865, a wealthy man paid £2-5-0d for himself and two other members of his family while a poor man paid £2-12-0d in pennies just for himself. Willoughbys, who ran Tranmere ferry, sold weekly and monthly tickets at 9d and 2/6d respectively. However the new boats were coal eaters, *Cheshire* consuming 11 cwt per hour, and working expenses rose alarmingly while traffic was increasing at a slower rate. A contemporary exercise revealed that *Prince* and *Lord Morpeth* consumed on average 26-27 tons per week while *Cheshire* used 57 tons to do the same work.

In the late summer of that year, the Commissioners debated the possibility of reducing the 10-minute service to a frequency of 15 minutes but this was rejected out of hand. It was then proposed to run the Woodside service with one large and two small boats from 8.00am to 8.00pm and two small boats during the night. A small boat might be replaced by a goods boat on occasions. The existing arrangement was to run two large boats and one small boat and the proposal provoked the submission of a 'memorial' by influential inhabitants, a reference back by the General Board and a return to the *status quo*. However, to cover additional expenditure, it was suggested that the annual contracts be increased from £1-5-0d to £1-15-0d with half-yearly and quarterly tickets at £1-5-0d and 17/6d. This was eventually toned down to

Coal Contract

Year	Contractor	Price per Ton	Yearly consumption in tons
1864 & 65	R Evans Co	9/6	10714
1865 & 66	R Evans & Co	9/6	12,850
1866 & 67	do	10/	14,195
1867 & 68	do	10/-	14,294
1868 & 69	do	10/-7½	11,982
1869 & 70	do	8/9	11,501 (also 243 Tons Slack for Rotary Furnace)
1870-71	do	8/9 & 9/	11,093
1871-72	do		11

Certificate of work done & cash received See Nov 13, 1892

Coal Contract

Year	Contractor	Price per Ton	Yearly Consumption in Tons
1856-7	Caldwell & Co	8/6	
1857.8	do	8/7	8370
1858.9	do	8/3	8415
1859.60	do	8/9	8074
1860.1	do	9/9	8350
1861.2	do	9/3	8005
1862.3	do	8/9	8331
1863.4	do	8/9	10,008
Till Oct 64 then	do	8/9	
	R. R. Evans	9/6	

Memo: 5 men are employed in discharging from the Flat on to the stage where our 2 men receive it & load the barrows — The 5 men are paid 6½d per Ton — of which Neilson pays 4½d and the Flatmen 2d., When the coal is put on the bank 7 men are employed & are each paid 1d a ton —

Coal was a substantial item in the ferries budget. The price of coal was lower in 1870 than in 1864 and these figures show how consumption increased dramatically when the new large boats were first placed in service. The arrangements for putting the coal ashore are of interest. The identity of Neilson has not been discovered but putting coal on the bank involved carrying bags up the slippery steps in the river wall south of Woodside landing stage.

£1-10-0d per annum. In the case of a man who went home for lunch daily, this worked out at three crossings for 1d — and still they grumbled. The financial results for the year ending April 1868 enabled £8,000 to be paid into the rate fund whilst 1869 provided £1,000 for relief of rates and enough to build up a new boat fund to £5,000.

In 1868-69, nearly six million people paid 1d, 29,000 night travellers paid 6d, over 1.5 million crossings were made on contracts and 10,000 crossed on passes of various kinds. The boats crossed the river 85,000 times. Increased contract rates brought in less than expected but the Ferries undertaking continued to prosper to the extent that a joint meeting of the Ferry and Finance Committees on 21st October 1870 agreed to reduced contract rates of £1-1-0d for a year, 15/- for six months and 10/- for three months, the rates for additional members of the same family being 10/-, 7/6d and 5/- respectively; these came into effect on 1st January 1871 and 628 additional annual contracts were purchased that year. By this time the contractors represented about 25% of the traffic but only 10% of the passenger revenue.

Until the old small boats were phased out, the contrast between the amenities of the old and the new caused many complaints. It was the custom to keep the new boats on the same timings and contractors, being creatures of habit, either got a new boat every time or never. At one time it was suggested that the allocation be reviewed to give everyone the chance of a sail in a new boat. The new boats were very clumsy to handle and were involved in numerous collisions with other vessels and each other.

The three great events of the 1870s were the Liverpool Landing Stage fire of 1874, Incorporation of the Borough of Birkenhead in 1877 and the extension of the railway to Woodside in 1878. To this list can be added the commissioning of the first purpose-built luggage boat in 1879 (see chapter 7).

The opening of the new George's Landing Stage on 27th July 1874 was greeted with great satisfaction by the ferry operators, all of whom had been experiencing congestion problems at the old stage which had been designed for the old, smaller vessels. Furthermore the completion, after many delays, of the Liverpool floating roadway promised much improved handling of vehicular traffic particularly for Birkenhead which already had its floating roadway. There was, therefore, great despondancy when, on the afternoon following its opening to the public, the stage was destroyed by fire. The Ferry Committee met immediately and was advised that on no account must the

Fog was both disruptive and dangerous for the ferries and, in a real pea-souper, it was quite common for the three-quarter mile passage to take 45 minutes or an hour. November 1858 appears to have been a dreadful month, with 102 hours of fog, though the total for the years 1858 and 1859 was little different.

Number of hours of Fog in the following months –

	1858	1859	1860	1861	1862	1863.	1864	1865	1866
January	–	16	14	34½	28	24¼	55¾	24¼	
February	18	–	–	¾	5½	5½	5	8	
March	8	–	7	4	–	4½	7	7	
April	–	–	–	5¾	3	–	23¾	9½	
September	–	–	1	9½	27	–	—	—	
October	36	31½	23½	12¼	8½	24½	—		
November	102	48½	15	-	53	–	6½		
December	14	78	39½	28¼	—	½	—		
	178	174	100	95	125	59¼	97½		

large steamers be grounded whilst using temporary berths. After a hurried meeting with the Dock Board, it was arranged that the Woodside steamers would ply to the stairs at George's Pier opposite the Baths, two barges being placed alongside to form a landing stage. A return to the hazardous practice of landing passengers on to slippery steps, only a distant memory for many regular travellers, was a severe setback and no doubt, many ladies were deterred from crossing the river during the period of exactly one year that the stage was out of action.

Meanwhile Woodside was gaining in importance as a terminal. A tramway connecting the ferry with their Docks Station was opened by the Hoylake Railway on 6th September 1873. The Commissioners laid two sidings on the north side of the ferry approach for which rent of £200 per annum was charged. The Hoylake Railway's tramway, whilst laid for the purpose of feeding the railway, also provided local transport along the Line of Docks. The Wirral Tramway Co Ltd obtained powers to lay a line from New Ferry to Woodside and this was opened on 28th March 1877 as far as Chester Street-Ivy Street corner, completion through to Woodside being prevented by the closure of Chester Street during the construction of the new railway tunnel. A line on to the ferry approach, again the property of the Commissioners, was opened on 19th January 1878, the original rent of £100 being subsequently reduced to £50. At this stage, none of the three separate tramway companies' tracks was physically connected at Woodside.

Birkenhead obtained its Charter of Incorporation as a borough in 1877 and the first Town Council was elected at the end of that year. However the Improvement Commissioners remained in existence until the Privy Council approved the transfer of their powers to the new Town Council. The Commissioners' Ferry Committee last met on 29th October 1879, the first meeting of the Corporation Ferry Committee being held on 5th November 1879. Nine boats were registered in the name of the Mayor, Aldermen and Burgesses—*Woodside*, *Liverpool*, *Lancashire*, *Cheshire*, *Prince*, *Queen*, *Oxton*, *Birkenhead* and *Claughton*, the latter two being further vessels of similar type to their three predecessors, built in 1872 and 1876 respectively. *Prince* and *Queen* were sold in 1881.

The Railway Reaches Woodside

The Joint Railways' decision to abandon the concept of a separate railway ferry was born of two factors. The first was their experience since 1868 of the cost and complexity of running a ferry and the second was the realisation that, with the advent of large steamers and the achievement of the standard of regularity and reliability being attained by Woodside, there was no need for a railway ferry. Large steamers with certificates for 1,500 passengers running every ten minutes could easily absorb a trainload of passengers without difficulty Accordingly powers for a new branch, mainly in tunnel, between Grange Lane and Woodside, were included along with several other items in the Great Western Railway (Additional Powers) Act 1871.

The station was to be an impressive structure with seven tracks, entirely covered by an arched glazed roof. The original concept was for the main entrance to face the river, as covered communication with the ferry was planned. The station was built like that and the booking office was sited accordingly but, despite several attempts, the covered connection was never built because, to avoid demolishing the ferries yard, the station site was moved a few yards inland. The 'main' entrance was never opened, access always being by the side entrance giving access to the ferry approach.

Rebates for the Railways

Before committing themselves to the Woodside scheme, the Joint Railways had made an Agreement with the Birkenhead Commissioners guaranteeing the future provision of a service at least as efficient as that provided at the date of the Agreement, especially between midnight and 5.00am. This Agreement, enshrined in the 1871 Act, constituted the only statutory duty to maintain a day and night service. The 1881 Act, which was passed to give general powers to the new Corporation, stipulated 'reasonable hours' which might have been construed as not requiring an all night service. As the railways were handing over to the Commissioners a considerable volume of traffic which could be virtually absorbed without additional cost, they not unreasonably felt that they were entitled to special terms and it was agreed that the Commissioners would pay the joint companies 33⅓% of the tolls paid by railway passengers.

As is so often the case, an apparently straightforward Agreement proved difficult to execute. During their tenure of Monks Ferry the railways had introduced contracts and through bookings to and from Liverpool landing stage and they were entitled to continue to do so in terms of the 1871 Agreement. Holders of through tickets were easy to identify, as there was a positive record of each transaction. However, there were many passengers who, for one reason or another, did not book through tickets, usually due to ignorance of the existence of a through facility. This applied particularly to passengers from Liverpool who paid their ferry fares and then booked a railway ticket at Birkenhead. The railway companies were entitled to one third of their ferry fare also. The North Staffordshire Railway and some other minor lines declined to issue through tickets to Liverpool via Birkenhead arguing that the route to Liverpool lay through Runcorn.

Talks started several months before Woodside station opened. The railways suggested that passengers carried by the railway boats should be used as a basis, but the Commissioners rejected this, proposing as an alternative the use of the Railway Clearing House returns of through bookings. This would have ignored the casuals and the railways countered with a suggestion that a fixed sum be paid in commutation of the 33⅓% payable. The Commissioners did not favour this but nevertheless agreed to pay £750 for the period 1st July 1878 to 30th June 1879 as an interim measure. After 31st March 1978 when Woodside station opened and Monks Ferry closed, the booking offices formerly placed upon the Monks Ferry boats were maintained, manned by railway staff, on the Woodside boats until 1st March 1879. It is not known for certain that the railway booking office on George's Landing Stage was opened on this date. Talks between ferry manager and railway officials continued and various complicated formulae were proposed. The railways still favoured commutation but indicated that they would expect £850 for the next twelve months as they had experienced an increase of 39,455 passengers (Liverpool and Birkenhead) since the opening of Woodside station. The basic formula was to ascertain the traffic in one

direction, double it and add 10% for the unidentifiable passengers. A special check was carried out in October 1879 and the results of this plus a 5% increase (not 10%) were eventually agreed by the Council on 3rd March 1880, almost two years after the opening of the railway extension. The logic was as follows:-

Total traffic by tickets actually collected	20,737	
Of these, passengers going to Liverpool totalled	13,830	
Difference	6,907	

As it is scarcely reasonable to suppose that 13,830 went into Liverpool and fewer than 7,000 came out, the proposal is to take 13,830 x 2

=	27,660
Add 5%	1,383
No. on which 33⅓% will be allowed	29,043

Other provisions were for the payment of £125 per annum for Excess Luggage and Parcels and £50 for fish and milk for the first three years, increased in total to £200 for the second three years. The calculation of rebates for railway passengers created an enormous amount of clerical work over the years. The first commutation agreements covering railway season ticket holders were made in 1895 and 1897. In 1915 the excess luggage and milk charge was increased to £750 per annum rising by £25 per year to £800 to cover the full use of the ferry for passenger train luggage and parcel traffic of all descriptions whether conveyed by passenger or goods ferry boats. The railway companies indicated their intention to run a parcels cart between Woodside and their Liverpool office in James Street, using the goods boat, special freight passes being issued by the ferries for this purpose.

By 1918, the availability of through railway tickets to and from Liverpool landing stage was sufficiently well-known to correct substantially the imbalance of 'to Liverpool' and 'from Liverpool' tickets and from 1st February 1919, it was agreed that the railways would receive 33⅓% rebate on the basis of tickets collected plus 5% to represent 'short-booked' traffic. At the same time a commutation of £30 per year was agreed for short-booked season tickets.

The 'Tunnel Railway'

A railway tunnel beneath the Mersey had been the object of many proposals during the nineteenth century. Powers for the line that was actually built were granted in 1871 but work did not commence until December 1879. As was to be expected, the Birkenhead Commissioners spared no effort to protect the ferry undertaking and, when it became clear that the railway would be authorised, they were successful in having a clause inserted in the Bill awarding them £20,000 compensation for loss of revenue, to be paid

The clumsy lines of the paddle steamer Claughton, with funnels athwartships, were well captured in this Illustrated London News engraving of an event during Queen Victoria's visit to Liverpool on 11th-13th May 1886. The old fog bell tower and device for hoisting cones during gales is well reproduced in this picture.

An emotive drawing by A. E. Emslie depicts a cross-section of travellers between Liverpool and Birkenhead in 1886. The ferries were always classless, though every Birkenhead steamer had a ladies' saloon.

by the Mersey Railway Company when the line opened. During the six years that the railway was under construction, the new Corporation radically improved the goods service (see Chapter 7), put its legal house in order by obtaining a wide range of statutory powers under the Birkenhead Corporation Act 1881 and upgraded several passenger steamers technically as described in chapter 11.

The first section of the Mersey Railway was opened between Green Lane and Liverpool (James Street) on 1st February 1886; there were intermediate stations at Birkenhead Central and Hamilton Square. A 10-minute service of steam-hauled trains was provided and there was considerable curiosity riding at first, 36,000 passengers being carried on the first day. On Easter Monday 1886, 50,000 passengers used the railway. The trains had the advantage, particularly in winter, of avoiding exposure to inclement weather and, being away from the river front, the stations were nearer to the business districts. Passenger traffic at Woodside had declined year by year as the mid-1880s were slump years. A record total of 12.04 million passengers had been carried in 1883-84 and this fell to 11.65 million in 1884-85 and 10.41 million in 1885-86, in which year the railway competed with the ferries for two months. In 1886-87, with a full year of railway competition, the passenger figures fell to 6.23 million and continued to decline until they hit a low point of 5.26

million in 1889-90, less than 44% of the peak figure of six years earlier.

Being capital intensive, it was difficult to effect economies on the ferry without making the service less attractive and a very worried Ferry Committee devoted much time to investigating possible solutions. The competitive situation was fluid as there were several developments during the ensuing five years. A new branch line from Hamilton Square to Birkenhead Park opened simultaneously with extensions of the lines of the Wirral Railway on 2nd January 1888, extending the railway's potential catchment area very considerably. The extension of the line from Green Lane to Rock Ferry, where a station was shared with the Joint Railways, on 16th June 1891, diverted less traffic from the ferry than might have been expected, as a cross-platform change and an immediate onward rail connection at Rock Ferry could potentially deliver the passenger at James Street before the alternative boat had left Woodside. The advantages at the Liverpool end were enhanced when the railway was continued on to Central Low Level station on 11th January 1892. Receipts from railway passengers using Woodside decreased from £979 in 1890-91 to £799 in 1892-93, the first full year of the Rock Ferry extension, a decrease of 18%. The railways made no attempt to encourage use of the underground railway at the expense of the ferry and a

N.º of

Hours the Boats are Under Steam
Woodside Ferry

1 Passenger Boat 24 hours daily = 8760 per year.
1 — " — " 21 — " — " — = 7665 — " —
1 — " — " 13 — " — " — = 4745 — " —
1 Luggage — " 11 — " — " — = 4.015 — " —
                                        25.185

Monks Ferry

1 Boat 15 Hours daily = 5475
1 — " — 15 — " Daily 313 days 4695   10.170
   Total hours per year.   35.355

An 1860s assessment of the number of hours the boats were under steam taken from Mr McKelvie's note book.

full range of through tickets was made available by both modes. The comparatively small loss of railway passengers to the ferry was influenced by two factors—railway traffic was increasing year by year and the Mersey was essentially a local traffic railway as was proved by the withdrawal of the privately owned Rock Ferry boats soon after its opening as described in Chapter 5.

The ferry still had certain advantages. Although the railway used condensing locomotives and installed expensive machinery to keep the tunnel free from smoke and steam, the equipment was imperfect and the atmosphere in the stations and trains became more and more polluted as each day progressed. The powerful locomotives, operating in confined tunnels, made a great deal of noise and this, combined with the darkness relieved only by flickering gas lights, resulted in an oppressive, even frightening atmosphere which contrasted strongly with the rhythmic splash of the paddle wheels and the comforting subdued beat of the steamers' engines. Whilst the speed of the railway's connections brought new passengers, many of the local passengers on whom the line depended, began to drift back to Woodside ferry on which passengers increased year by year until they reached 7.98 million by 1897-98.

Proposed Combined Service

A five-point plan, put forward by the full Council in April 1886, was rejected after detailed examination by a sub-committee. Whilst the passenger and goods ferries had always been considered as completely separate, the plan suggested a measure of integration as had been proposed by G. F. Lyster, the MDHB Engineer, in 1866 and as was practised by the majority of British ferries across major estuaries. It was the volume of traffic, the need for high frequency (to some extent the result of competition from

the privately owned ferries) and the excessive loading and unloading times of the goods vehicles, until the floating roadways were installed, which led to separation of the traffic on the Mersey. The plan now envisaged doubling the goods service from every half hour to every fifteen minutes, reducing the passenger service from every ten to every fifteen minutes and allowing passengers to use the goods boats. This arrangement would have used the same number of boats but only two would have been slow, coal-eating paddlers instead of three.

There were proposals to cancel the night service and run only passenger boats on Sundays. All these suggestions were found to be impracticable or undesirable for one reason or another but the debate continued and the idea of combining the two services had taken root. On 14th February 1887 the Committee took note that the ferry had 'run at a pecuniary loss' during the previous three months and, that same month, a formal proposal was made to run one class of boat for both goods and passengers, subject to suitable berthage being arranged at Liverpool. The three new goods boats would be converted at a cost of £500-£600 each and a new combined boat ordered. No plans of the intended conversion have been traced but one can envisage the addition of an upper deck with direct high level gangway access. A sub-committee, concerned mainly with studying the problems of handled goods,

These notes explain how the contractors' gate and turnstiles at Woodside were manned. It is undated but probably the arrangements were little altered during the nineteenth century.

Mens Time

Contract Gate. 5 AM to 12.15 Midnight—
Relieve at 9 AM & 2 & 7 P.M.
Man leaving at 7 P.M. takes first morning duty.
Change every Sunday evening
Sunday. 2 P.M. to 12 15 Midnight—

At Stiles— 7 Collectors are employed—
Down Stiles
1 Man 5 AM to 2 P.M   9 Hours
1 — " — 2 — " to 12 — "   10 — "
The man on morning duty comes down for an hour between 5 & 6 P.M.
Up Stiles
2 Men 5 AM to 2 P.M   9 Hours
2 — " 2 P.M. to Midnight   10 — "
Night Stiles— Up & down are worked by one Man
All change Weekly— each is one week on night duty every Six weeks.

Woodside landing stage from the river about 1880 with 1860s twin-funnel steamer moored.

suggested a 20-minute goods service and a 20-minute passenger boat service, all carrying passengers and pointing out that it was the time taken in handling loose packages which prevented a 15-minute goods service being run. *Cheshire*, converted back to passenger service, was laid up and eventually sold, a new paddle steamer of the same name being ordered from Canada Works in 1888.

Various changes were made to the passenger fares. Early in the decade there had again been agitation for monthly contracts. There were already books of 25 'pass tickets',

available before 8.00am, sold for 2/-. In 1882, the three monthly contract was reduced from 10/- to 7/6d with a half-price contract for schoolchildren, but the Corporation dodged the monthly issue by saying that they had no Parliamentary powers. This was an excuse, as the 1881 Act laid down only maximum fares, all of which were roughly double what was being charged. From 10th January 1887, 9d weekly contracts were issued to combat the railway fare between Hamilton Square and James Street of 1½d single, 2½d return, and a proposal to withdraw them from 1st

The ferry approach at Woodside towards the end of the nineteenth century. Erection of the drinking fountain and ornamental lamp marked completion of the ferry modernisation scheme in 1864. The three horse-tramway lines were originally unconnected and the centre one, the Wirral Tramway Company's New Ferry line to the right of the cabs, was still separate until electric tramway days.

January 1888 in favour of a 2/6d monthly contract was rejected by the full Council.

However it was eventually realised that salvation lay in improving the service and reducing the costs. Various organisational and staff economies were made and recommendations to modernise the ferry fleet with screw steamers were heeded. Two new steamers were ordered in 1889, *Birkenhead* being sold by auction through C. H. Kellock & Co for £600 and broken up at Tranmere. TSS *Mersey* and *Wirral*, built by J. Jones and Sons, had twin 3-cylinder triple expansion engines. They were smaller than their predecessors with Board of Trade certification for 1,214 passengers. Above all they were fast, (*Mersey* achieved 13.06 knots average on her trials) and economical, consuming 5¼ cwt of coal per hour compared with the 9 cwt of the paddle boats. Furthermore, the 10-minute service could be maintained by two boats instead of three. The economies in fuel and wages were enormous and the action of the Council in ordering a further paddle steamer *Birkenhead* in 1894 is inexplicable. The two new boats put Woodside on the road to recovery from the effects of railway competition and there is no doubt that without this stimulus, the ferries management would have been content to continue the practices of earlier years indefinitely.

New Management

Capt. Pinhey had been appointed ferry manager in 1871 at £400 per year, subsequently increased to £500. In July 1887 all the officials agreed to accept reduced salaries, Pinhey's being halved to £250 pa but this had been increased to £300 by 1890. In January 1892, there was a scandal in the Council when the chairman of the Ferry Committee, Counc. T. H. Jackson and his brother Ald. William Jackson resigned following a revelation by a Liberal councillor, Cecil Holden, that they had not declared an interest when certain contracts had been awarded by the Council. Cllr. Holden appears to have made himself very unpopular by waging war against the 'establishment'. The contracts concerned were the Woodside coal contract with Bettisfield Colliery, Flintshire, and the Gas Works contract with the Clay Cross Company. The Jacksons had a special relationship with the Gas Works as their father, the late Sir William, had sold the undertaking of the Birkenhead Gas & Water Co to the Commissioners in 1853. It seems that Counc. Holden had detected some irregularity in the coal supply at Woodside and initiated a prosecution against Bettisfield Colliery. When the matter came up for hearing in the Borough Police Court on 23rd December 1891, the delivery notes could not

Wind and driving rain drench these Victorian passengers, hurrying from the Woodside boat along the George's Landing Stage. The two-funnelled steamer is a Wallasey boat on the Seacombe service.

be found. On 2nd March the Council delegated five members to enquire into (1) the alleged misconduct of Capt. Pinhey and (2) the destruction of 'tickets' and especially the particular ticket required by Counc. Holden in his prosecution. At their next meeting, the Council resolved that the report of Capt. Pinhey and the declaration of Mr. George Mowll, Day Inspector, dated 19th January 1892, 'be expunged from every record of the Council'. The blank pages can be seen in the minute book to this day which is unfortunate, as these documents would obviously have added piquancy to the story.

The Council cocked a snook at the critics by again awarding the Woodside coal contract to Bettisfield Colliery from 1st July 1892. The Council decided to re-organise the staff structure of the ferry as a result of which Pinhey, Mowll and Thomas Nichols, the accountant, (who was 74, with 44 years' service), all resigned on 19th October 1892 being appointed 'Assistants' which, in the days before superannuation in municipal service, was the equivalent of a pension. Capt. Peter McQueen of Douglas, IOM took over as manager on 20th January 1893 at £350 pa and held the job for 21 years.

It is of interest to note the almost complete absence of staff turnover in those days. Appendix 3 shows that the average length of service of all employees in 1892 was 16 years. The most junior captain had served for eighteen years and, of ten engineers, eight had service of 20 years or more.

The financial recovery of Woodside ferry during the 1890s was, to some extent, the product of arrogance on the part of the Mersey Railway directors who increased fares and discontinued the through carriages across Birkenhead Park Station after quarrelling with the Wirral Railway. An increase of rail fares on 1st December 1893 was followed by substantial passenger resistance, resulting in a loss of traffic of £150 per week and a reversion to the old scale within three months. The company demanded a deposit of 5/- on contracts as a precaution against misuse and this sent many passengers back to the ferry as a matter of principle. A press report mentioned a 'reduced number of trains and bewildering irregularity from hour to hour'.

Ninepenny weekly contracts were discontinued at Woodside on 19th May 1895 in favour of books of twelve tickets at 8d, valid only during week of issue. This prevented the four-journey a day man, of which there were many, from travelling at weekly contract rates.

The 'nineties were years of recovery and consolidation. Schemes for covered walkways between the station and the ferry terminal were considered more than once but nothing was done. Other proposals to modify the tramway terminal layout and erect passenger shelters were overtaken by municipal plans to purchase and electrify the horse tramways and the only progress in the provision of passenger amenities was the building of a waiting room on the landing stage. In 1897, the ferry undertaking was being expanded by the acquisition of New Ferry and the intended building of a pier at Rock Ferry. Two years later two new twin screw steamers *Lancashire* and *Claughton*, the largest yet (150ft. by 41ft. by 11.3ft.) of 1200 ihp, took over at Woodside, relegating the last of the paddlers to reserve status.

The operating methods evolved during the last years of the century continued for many years. Woodside required four boats, two on service (augmented on fine summer Bank Holidays), one on survey and one in dock, in steam, to cover any mishap. In later years, the spare boat was berthed in Morpeth Dock where Wallasey ferries established a workshop but the Birkenhead ferry workshop was 'on the bank' south of Woodside and machinery was craned up for maintenance.

WOODSIDE FERRY STEAMER.

"The Unique Series.

The Woodside steamer **Lancashire** *of 1899, viewed from the deck of a luggage boat moored at Woodside stage. This steamer was fairly typical of its generation with a narrow promenade deck, not extending right across the main deck, except for gangway access.*

4 TRANMERE & BIRKENHEAD FERRIES

Until the early nineteenth century, Tranmere with a population of about 350 was the second most populous settlement in Wirral. It comprised several groups of dwellings with a village on the hill (the present day Church Road), the hamlet of Hinderton with its stone quarries and the riverside cottages whose inhabitants carried on fishing and other maritime pursuits. From its medieval origins, the place had the natural advantage of a sheltered bay but the muddy, shallow water restricted easy embarkation and landing to the times of high water. It is not known when the first slipway was built but it doubtless comprised sandstone from the nearby hillside. The ferry rights vested in the Manor of Tranmere and there were many lessees throughout the years.

With the coming of the coaching era Tranmere ferry became a serious rival to Woodside. The river passage was very little longer and the route to Chester was easier, avoiding the worst part of the climb over Tranmere Hill. In the early 1800s there was great competition between the two ferries. The proprietor of Tranmere was W. Roberts who experienced a large and increasing business. Whilst coach travel was normally undertaken only as a matter of necessity, its sightseeing aspects were stressed in an advertisement on 9th October 1805 viz:-

'The Commercial Coach leaves Poole (Tranmere Ferry) every evening at five o'clock through Chester and Wrexham, passing near the grand aqueduct across the Dee at Pont Cysyllte, to Chirk, where it meets the coaches from Shrewsbury to Holyhead, by way of the Lord Penrhyn New Inn at Capel Curig. The peculiar advantage of travelling this way must be apparent, when it is considered that, besides obviating the inconvenience of several steep and almost inaccessible hills, passengers avoid by this conveyance the ferry at Conway, and have the advantage of sleeping one night on the road at Capel Curig, which for extensive and convenient accommodation as an inn, and romantic and beautiful scenery in the neighbourhood, it is not to be excelled in the Principality.'

One would have thought that October was a little late in the year for that sort of thing and, presumably, it was the second night that was spent at Capel Curig as darkness would have fallen by the time the vehicle reached Chester.

In June 1808 Tranmere was the terminus of the Royal Mail coach to Chester and Holyhead daily at 6.00am and the previously mentioned Commercial coach now following a different route through Neston, Chester, Whitchurch and Wem to Shrewsbury and a coach three times weekly at 9.00am to Wrexham and Oswestry. A boat every morning at 8.00am from Liverpool was specifically advertised as a coach connection but no doubt there were other boats throughout the day. Mr Roberts suffered a slight setback in November 1808 on the 7th of which the following advertisement appeared:-

'The Postmaster has been pleased to order that the Mail Coach between Liverpool and Chester shall proceed by the direct road by Thornton and Sutton and that the mails should, in future, cross the Mersey to and from Woodside Ferry instead of Tranmere. The public are informed that the arrangement started yesterday and that the Post Office will be kept open for Ireland, North Wales and Shropshire till 3.0 p.m. The Mail Boat to carry Mail Coach Passengers only.'

No doubt Mr. Roberts was not as pleased as the postmaster but the change did not appear to have had such an adverse effect on his business as might have been expected. In 1810 he advertised as follows:-

'Tranmere Hotel, Cheshire. A Daily Post Coach (the Eclipse), by Sutton, to Chester, every afternoon at 5; returns next morning at 7 The Commercial Coach to Chester and Shrewsbury, every morning at 9 (to Shrewsbury same day). Boats every morning at 8, for the Commercial and at 4 every afternoon, for the Eclipse, for Chester, etc. Passengers and parcels booked at the Commercial Tavern, High Street, Liverpool; or at Robert's the Tranmere Hotel. Performed by WILLETS, ROBERTS & CO.'

By 1816 there was a regular daily coach from Tranmere to Parkgate for Flint and in June of the following year a steam packet *Ancient Briton* was put into service across the Dee between Parkgate and Bagillt, thus increasing the importance of the Tranmere-Parkgate coach service as a link in the chain of communication to the North Wales coast.

In 1818 the Parkgate coach bore the name 'Traveller's Friend' and left Tranmere 'every day at one hour's flood, to be at Parkgate in time to cross the River Dee at the same tide'. There was a coach connection on the other side for Holywell, St. Asaph and Denbigh.

Meanwhile a group of local men formed a syndicate to build a steam boat to enter ferry service on the Mersey. The active partners were William Batman and George La French, described as a boarding house keeper at Birkenhead. Batman approached Liverpool Corporation in February 1817 with a view to securing a landing place for this vessel and 2,000 yards of land was duly let to Batman and Company at £60 per annum. A new slip was built to the west of Queen's Dock Graving Docks. As steam boats were still being viewed by the authorities with some suspicion, Batman supported his application by a

The handbill advertising the commencement of the first steam ferry on the Mersey in April 1817. The picture at the top was apparently a printer's block and not intended to be a representation of *Etna*.

ETNA, TRANMERE FERRY
Steam Packet.

THIS Packet (as was originally intended) will commence running from the New Slip, at the west side of the Queen's Dock Graving Docks, on Thursday Morning, the 17th April, at Eight o'Clock, where every convenience will be found for taking on board and discharging Horses and Cattle of every description going to and from Cheshire, without the trouble that has hitherto been experienced in the common Sail Boats, and which it is the intention of the Proprietors as much as possible to obviate. This Vessel remaining at each side only Ten Minutes, the certainty with which Passengers may calculate upon crossing, at all times of the day, will be an advantage that never yet has been afforded to those whose business or pleasure lead them to cross the River.—The Fares for Passengers, &c. will be precisely the same as customary by other regular Boats. Due notice will be given when Carts and Carriages of every description will be conveyed over, which will be in a very few days.

Performed by BATMAN, FRENCH & Co.

April 15th, 1817.

J. GORE, PRINTER.

certificate worded as follows:-

'We, the undersigned, having seen double Steam Boats for crossing Rivers, beg to certify that in our opinion they are perfectly safe for passengers, carriages and cattle and that in point of accommodation they are much superior to Sail Boats.'

Signed Alex. McGregor, Jno. Richardson, Thos. Davidson, Jas. Butler Clough, Thos. Thornely.

Just where these worthies had seen 'double steam boats' is not known as the vessel, said to have been designed by La French, was quite unique. It was built by Dawson and Co and consisted of two flats side by side, connected by beams and decked over. A 22hp engine, supplied by Fawcett and Littledale, drove a wheel placed between the two hulls. This was Fawcett's first venture into the field of marine engineering and laid the foundation for the recovery of his fortune after his 1810 bankruptcy. The engine is said to have been in one hull and the boiler in the other. The vessel was about 64ft long and was launched on 7th March 1817.

It was named *Etna* (sometimes spelt *Aetna*) and was advertised as entering service on the Tranmere crossing on 17th April 1817. However a press announcement on that day postponed the event so that 'additional improvements could be made to the engine and water wheel' and the steamer entered service at 7.00am on

A reproduction of a copper token sold for use as fare money on the pioneer steam boat *Etna*. It was the custom to sell these in bulk at a discount to minimise peculation of the fare money.

Saturday 26th April 'when every convenience will be found for taking on board and discharging carriages, carts, horses and cattle of every description going to and from Cheshire without the trouble that has hitherto been experienced in the Common Sail Boats and which it is the intention of the Proprietors as much as possible to obviate. This vessel being peculiarly adapted for carriages etc. to drive on board without the trouble of unharnessing will be found a most eligible and safe conveyance.'

As the original notice had excluded carts and carriages it is presumed that the extra days were spent in improving the loading and unloading arrangements at each side of the river. The almost rectangular construction of *Etna* without protruding paddle boxes made it suitable for wheeled traffic whereas for many years it was necessary to load carts and horses separately on other vessels. The *Liverpool Mercury* commented on the 'peculiar advantage of this packet that in crossing the river in a calm, or in any state of wind and tide, the passage will always be very short and the inconvenience to passengers and the risk to carriages, horses etc. which is inseparable from the use of sailboats, will be almost entirely removed.'

Passengers were charged 3d on weekdays and 4d on Sundays and the remainder of the tariff was as follows:-

4-wheel carriage with two horses and passengers	10/-
Gig and horse with passenger	4/-
Cart and horse	4/-
Large cart and 2 horses	5/6
Extra horses	1/-each

(If any of the above return same day, half price will be charged)

Horse and rider	1/6d
Cattle per head	1/-
Sheep per score	3/-
Pigs and calves	3d
Corn, flour, Meal, Bran etc. per sack	2d
Market people allowed to carry 3 baskets or hamper without extra charge	3d

Within a month, passenger fares were increased after 6.00pm to 4d on weekdays and 6d on Sundays and there had obviously been difficulty in collecting tolls on board in what were probably very crowded conditions at times, as the novelty value was considerable at first. A notice dated 28th May read:-

'Great inconvenience having arisen in the collection of fares both to Passengers and Proprietors, they respectfully inform the public and their friends that the fares will be received in future on the new Slip at the Liverpool side.'

The same notice advised that on the packet's arrival at Liverpool after 12.00 noon, she would stop for 20 minutes for the men belonging to her to dine but for the rest of the day she would tie up for only 10 minutes thus enabling a half-hourly service to be maintained.

It can be deduced from various contemporary reports that Batman, French and Co regarded their enterprise as a Liverpool-based ferry in competition with the established ferry. Different landing facilities must have been used in Tranmere Bay as carriages could not have been driven on and off the slipway. James Ball, who took over Tranmere Ferry about 1817, countered the competition by acquiring a steamer *Regulator* a wooden paddler of which no more is known. It probably worked to and from the Parade Slip, Liverpool which to most people was a more convenient landing place than Queen's Dock.

A second steamer, probably also twin-hulled, *Mersey* of about 80 GRT, was placed in service by La French and Co in 1819 (Batman seems to have disappeared). *Field's Diary 1821* described it as a 'single vessel almost as wide as long, very slow and occasionally employed towing'. Its 20hp engines were built by Fawcetts. *Etna* was reboilered in 1821 and remained in the river until about 1832.

Although no positive evidence has been found, it seems possible that trouble over the use of Tranmere Bay by a rival Liverpool ferry was the reason for the establishment of Birkenhead Ferry in 1820 by permission of the Lord of the Manor of Birkenhead, F. R. Price (see page 53). La French was no longer involved with Tranmere, but he must have reached some sort of accord with Ball who was also concerned with Birkenhead by 1827. His place at Tranmere Hotel was taken by one Pearce but there is no certainty that the latter leased the ferry.

The Willoughbys

With Woodside still using sail, the years 1818-22 were undoubtedly the zenith of Tranmere's prosperity and, despite some competition from the new Birkenhead Ferry, which enticed some coaches away, Tranmere continued to do well for a few more years. The building of the causeway across the Tranmere Pool and the completion of Brassey's New Chester Road in 1833, coupled with the improvements at Woodside, eroded Tranmere's popularity and this was accelerated by the opening of the railway from Chester in 1840. The coaching trade was eclipsed and by 1844 only three coaches remained, none of which used Tranmere. No right-minded railway passenger would back-track to make use of this passage when he had the choice of three others, much better placed in relation to the railway terminus in Grange Lane. The ferry had been leased by William Willoughby and Son (later Edward and Seymour Willoughby) in 1838 but was closed for some years in the 1840s; it was reopened in 1848 by the same lessees. After they had taken over the lease of Birkenhead ferry in 1851, they attempted to run both ferries as one with the aid of a wooden bridge across the Pool (see page 56). The Willoughbys started a cartage business and, until Wallasey established its own goods ferry about 1862, they secured the Wallasey traffic despite the long detour necessary to by-pass the Wallasey Pool.

In their early days, Willoughbys owned at least six steamers, all iron paddlers except the second *Abbey* built by Humble and Millcrest in 1833. The others were the second *Mersey* (1841), *Birkenhead* (1846), the second *Britannia* (1847), *Royal Victoria* (acquired 1846) and *Curlew* (acquired 1855). By the 1840s, ferry steamers were exceeding 100ft. in length, starting a trend which continued for almost a century. In the 1860s they operated

Star (acquired from Hetheringtons in 1865), *Woodside*, and *Seymour*. After closure of the Birkenhead Hotel in 1850, the Parkgate coach was replaced by an omnibus, at first worked by John Wright but by 1853, by Thomas Johnson, to and from Rock Ferry. In 1862 it was operating to and from the Tranmere Hotel on Tuesday and Saturday only, the change of ferry probably following some unreliability in the running of the Rock Ferry boats. The bus left Parkgate at 8.00am, returning from Tranmere on arrival of the 4.30pm boat from Liverpool. This service seems to have survived, at least in summer, until the opening of the Parkgate branch railway in 1866. Joseph Reilton's boat to Bagillt was still extant in 1860 but was withdrawn soon afterwards because of railway competition. Pleasure trips by omnibus to Parkgate and Chester Races continued to run from Tranmere Ferry on special occasions for many years but they had little effect on the ferry revenue.

One of the events of mid-19th century Tranmere was the Whitsuntide Wakes which became notorious for rowdyism, drunkenness and violence. The celebrations were held in fields near the ferry and it was said that in one year 40,000 people had come from Liverpool by ferry 'the idle and dissolute from all over the county under circumstances so subversive to all order, morality and security as loudly to call for the prompt and energetic interposition of the justices .....' Tranmere Ferry could not cope with such numbers and doubtless Birkenhead and Woodside got their share.

Dependent entirely on local traffic, the ferry had to be highly competitive. In the 1860s the Willoughbys were offering weekly tickets at 9d and monthly contracts at 2/6d at a time when the minimum period for a contract at Woodside was three months. Tranmere was undoubtedly the pioneer of weekly contract tickets on the Mersey. The

Provisional Agreement

made this seventh day of July — one thousand eight hundred and seventy four **Between** *The Rock Ferry Company Limited of the one part and The Tranmere Ferry Company, Limited of the other part* **Whereas** *the said Rock Ferry Company are seized in fee of the pier slip pay Gates Ferry house office Warehouse and the approach thereto situate at Rock Ferry in the Township of Higher Bebington in the County of Chester and they are also possessed of four paddle wheel Steamers known by the names of the "Fairy Queen" "Gypsy Queen" "Ant" and "Bee" and the said Company have for a number of years now last past carried on and worked the said Ferry both for passenger and Goods traffic to and from Liverpool and also used their said Steamers as Tenders for Sea-going Steamers and Vessels* **And whereas** *the said Tranmere Ferry Company are possessed of or well and sufficiently entitled to the pier slip pay Gates, ferry houses office, Warehouse and the approach thereto situate at Tranmere in the County of Chester under and by virtue of a Lease thereof to them for a term of ninety nine years from the twenty fifth day of March one thousand eight—*

The first page of the abortive agreement between the Rock Ferry Company and the Tranmere Ferry Co intended to pool their resources in the interests of economy. The two companies could not agree on a modus operandi and the agreement was cancelled.

ordinary fare was 1d (½d for children under 12). It was 'the longest sail on the river for 1d'.

After attaining Local Board status in 1860, Tranmere went to Parliament for various powers. An official notice, published on 23rd November 1861, announced the Board's intention to apply for powers 'to acquire by compulsion or agreement Tranmere Ferry and all or any rights or interests and to extinguish all existing rights and privileges'. This was somewhat radical for the times and the Tranmere Improvement Act 1862 was toned down, giving the Local Board power to purchase the ferry but not compulsorily. Nothing was done and when the Willoughbys' lease expired on 29th June 1872, the ferry closed.

The ferry rights were acquired by Samuel Davies, land agent of Mollington, who saw an opportunity to cash in on the growing port activities in Birkenhead following the opening up of the docks. Tranmere Ferry Co. Ltd. was incorporated on 31st January 1873 with a nominal capital of £25,000. The principal shareholder was Davies who held 200 £5 shares, and other Davies's held another 100. Local shareholders were John McGaffin, engineer, of Holt Hill; Henry Charles Gerard and David Smart, spirit merchants; William Wolliscroft, accountant, of Egerton Park; Henry Jennings, provision merchant also of Egerton Park and David Anderson, luncheon room proprietor of 8 Holt Road. The secretary was originally Daniel Thwaites of 26 Old Chester Road, which was initially the registered office, but within a few months this had moved to Tranmere ferry and Anderson had taken over as secretary. In 1878 he was also secretary of the Tranmere Shipping Co in which Samuel Davies held 468 of the 1,680 shares. It seems likely that the two businesses were run as one.

Samuel Davies granted a lease of the ferry properties for 99 years from 25th March 1873 at a progressive yearly rack rental and the company commenced trading in May 1873, one report says on 1st, another 30th. Vessels placed in service in 1873 included an old Woodside steamer, *Lord Morpeth* and *Superb*, built at South Shields in 1853. *Kingstown* of 1865 came into the fleet in 1876. The draft agreement with the Rock Ferry Co (see below) credited the Tranmere company with six vessels but it is clear that so many were not needed for ferry service.

A Failed Amalgamation

In 1874, talks were held between the Tranmere Ferry Co Ltd and the Rock Ferry Co Ltd with a view to running the two ferries as one undertaking and a provisional Agreement was drawn up on 7th July 1874. By this time the Tranmere company had decided to erect 'a high level pier with swing bridge and to connect the same with a floating landing stage in the tideway' whereas the Rock Ferry was still using a stone slipway. The Agreement was to run from the date of completion of the new pier at Tranmere until 25th March 1903 and there was to be a joint board of directors, comprising four directors from each company. These directors were to determine what portion of the business of the two companies, beyond that of the ordinary ferry traffic, should be assumed jointly and this referred to the towing business which made up a large proportion of the Tranmere company's business.

The Joint Board was duly elected and a series of meetings was held between November 1875 and May 1876 but agreement on the shares of the two companies could not be reached. The nature of the problem is not on record but it is not difficult to imagine that the Tranmere company, with its new pier already under construction and its towing business, demanded a greater share than the Rock Ferry company was prepared to concede. The Agreement was formally cancelled on 18th July 1876, after special meetings of both companies had been called. The new pier and landing stage was completed in 1877. Technical details have not been traced but the 1899 Edition of the Ordnance Survey shows that it was built immediately alongside and to the south of the stone slipway. It was 750ft. long and connected by a 120ft. bridge to a floating stage about 144ft. long. All measurements are approximate.

Both Willoughbys and the new company had had a profitable contract with the MDHB for towing mud barges for dumping at sea but when the MDHB acquired their own hoppers in 1879, revenue fell substantially and it became apparent that the 10% dividends recently paid had been derived from this activity rather than the ferry. The quarter-hourly peak hour service was reduced to half-hourly from 1st March 1879, saving £2,000 per year.

Contractors were offered a refund if the new service did not suit them. In May 1880, a Petition was presented to wind up the company and a liquidator appointed but the shareholders had second thoughts and the Court agreed to the withdrawal of the Petition. A storm on 3rd March 1881 broke the bridge away from both the pier and the stage. It was thought at first that this would be the end of Tranmere ferry but repairs were made and the service resumed on 11th April 1881.

Tranmere had been absorbed into the new Borough of Birkenhead in 1877 so the powers of acquisition had lapsed. As the Tranmere ferry was considered to be an amenity worth retaining, clauses were inserted in the Birkenhead Corporation Act 1881 giving the Corporation power to acquire Tranmere ferry and to apply to it all provisions applicable to Woodside, but only by agreement. The rights of Birkenhead Ferry were not to be prejudiced. The Corporation could also arrange with tramway, omnibus and cab proprietors for use by them of the ferry premises. Maximum tolls, well in excess of those being currently charged, were laid down in the Act as follows:-

Contracts

	1 year	6 months	3 months
1st Contractor	£2-5-0d	£1-10-0d	£1-0-0d
Additional Member of Family	£1-2-6d	15-0d	10-0d
Single Tickets in packets of not less than 12			
Day Fare	2d	Night Fare	6d

A horse tramway between New Ferry and Woodside was inaugurated by the Wirral Tramway Co in March 1877. Although the cars passed the ferry approach, passengers could ride to Woodside for the same fare as to Tranmere and, in inclement weather, people preferred to use the more weatherproof facilities at Woodside. Various plans for tramway sidings came to nothing. The Mersey Railway was opened between Liverpool (James Street) and Green Lane, very close to the ferry approach, on 1st February 1886 and extended to Rock Ferry in 1891. Traffic on all the ferries was seriously affected and it was only because people objected to the noxious fumes in the railway tunnel that ferry traffic began to recover in the mid-1890s.

The pier and bridge were damaged again in a severe gale on 1st November 1887 when two schooners drifted down and broke through them. Once more, repairs were effected and the ferry re-opened on 2nd June 1888 with a half-hourly service from 6.30am (10.00am on Sundays) to 9.30pm. The fare was still 1d and the monthly contract was reduced from 2/6d to 2/-.

In its later years, Tranmere Ferry was worked by the iron paddle steamer *Mollington*, named for Samuel Davies' home village. This may not have been her official name as it cannot be found in *Lloyds List*. She was built in 1879 by Jn. Reid and Co of Port Glasgow, allegedly as a yacht for which the order was cancelled. 128.2ft. long, 15.1ft. broad and 6.1ft. deep, she had a gross tonnage of 97.57 and developed 50 nhp; she was acquired in April 1882. There was a saloon abaft the paddle boxes and a raked funnel, yellow with a black top.

The relief steamer was *Harry Clasper*, purchased in 1879 from the Tyne General Ferry Co and named after a rowing champion well known on Tyneside. Built in 1861 by J. Rogerson and Co, St. Peters, Northumberland with engines by Hawks, Crayshaw and Co of Gateshead, she was double ended with a rudder at each end. She was 115.6ft. long, 16.7ft. in beam and drew 7.5ft. Her gross tonnage was 103 and her 40 nhp engines had two cylinders, 24in. and 36in. Contemporary reports suggest that she was underpowered and had great difficulty getting across from Liverpool on the ebb tide, hugging the dock wall until almost opposite Rock Ferry before crossing the river. She was nicknamed 'Harry Go Faster' and was finally scrapped by T. W. Ward Ltd at Preston in 1898.

The ferry service became seasonal about 1890, probably as a result of Mersey Railway competition. It was advertised as reopening to passenger traffic on 25th February 1893 in which year the MDHB purchased the foreshore at Tranmere for £115,000 to frustrate a scheme for a rival cattle market and in 1895 the Tranmere Ferry and adjoining properties were also acquired for £70,000. John Davies, W. J. Little and David Anderson were appointed liquidators of the Tranmere Ferry Co and the Chancery Court ordered the liquidation to take effect from 3rd April 1894. John Roberts purchased the assets and continued the service but he died almost immediately and John Davies is credited by Duckworth and Langmuir (*West Coast Steamers*) with maintaining a ferry service in 1895; *Mollington* apparently reverted to Samuel Davies, as it passed by will in the same year to James Orr, who may have been a son-in-law. He continued seasonal operations until his death in 1904 and the ferry closed down in March of that year. The assets passed to his wife, Isabella, who sold *Mollington* to Portuguese owners. The pier was demolished almost immediately and the Pool enclosed to accommodate extensions to Lairds' shipbuilding yard.

As late as November 1898, Birkenhead Corporation considered taking over Tranmere Ferry, which it could have worked in connection with New Ferry, but it decided that it was 'undesirable at the present time to approach the owners ...'. Instead it embarked on an expensive scheme to revive Rock Ferry.

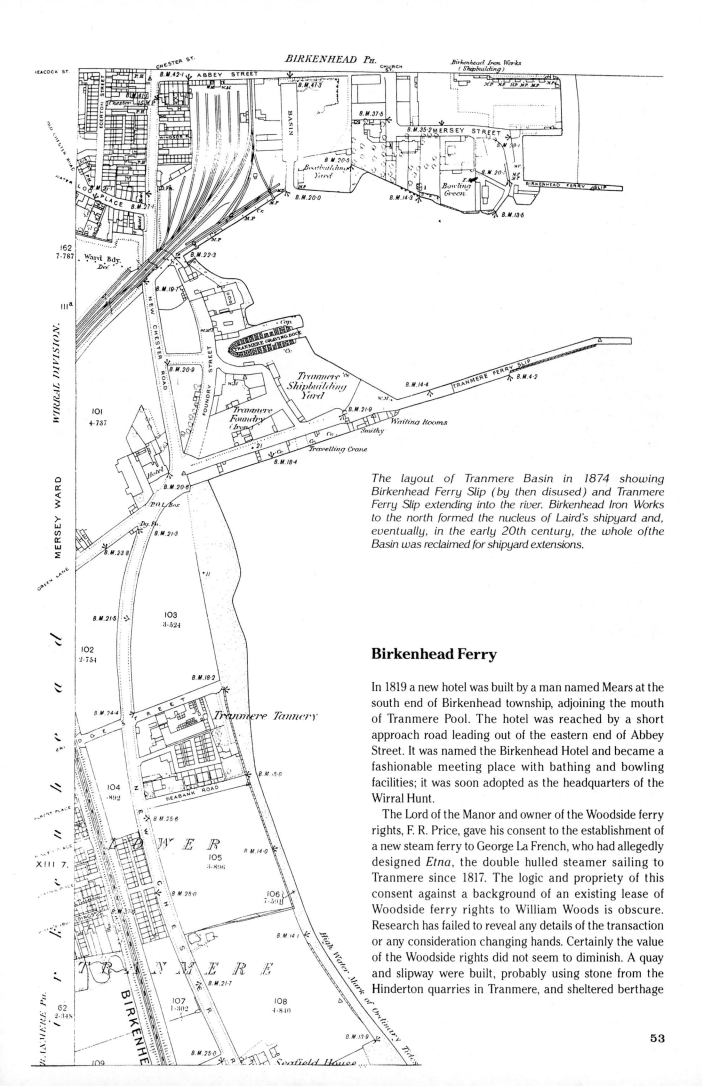

The layout of Tranmere Basin in 1874 showing Birkenhead Ferry Slip (by then disused) and Tranmere Ferry Slip extending into the river. Birkenhead Iron Works to the north formed the nucleus of Laird's shipyard and, eventually, in the early 20th century, the whole of the Basin was reclaimed for shipyard extensions.

Birkenhead Ferry

In 1819 a new hotel was built by a man named Mears at the south end of Birkenhead township, adjoining the mouth of Tranmere Pool. The hotel was reached by a short approach road leading out of the eastern end of Abbey Street. It was named the Birkenhead Hotel and became a fashionable meeting place with bathing and bowling facilities; it was soon adopted as the headquarters of the Wirral Hunt.

The Lord of the Manor and owner of the Woodside ferry rights, F. R. Price, gave his consent to the establishment of a new steam ferry to George La French, who had allegedly designed *Etna*, the double hulled steamer sailing to Tranmere since 1817. The logic and propriety of this consent against a background of an existing lease of Woodside ferry rights to William Woods is obscure. Research has failed to reveal any details of the transaction or any consideration changing hands. Certainly the value of the Woodside rights did not seem to diminish. A quay and slipway were built, probably using stone from the Hinderton quarries in Tranmere, and sheltered berthage

53

The Birkenhead Hotel and ferry slipway, probably about 1840.

was thus provided. At the time of the transaction, La French was running Tranmere Ferry which he gave up, and the Birkenhead Ferry started operating in 1820. Some of the stage coaches transferred to the new hotel which was taken over in 1827 by James Ball from Tranmere. The hotel and ferry became one undertaking and accessibility from Liverpool was an important factor in attracting custom to the hotel's amenities.

Abbey, built by Grayson, entered service in March 1822 and *Vesuvius,* from Gladstone and Foster's yard, followed in 1832, between them providing a half-hourly service to and from Parade Slip. It is possible that *Etna* and *Mersey* served the Birkenhead Ferry after La French withdrew from Tranmere. The involvement of Ball in more than one ferry has led to confusion as to exactly which vessels were used on Birkenhead Ferry at this time. Four wooden paddlers are recorded as being in his ownership about this time; *James* built by Mottershead and Hayes in 1826; *Hero* built at Tranmere in the same year and engined by Foster and Gladstone; *Britannia* (1827) and *William Fawcett* (1829) both built by Mottershead and Hayes.

The fears of Liverpool Corporation about the potential of Birkenhead as a rival port were still playing a part in local politics, although the scheme for a ship canal between the Wallasey Pool and the Dee had been snuffed out by earlier land purchases. In 1839, discussions were going on between Liverpool Council and agents for F. R. Price who, as absentee landlord, was gradually divesting himself of his Birkenhead lands. A sub-committee was appointed to

consider the purchase of the 'Birkenhead Estate' comprising the Birkenhead Hotel, a dwelling house, land along the shore and the undisputed right to the ferry. The whole estate measured 43,000 sq.yds. (about nine acres). There was room to build a dock measuring 300yds. by 110, adequate space for expansion and plenty of stone for dock walls available near to hand. Liverpool Corporation's negotiators obtained an option to buy for £65,000 which was to lapse if the Council did not confirm the purchase by 6th February 1840.

An editorial in the *Liverpool Courier* reflected local approval to the deal going through as it was felt in many commercial circles that the line of docks was long enough and it made more sense to build future extensions on the Cheshire shore. The purchase was approved by Liverpool Council on 15th January 1840.

Liverpool's Ferry

The decision was influenced by the imminent opening of the Chester and Birkenhead Railway, the terminus of which was to be at Grange Lane. Having itself had a railway for almost ten years, Liverpool knew the catalytic effect of the iron road on the expansion of trade and the increase in land values. Vested interests in the Tranmere and Birkenhead Ferries had succeeded in binding the railway company to build branch railways to those ferries before any extension to Woodside could be constructed and, as has already been recorded, Liverpool Corporation was successful in thwarting the railway company in an attempt to set these conditions aside in order to reach Woodside later that year. After obtaining the necessary Parliamentary powers, Liverpool Corporation purchased the land and ferry in 1841 for £73,800.

Liverpool thus became the first British municipality to be involved in passenger transport operation but it was never an enthusiastic ferry proprietor and stood by apathetically while Birkenhead secured statutory ferry rights in 1842. At the time of acquisition, the ferry was leased to Hetherington and Grindrod until 1846. Two Hetheringtons were among the founding Improvement Commissioners, appointed in 1833. It seems that in the competitive situation which prevailed in 1846, Liverpool Corporation was unable to find a lessee and there was a period of direct operation. A ferries sub-committee of the Town Council's Finance Committee was appointed and

the ferry was probably run with a chartered vessel to begin with as the first record of a boat owned by Liverpool Corporation is in 1848 when *Fanny*, an iron paddle steamer built at Renfrew two years earlier, was acquired. In October 1848, the Council approved the provision of landing facilities at the south end of Liverpool but nothing was done despite agitation by some councillors who were keen to see Liverpool become an important ferry operator. A later suggestion for building ferry landing facilities at the north end was also disregarded.

With the railway traffic using Monks Ferry and most of the town traffic crossing by Woodside, very few passengers used the Birkenhead Ferry which embarrassed Liverpool Corporation by incurring an annual loss of £5,000-£6,000. Following the temporary abandonment of dock construction at Birkenhead in 1847 when funds ran out, hundreds of workers left the town, leaving behind

An artist's impression of Birkenhead Ferry, the Birkenhead Hotel and the Priory Church dating from about 1845, by which time the ferry's palmy days were already over. The diminutive paddle steamer was typical of the ferry boats of the 1840s.

empty and uncompleted houses. The reduction of the ferry fare from 2d to 1d has been attributed to the agitation of Joseph Craven, an estate agent, who believed that the salvation of Birkenhead lay in making it attractive as a dormitory town for Liverpool. It was certainly Liverpool Corporation which took the initiative in June 1848 in an attempt to attract passengers from Woodside and Tranmere, but as these ferries immediately followed suit, the short term result was to increase the losses.

In 1849, Liverpool Corporation took delivery of two more steamers, *Cato* and *Vernon*, both named after their respective builders, Cato, Miller & Co and T. Vernon. Both were engined by Fawcett, Preston & Co.

On 1st May 1850 Liverpool Town Council considered a recommendation of the Finance Committee to let Birkenhead ferry with its three steamers. A motion was put 'that the Finance Committee be instructed to cease running boats to the Birkenhead Ferry .... and that until the ferry be let, the steamers .... be laid up or sold and that the Corporation maintain the right of ferry by employing a row-boat to take passengers and also that all steam or other boats be allowed to use the slip free of charge ....'. The motion was lost.

A record of a meeting on 2nd August 1850 of the sub-committee on the Management of the Birkenhead Ferry has survived. The chair was taken by James Nelson Ward, the others present being James Procter and William Purser Freme. A letter was read from one Richard Marrack, complaining of irregularity in the departure of the boats, the Water Bailiff being instructed to investigate. The latter gentleman reported on a collision between *Fanny* and another vessel, *John Bull*, the *Fanny's* master, George Train, being sacked. Other routine business transacted included the refusal of a request by Rev. J. R. Connor for the 52nd Regiment to pass over the ferry free and a resolution that all charity school children be allowed to go to Birkenhead and back for 1d. This ecclesiastical involvement in military matters is mysterious, though in August 1848, the Birkenhead Commissioners' ferry manager had reported that Birkenhead ferry boats were in the habit of using Monks Ferry slip for the embarkation of troops and the receipt of the Dublin morning mail which arrived by train. After legal opinion had been obtained, the Commissioners had correspondence with Willoughbys who were granted permission to continue these activities on payment of £10-10-0d for the half year as acknowledgement of ferry rights. A possible explanation is that a Willoughbys' boat ran the Birkenhead Ferry until the arrival of *Fanny* in 1848. However the practice was still in force in July 1850 when the Committee noted that Willoughbys had not paid the fee of £21 for landing mails and decided to sue unless they did so forthwith. Willoughbys' involvement with Birkenhead ferry was inexplicable as there would be an obvious conflict of interest.

Birkenhead Hotel closed in 1850, the last stage coach, the 'Princess Royal' to Parkgate, being withdrawn at the same time.

Birkenhead Ferry was leased to the Willoughbys for 14 years from 15th February 1851 and they acquired the three Liverpool Corporation steamers. A few months later, they approached the Commissioners for their approval of the building of a wooden bridge across the mouth of Tranmere Pool connecting the slipways of the Birkenhead and Tranmere Ferries so that the same steamers could serve both ferries. The Commissioners, feeling that it was outside their jurisdiction, declined to comment. The precise details of this structure have not come to light. As small steamers were being built in Tranmere Bay, it was potentially obstructive to shipping and dreadfully exposed to the elements. That it was built, or at least started, is certain as the work was reported to the Commissioners' Ferry Committee on 2nd January 1852. One would have expected the Conservator of the Mersey to have opposed it as a hazard and perhaps that is what happened for, if the bridge was ever completed, it was not in use for long. By 1860, with Woodside Ferry being extended and equipped with a floating stage and the railway traffic using Monks Ferry, Birkenhead Ferry, remote from all public transport, was in decline. It was offered at auction on a 999 year lease on 9th August 1870 but there were no bidders and the ferry closed. In 1872, its installations were removed to make way for an extension to Lairds' shipyard and the hotel buildings met the same fate in 1904. The dormant existence of the Birkenhead ferry rights was recognised in the Birkenhead Corporation Act 1881.

Liverpool Corporation had begun to sell its land in Birkenhead in 1844. The formation of the Mersey Docks and Harbour Board in 1858 ensured the unity of the port and the disposal of Birkenhead Ferry was the last stage in the Corporation's disengagement from the Cheshire shore.

Fanny was advertised for sale in February 1857 but *Cato* and *Vernon* continued in service until the ferry closed. Their ultimate fate is unknown.

5 THE SOUTH END FERRIES

Rock Ferry

Rock Ferry, being further south, was less directly competitive than the other ferries. As has been related in Chapter 1, it attracted its share of the coaching trade, Rock Lane, its main approach road in olden days, being part of the turnpike road system.

Three attempts were made at different times to link it with points in the south end of Liverpool, the first of which was in 1776. By 1800, the ferry was in the possession of Joseph White of the Manor of Higher Bebington who promoted successfully, despite the opposition of Liverpool Corporation, an Act of Parliament in 1805 'for improving the passage between the Town of Liverpool and the County of Chester at the Rock Ferry on the River Mersey and for charging tolls on vessels using the same'. The Act stated that White 'possessor of Royal Rock Ferry intends making or extending a pier, slip or quay into the River Mersey so that persons, horses, cattle carts and other carriages may be expeditiously and safely conveyed in boats across the said river at all periods of the tide and particularly at low water which at present cannot be done at this or any other ferry on the said river and the said Joseph

White is also possessed of a house and lands at Harrington in Toxteth Park .... where he also intends to erect another pier, slip or quay'.

The 1805 Act became the statutory authority covering ferry rights between Rock Ferry and Liverpool and was never challenged. White was authorised to take tolls but only so long as the piers etc. were kept in good order. Toxteth Park was then a separate local authority, not a part of Liverpool, and the Harrington estate was being developed as a rival port to Liverpool. Originally it had been intended to call the place 'New Liverpool' but the name Harrington was adopted as a compliment to the Countess of Sefton whose father was the Earl of Harrington. The establishment of a South End ferry seemed sound in those days as the docks which had been constructed were all south of Liverpool town centre. However, from 1796, when Queen's Dock was completed, the Napoleonic Wars put a stop to construction which was resumed only in 1821 when the Prince Regent (later Prince's) Dock was opened north of the town centre.

It is not known how long White's enterprise survived but the slipway, which still exists, was not built until about 1820. The ferry rights passed to Thomas Morecroft who is

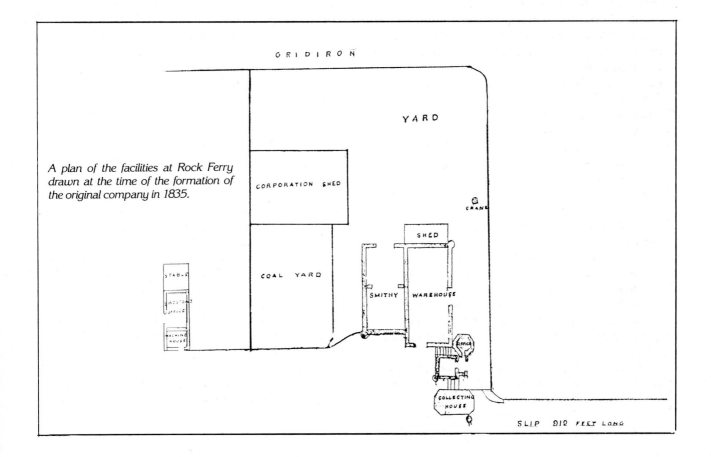

A plan of the facilities at Rock Ferry drawn at the time of the formation of the original company in 1835.

believed to have started running the service in 1831.

In 1835, when the Birkenhead Commissioners thought they might like to buy it, the ferry was reported as being closed but this was probably seasonal. On 5th July 1836 an indenture was drawn up forming the Royal Rock Ferry Steam Packet Company with a capital of £35,000 in £20 shares. Morecroft and others received £25,000 for the ferry and the steamer *Aimwell*, a wooden paddler built at Dumbarton in 1825 and acquired by Morecroft about 1832. Two more vessels were purchased and these were probably *Alexandra* and *Cheshire Witch*, both iron paddlers 84ft. long. There were in all 157 proprietors but the principal promoters were John Nelson Wood, William Dowson, Anthony Nichol and Henry Jenkins, who were joined as directors by John Fletcher, William Wilson and Henry Hutchinson. The directors were precluded from having any connection with another ferry within two miles. Notable among the shareholders were William Jackson (one share) and the coach proprietor Bartholomew Bretherton Jnr (15), whose services made extensive use of Rock Ferry. Morecroft retained a considerable interest.

The objectives of the company were to maintain a ferry or passage for passengers, carriages and live and dead stock; and towing, removing and assisting vessels. The company also acquired Rock House and Rock House Farm. The undertaking was immediately mortgaged to Christopher Bullen and Thomas Berry Horsfall, Liverpool business men.

In 1837, a Sunday service was being operated to Herculaneum Pottery Ferry directly across the river from Rock Ferry and it was intended to run a daily service if there was sufficient demand; the Sunday service was not a success so the weekday sailings never started. The nature of the landing arrangements at Herculaneum are not known.

The opening of the railway in 1840 and the rapid demise of the stage coaches removed an important source of revenue from Rock Ferry. In 1844 there were only the 'Lord Mostyn' coach to Holywell and the 'Leeswood Arms' coach to Mold and Ruthin, both leaving the Royal Rock Hotel every weekday afternoon. Both had gone by the following year when the only coach serving the district was the 'Princess Royal' between Parkgate and the Birkenhead Hotel. When the latter closed in 1850, it was replaced by John Wright's omnibus to Rock Ferry. By 1853 the Parkgate omnibus was being run by Thomas Johnson, a farmer, whose land lay behind the Pengwern Arms, later known as the Boathouse Inn. He ran once daily to Chester and three times a day in summer and once in winter to Rock Ferry but by 1860, Rock Ferry was being served only on summer Tuesdays and Saturdays, the majority of passengers preferring to use an alternative feeder omnibus to Hooton Station which ceased when the railway reached Parkgate in 1866.

By the end of the 1840s the company was in difficulties. From 18th May 1850 the ferry was leased to John Crippen (who had tugs and excursion boats at Runcorn), and William Robinson Foster, engineer, jointly for five years. The terms of the lease were £400 for three years, £450 for the fourth year and £500 for the fifth, with an additional £50 if the revenue reached £6,000. At that time, the ferry consisted of a 912ft.-long slip, a gridiron facing north and several sheds, warehouses and offices.

On the expiry of the lease to Crippen and Foster, a new one was granted to T. F. and R. Hetherington and, as population growth brought more traffic, they appear to have prospered. By 1861 the Rock Ferry Family Hotel, Gardens and Pleasure Grounds, which advertised a separate entrance for ladies, had been established. The proprietor was William Huntriss who was fined on one occasion for giving short measure.

The Steam Packet Company's annual meeting in 1864 reported the best results ever, paying a dividend of 5/- per share. At the same meeting complaint was made that the cabin of the steamer *Nymph* was leaking and there was speculation about how much profit the Hetheringtons were making in view of the company's prosperity.

The same meeting resolved to replace the old company with a limited liability company, a move facilitated by recently passed legislation. Accordingly, the Rock Ferry Company Ltd was formed on 10th September 1864 with capital of £35,200 which was increased by 50% to £52,800 on 24th January 1865. Principal shareholders were W. F. Morecroft, solicitor (both in his own right and as an executor of Thomas Morecroft) and Robert Hetherington. The registered office was at the Rock Ferry Hotel. The company proceeded to develop Rock Park as a select residential area.

The opening of New Ferry with its pier and floating landing stage in 1865 inevitably affected traffic at Rock Ferry with its spartan 900ft. slipway. A landing stage of sorts was added but this was probably a landing boat and the facilities could not be compared with the much safer and more comfortable landing arrangements of its neighbour. Towing and peripheral activities augmented declining passenger revenue. In 1873 the company signed a provisional Agreement with the Tranmere Ferry Co Ltd for the joint working of the two ferries but the parties fell out. Under the terms of the Agreement a Joint Board was elected and, despite several meetings between November 1875 and May 1876, differences could not be resolved and the Agreement was cancelled on 18th July 1876. The Rock Ferry Company struggled on and finally granted a lease to Thompson and Gough from 1st January 1879. These two already leased Eastham and New Ferries and announced the start of a service leaving New Ferry for Liverpool at 7.00, 8.00am and every 30 minutes until 9.30pm calling at Rock Ferry. The fares from either place were 2d single or 5/- per month (4/- for artisans) and there was a wide range of concessionary tickets offered. On recommencement of the seasonal Eastham ferry, these boats, too, called at New Ferry and Rock Ferry. Thereafter the history of the ferry is linked with New Ferry.

Thompson and Gough gave up Rock Ferry after the New Ferry landing stage was carried away in a gale in May 1887. Rock Ferry seems to have closed for a time but was re-opened in 1889 and operated by R. A. Macfie, in conjunction with New Ferry. The terms of this arrangement have not come to light but there was obviously a formal sale as, later on, Macfie's trustees were able to sell the ferry rights to the Corporation. The company rendered no statutory returns in 1888-89 and a letter from the Registrar of Companies dated 13th October 1890 was returned marked 'Gone—no address'. Finally there was a winding up meeting on 29th October 1895, the proceedings being handled by William F. Morecroft and Co. solicitors, of Castle Street, Liverpool. Both Morecroft and Hetherington were still shareholders in 1887 and probably to the end.

Macfie abandoned Rock Ferry following extension of the Mersey Railway to Rock Ferry on 5th June 1891.

New Ferry

It is not known exactly when New Ferry was founded or how it came by its name instead of bearing that of Bebington (or Bebbington to use the older spelling) as one might have expected. As with Rock Ferry, the ferry gave its name to the surrounding district which still carries that name long after the pier and boats have disappeared.

The first mention which has been traced was in 1774 when its tenant was one Englefield Lloyd. A coach was advertised to set out from the New Ferry House every day at half past nine in the morning for Chester, the Pyed Bull Inn, Northgate Street and return the same day. Each passenger paid 4/- inside or 2/- outside. By applying to Richard Davenport at the Friendship Coffee House, Strand Street, Liverpool, passengers could be 'accommodated with

boats to the said ferry on the shortest notice'.

New Ferry had considerable advantages at that time for the road to Chester was shorter than from Birkenhead and the difficult and hilly road over Tranmere Hill was avoided. This road was in use until 1790 when the present Old Chester Road was improved and diverted at Dacre Hill. The direct road dates from 1833. Another advantage was that the voyage was shorter than to Eastham and it avoided the troublesome sandbanks in the river there which made navigation for sailing boats both difficult and dangerous.

The improvements to the Chester road deprived New Ferry of the coaching traffic in the heyday of the coaching era. It was little more than half a mile upstream from Rock Ferry and duplication of facilities so far up river could not be justified. It is doubtful if regular ferry services were provided continuously though it is believed that sailing boats were in use in 1846 and New Ferry is thought to have been the last Mersey ferry to use sail. The landing facilities were primitive, comprising a clay bank raised almost two feet above the sloping shore and covered with loose stones.

In 1863, Herculaneum Dock opposite New Ferry was under construction and the Dock Board agreed to the lease to the Mersey River Steamboat Co of a piece of land running from Sefton Street to the Herculaneum Estate. This land, 213yds. long by 8yds. wide, was to be used solely for the purpose of a private road to the floating bridge leading to a landing stage proposed to be constructed and fixed by the company. This landing stage was intended to be used by a ferry thence to New Ferry and elsewhere and

Design details from the original New Ferry and New Brighton piers, showing how the bridges were flexibly suspended so that no stresses were produced by the movements of the floating stages. Both piers were built from the same plans.

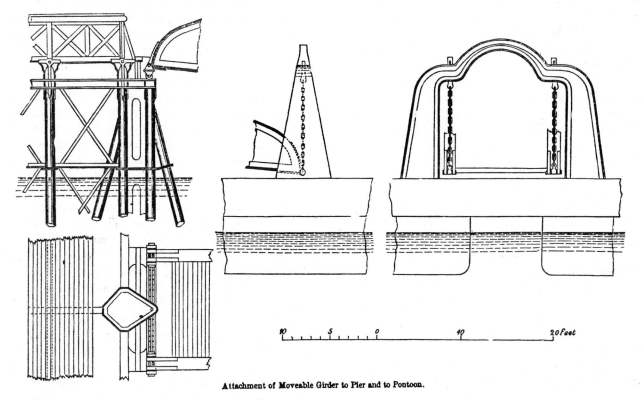

10   5   0   10   20 feet

Attachment of Moveable Girder to Pier and to Pontoon.

the company was empowered to land goods etc. at the steps at the entrance to Toxteth, Brunswick and Coburg docks and abreast the Tobacco warehouses. The nominal tenancy at £100 rent p.a. was 21 years but terminable by six months notice. The company was bound to permit boats from other ferries to land at this stage and no fare was to exceed the maximum Woodside fare.

In the meantime, New Ferry had been acquired by R. A. Macfie, a wealthy Liverpool sugar merchant and MP for Leith. A prospectus for the Mersey River Steamboat Co Ltd was issued in September 1863 with a capital of £20,000 in £5 shares. The Chairman was Matthew Gregson of Toxteth Park. An Agreement was made with Macfie, who undertook to build a new pier and landing stage and lease it to the company for 'a long term of years'. The rent was to be the same as the dividend paid to shareholders and if the company did not make a profit, Macfie would receive nothing that year. A piece of land, part of the foreshore and bed of the River Mersey, was leased by the Commissioners of Woods and Forests to Macfie for 80 years from 5th April 1865 at £20 per year and formal ferry rights were acquired from the same source on 23rd October 1865.

The wrought and cast-iron pier and pontoon was designed by the Scottish engineer, James Brunlees, later to be knighted for his work on the Mersey Railway. He based the design on his successful and much-imitated Southport pier, using cast-iron tubular columns on screw piles; 30 men on long capstan bars screwed the piles six to ten feet into the river bed until they stopped in hard clay. Three parallel rows of wrought iron girders linked the tops of the columns, arranged above the timber deck of the pier so as to act as parapets segregating the up and down traffic along two roadways each nine feet wide. The 850ft.-long pier consisted of 14 60ft. spans. The same plans were used for New Brighton ferry pier and identical stone 'horse-shoes' at the shore ends can still be seen even though both piers have long disappeared.

The floating pontoon at the end of the pier was of wrought iron, 100ft. by 22ft. and tapered at each end; it was divided into five watertight compartments and carried two waiting sheds for passengers. Landing steps were provided for small boats at the back of the stage and four heavy chains ran to anchors in the river bed. Linking the pontoon to the pier was a 10ft.-wide bowstring bridge, 158ft. long. It rested on a single pivot at the landward end and at the bottom of the slope, it was suspended by two chains from a strong arch made of wrought iron; this arrangement permitted the pontoon to pitch and roll without straining the bridge. On top of the arch was a dioptric navigation light and the whole structure was lit by gas.

Even at low water springs, there was never less than seven or eight feet of water in front of the stage. With floating stages at all three of their termini, the New Ferry steamers could now work with greater regularity and safety. Including £1,063 for the approaches, where the two payboxes stood, the whole pier and stage cost Macfie some £11,477. W. J. Galloway and Sons were the contractors and the engineer in charge was Henry Hooper, who had also put up Brunlees' pier at Southport.

South End Landing Stage

On the Liverpool side, the company provided a floating stage built by the Seacombe shipbuilders, Bowdler, Chaffer and Co and moored in the South Ferry basin down river from Harrington Dock. It was registered as a ship, *South End*, and comprised one pontoon of ¼in. wrought iron plates, 120ft. by 30ft. by 7ft. 9in. deep, stiffened with iron angle frames, bulkheads and flooring plates. The deck was 3in. pitch pine with a camber of 7in. It was moored to the dock wall by 1¾in. chains and connected by a 150ft. wrought iron bridge built in Liverpool by Graysons. There were two bowstring plate girders 8ft. apart, 152ft. long by 7ft. 6in. deep in the centre.

The opening of New Ferry Pier was celebrated by a 'déjeuner' laid out in a marquee pitched nearby, the cost being borne jointly by Macfie and Galloways. As a contemporary report described it 'The company was very numerous and included a number of ladies. Mr Macfie occupied the chair, Mr Matthew Gregson .... taking the vice-chair. Among the guests were His Worship the Mayor of Liverpool, Mr E. Lawrence and many other gentlemen of local influence. In the evening the landing stage was brilliantly illuminated'. The Mayor's role was a dual one, as he was a director of the company.

From 4th April 1865, a service was inaugurated between New Ferry and the South End, using two identical iron paddlers, *Sylph* and *Sprite*, built by C. & R. Miller, with 35 nhp engines by Fawcett. They were 126.7ft. long, 16.6ft. broad and drew 8.3ft. An application to call at Woodside was turned down in May 1865 on the grounds that there was no room at the landing stage.

However, within a few weeks, a berth was made available at the south end of the Prince's Landing Stage and a triangular service was inaugurated which met with such success that, on 11th August, a meeting of the contractors was called at the new refreshment room at New Ferry Pier. The chairman referred to the great increase in traffic since the boats had been 'compelled to go to the Prince's Landing Stage' and 14/- was then returned to every yearly contractor and a proportionate amount to those holding contracts for shorter periods. This unusual act of generosity may have been designed to attract additional custom by reducing contract rates. It was also revealed that a third boat, similar to the original two, had been ordered for delivery in October. This was *Syren*, built at Preston and launched in December 1865.

The success of the triangular service was short-lived and it is suspected that fewer and fewer sailings called at South End as time went on. In 1867, the fleet was bought by Henry Gough of Eastham, who probably worked New Ferry in connection with Eastham Ferry. He disposed of *Syren* and mortgaged the other two boats to Macfie. Soon after, he went into partnership with T. W. Thompson. It is not known when sailings to and from South End finally ceased but the stage and bridge were acquired by the Wallasey Local Board on 20th January 1876 for temporary use at Seacombe during the reconstruction of that ferry, which was not completed until January 1880. They were then broken up. *Sylph* and

An engraving of New Ferry pier as built in 1865.

Sprite, together with two Tranmere boats, were hired by Wallasey at the same time, to extend the temporary stage further into the river. Thereafter the service was run by the Eastham steamers *Wasp* and *Fairy Queen* and later by *Gipsey Queen*.

From January 1879, the New Ferry boats also served Rock Ferry and from April, an additional hourly direct boat was put into service for the summer season between New Ferry and Liverpool, starting at 11.15am from Liverpool. Rock Ferry and New Ferry contract holders could travel from Liverpool to Eastham at half fare on production of their tickets.

According to a report made to Birkenhead Corporation in 1909, there were problems with the New Ferry stage and it was replaced by a larger one of unknown origin, possibly about 1870. The old stage lay on the beach for about 15 years but the second landing stage was carried away in a severe gale on 20th May 1887, bringing the Thompson-Gough tenancy of both ferries to an end. Macfie arranged for the old stage to be completely renovated at Canada Works at a cost of £2,134 and he re-opened both New and Rock Ferries on a date which has escaped the record but was almost certainly in 1889. As recorded elsewhere, Rock Ferry was closed in 1891 but the New Ferry service continued, using *Firefly*, a steel steamer built by J. F. Waddington and Co, Seacombe in 1887. This was the only vessel owned by Macfie. An hourly service was run, starting at New Ferry at 8.00am on weekdays and 1.30pm on Sundays; it ran until 7.30pm in winter and 8.30pm in summer, the last boats from Liverpool being at 8.00pm and 9.00pm respectively.

An annual contract issued for travel between New Ferry and Liverpool under Macfie's ownership. Miss Dean would have had a lengthy walk from Parkfield to the boat at the end of the 1000ft. pier.

YEARLY CONTRACT
1891.

Name *Miss M Dean*

Address *20 Parkfield*

THIS TICKET IS NOT TRANSFERABLE.

And must be shown when demanded, and is issued subject to the following Conditions:—

The Proprietor shall not be bound to run on Sundays, and shall be at liberty to alter the times of sailing as may appear expedient; also he will not bind himself to run any boat if prevented by weather, or to be liable for any stoppage caused by weather, casualties or any other preventable circumstance; and should the ferry be stopped for any reason more than three days in succession, he will return a proportionate amount of the contract money paid.

Municipal Purchase

Public agitation for the re-opening of Rock Ferry was manifest as early as the autumn of 1892. *The Advertiser*, in a leader on 5th November 1892, reported on the proceedings of a properly constituted Town's Meeting which was highly critical of the conduct of the directors of the Mersey Railway for raising their return and season ticket prices. Rumours that Macfie would re-open the ferry in 1893 proved to be unfounded and the Corporation was reluctant to take on additional ferry commitments which would require high capital investment. Macfie died on 16th February 1893 and his trustees continued his policy. Rock Ferry was for sale but only together with New Ferry.

'Memorials' for and against purchase were signed, the anti-purchase lobby warning of an 8d or 10d rate such as the ratepayers of Wallasey suffered for many years. The supporters of municipal purchase were reminded that Rock Ferry had ruined everyone for the last 30 years and reports that the late Mr R. Hetherington had made £10,000 out of it were only a myth; he had made his money out of towing and providing tenders for the Collins Line.

By 1895, the public clamour was such that the Council entered into preliminary negotiations with Macfie's trustees and a Bill, at first known as the South End Ferries (Purchase) Bill, was drafted. At the first attempt, the ratepayers threw it out, but a special Council meeting on 11th September voted 29-10 in favour of purchase and this was confirmed unanimously at the ordinary meeting on 28th October after six dissenting members, who declined to vote, had left the chamber. A handbill issued in advance of a Ratepayers' Meeting on 11th November asserted that the rateable value of property in the Rock Ferry district had declined from £20,065 in 1884 to £17,683 in 1894, as a direct result of the closure of the ferry. Whilst large sums had been spent on Birkenhead Park and Bidston Hill, which benefitted the North End, Rock Ferry had acquired no amenities whatsoever and its ratepayers merely helped to pay the bills for the town as a whole. It went on to say:-

'The Dock Board have bought the whole of the land and river frontage from Birkenhead Ferry right up to Rock Ferry for Docks, and paid, it is said, **nearly a quarter of a million** for it. Practical people will realise what the construction of the Docks and works will cost in addition and the effect on the Ferry. It ought to pay as well as Woodside. The cost of the property, £20,000, is trifling compared with the value to the Borough. Why, the old Rock Company laid out **double** as much on Rock Ferry alone as the Corporation are paying for **both** ferries. The amount can be borrowed by the Corporation at 2¾ per cent, and the present **profit** of New Ferry alone (£1,300 or £1,400) is sufficient to pay for the interest, and a **Sinking Fund** to pay off the principal without loss to the Ratepayers. The Commissioners paid £71,000 for Woodside as a losing concern and see it now. The average income of the Rock Company for the last ten years of its existence was £8,123 and half this amount, a low

estimate, is ample to pay all expenses with economical boats like the *Firefly*, *Wirral* or *Mersey*, and leave a fair profit, besides developing the neighbourhood and consequently reducing the rates over the whole Borough.

Not even a new boat is **absolutely** necessary, notwithstanding the £20,000 odd reserve now standing to the credit of the New Boats Fund Account of the Woodside Ferry account, if the Committee are disposed to work carefully, for the Corporation have **four boats at present**, and the inclusion of the 'Firefly' in the purchase will allow two boats for Woodside, **two** for the South Ferries, and **one as a stand by**.'

Alderman Willmer and Cllr. Benedict Jones painted a rosy picture of the prospect of the purchase of both ferries. The New Ferry service was making a profit and Rock Ferry could develop substantially given a reliable ferry service just as Birkenhead had done half a century earlier when Woodside had been purchased.

The Birkenhead Corporation Act 1897 transferred the township of Rock Ferry from the Wirral Union to the Birkenhead Union and reinforced existing powers for the Corporation to take a lease or become tenants of Tranmere ferry, as the protagonists of the purchase were still thinking in terms of a service from New Ferry to Liverpool calling at Rock Ferry and Tranmere. The purchase was authorised by a separate Act, the Birkenhead Corporation (Ferries) Act 1897, which transferred the freehold Rock Ferry, the leasehold New Ferry and the steamer Firefly to the Corporation for £20,000. The Corporation was bound to run a service between New Ferry and Liverpool at least equal in all respects to that provided by the previous owners, for a period of 30 years from the date of transfer which was 22nd September 1897. In addition, the New Ferry service was not to be less frequent than that provided from Rock Ferry.

The Corporation Takes Over

The Mayor and Committee formally visited and took over the two ferries on the appointed day without ceremony. The Corporation continued the hourly service with one boat as run by Macfie's trustees until 1st May 1898, after which a two boat half-hourly service was put on from 8.00am to 9.00pm using the former Woodside steamers *Wirral* and *Mersey* with the *Firefly* in reserve until sold in 1904. The staff of New Ferry was retained at the same wages except the manager, George Robinson, whose services were terminated with £50 compensation. In the meantime, a Consulting Engineer had been engaged in 1896 to prepare plans for the proposed new pier and landing stage at Rock Ferry and on 1st April 1898 the tender of Jenkins Bros of Birkenhead was accepted. Almost a year later, the contractor was being chased because of delays and slow progress. In June 1898, it was agreed that the pay office at Rock Ferry should be increased in size, four turnstiles being provided instead of three and that the level of Bedford Road at the ferry

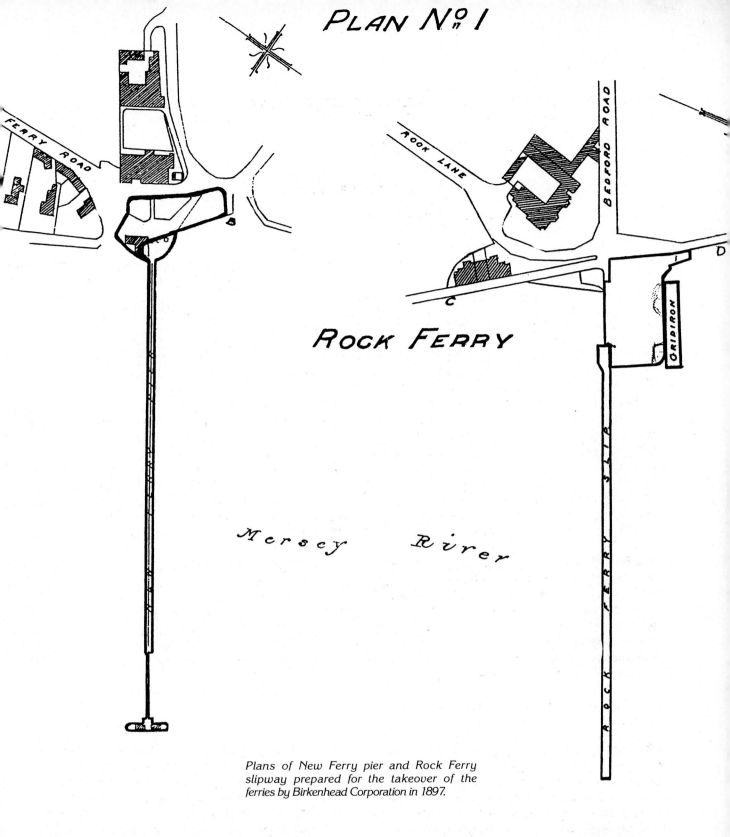

ROCK FERRY

Mersey River

Plans of New Ferry pier and Rock Ferry slipway prepared for the takeover of the ferries by Birkenhead Corporation in 1897.

approach should be raised 'above the influence of the tide'.

The pier was 780ft. long and 18ft. wide, being built alongside and to the north of the old slip. It was built in four sections each of three spans and supported on 14in. cast iron columns, suitably braced. A cluster of columns at the end connecting the pier to the bridge, rose from 24 bases sunk 4ft. into solid rock, the excavations being filled in with concrete for extra strength. The sub-contractor for wrought iron and steel work was J. Gordon Alison and Co of Birkenhead; the girders weighed about 100 tons and the

8ft. by 5ft. rolled steel joists forming the floor, weighed a further 35 tons. The pier decking was of Baltic redwood. Shelters 16ft. long were provided half way along and at the river end of the pier.

A substantial red brick terminal building, surmounted by a clock tower, was erected at the landward end facing Bedford Road. The stage, 150ft. long and 45ft. wide at the widest part, floated on 10ft. x 10ft. wide and 5ft. deep pontoons, four of which were 45ft. long and six were 30ft.

The moorings consisted of six Woods' patent stockless anchors, three at each end and secured with 1½in. studded

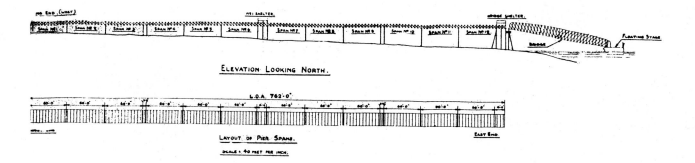

ELEVATION LOOKING NORTH.

LAYOUT OF PIER SPANS.

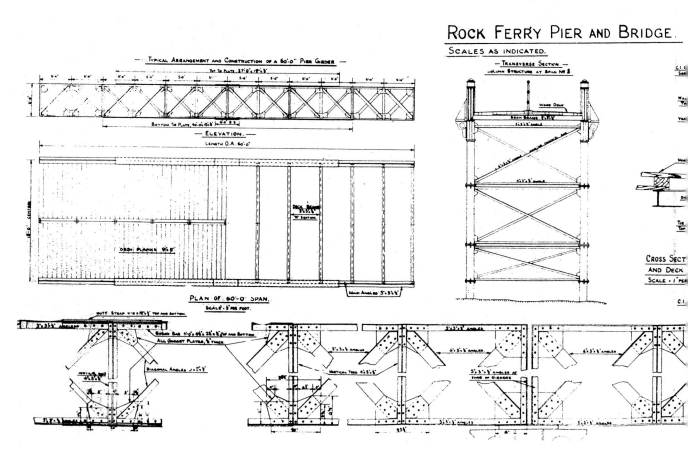

ROCK FERRY PIER AND BRIDGE.

SCALES AS INDICATED.

Design details of Rock Ferry pier built in 1899.

cable chain. The pontoons were connected by strong wrought iron kelsons weighing about 120 tons, over which the floor was laid with wrought iron joists covered with 3in. greenheart planking. There was a waiting room, stagemen's shelter and two small landing gangways for small boats at the back. The average depth of water at low tide was 11ft. The stage was floated out of dock and put in position on 7th June 1899 and, on the same day, the bridge was lifted by the floating crane *Atlas* and placed across two barges, which were towed by the tugs *Hotspur* and *Warrior* from the Great Float to Rock Ferry. It was placed between pier and stage two days later. The bridge was 160ft. long, 10ft. 6in. wide and 16ft. deep at the centre; its decking was of elm and it weighed 60 tons. The cost of the whole work was £18,602-9s-5d.

Rock Ferry was formally opened by the Mayor, J. T. Thompson Esq, with the Chairman of what was now termed the Ferries Committee, Ald. Shaw, at 5.30pm on Friday 30th June 1899. The official party sailed to Liverpool and back on *Mersey* and a public service started about 6.30pm, when the official party went for dinner at the Royal Rock Hotel. Pain's of London, the 'well known firm of firework manipulators' were engaged to illuminate the pier and bridge with several thousand coloured lights between 6.00pm and midnight. Residents of Rock Park let off rockets and other fireworks.

A half-hourly service was run between New Ferry and Liverpool, calling at Rock Ferry seven minutes later. The hours of service were extended to 5.15am to 10.0pm, slight adjustments being made to the early morning times from 1st August. The fare was 2d single (or 2d return up to 8.30am). Henceforth the two ferries were collectively known as the South End Ferries and separate accounts were prepared annually.

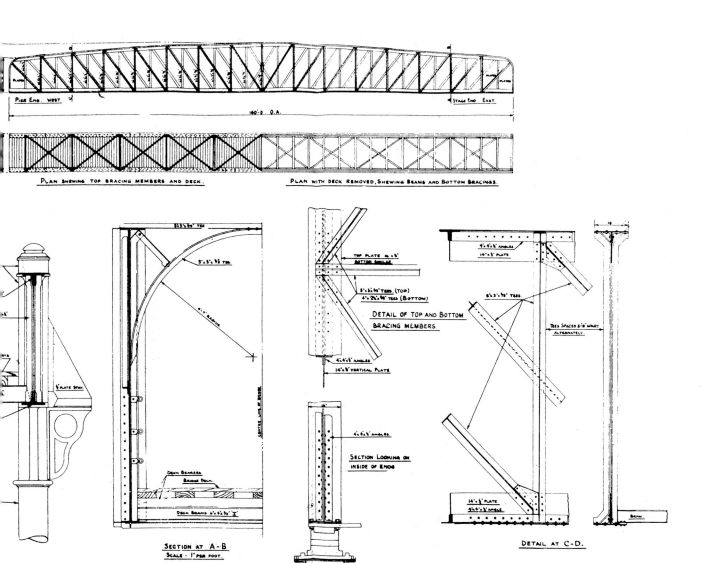

PIER END. WEST.

160'-0" O.A.

STAGE END. EAST.

PLAN SHEWING TOP BRACING MEMBERS AND DECK.

PLAN WITH DECK REMOVED, SHEWING BEAMS AND BOTTOM BRACINGS.

DETAIL OF TOP AND BOTTOM BRACING MEMBERS.

SECTION LOOKING ON INSIDE OF ENDS

SECTION AT A-B
SCALE - 1" PER FOOT.

DETAIL AT C-D.

The Corporation soon found that the protagonists of the acquisition of New Ferry and the development of Rock Ferry had been grossly over-optimistic. Macfie had made no provision for depreciation on *Firefly* or the New Ferry pier and stage, which were 35 years old and the profit of £1,372-14-6d for the last year's working was illusory. Both piers were remote from public transport and the electrification of the tramway between New Ferry and Woodside, from 4th February 1901, influenced many regular passengers to use Woodside. No doubt more would have done so if the tramway service had been adequate but, in the early years, the single deck cars made necessary by a low bridge in Chester Street, were too small to handle all the traffic. The Rock Ferry-Liverpool fare was reduced from 2d to 1d from 18th March 1902 and this reversed a falling trend, attracting £1,015 (30%) additional revenue in the ensuing year. Electrification of the Mersey Railway

from 4th May 1903 reduced the takings at Rock Ferry but did not have the disastrous effect which some councillors predicted.

The MDHB did nothing to develop the Tranmere-Rock Ferry foreshore, having bought it only to block development by rival interests, and the ferry traffic all but stagnated. Whilst Woodside Ferry and the Mersey Railway provided reliable services at all times, the South End ferries were prone to delays or suspension due to fog and lack of water on both sides of the river. The Dock Board would not dredge at New Ferry and the Wallasey UDC dredger *Tulip* was engaged to improve the depth of water in September 1899. The Manager's report, dated 13th January 1904, stated that there were two evenings when passengers were landed and embarked at the goods stage at Liverpool. In March 1904 he reported the curtailment of boats at Rock Ferry at low tide; on other occasions boats could approach

Birkenhead Corporation Ferries.

New Ferry, Rock Ferry & Liverpool Service.

On and after 1st AUG. next (until further notice) the Steamers will sail as under (Sundays excepted):—

To LIVERPOOL From NEW FERRY		To LIVERPOOL From ROCK FERRY		From LIVERPOOL For NEW FERRY calling at ROCK FERRY	
5 15 a.m.	1 30 p.m.	5 22 a.m.	1 37 p.m.	5 35 a.m.	2 0 p.m.
6 10 ,,	2 0 ,,	6 17 ,,	2 7 ,,	6 30 ,,	2 30 ,,
6 55 ,,	2 30 ,,	7 2 ,,	2 37 ,,	7 15 ,,	3 0 ,,
7 15 ,,	3 0 ,,	7 22 ,,	3 7 ,,	7 35 ,,	3 30 ,,
7 40 ,,	3 30 ,,	7 47 ,,	3 37 ,,	8 0 ,,	4 0 ,,
8 0 ,,	4 0 ,,	8 7 ,,	4 7 ,,	8 30 ,,	4 30 ,,
8 30 ,,	4 30 ,,	8 37 ,,	4 37 ,,	9 0 ,,	5 0 ,,
9 0 ,,	5 0 ,,	9 7 ,,	5 7 ,,	9 30 ,,	5 30 ,,
9 30 ,,	5 30 ,,	9 37 ,,	5 37 ,,	10 0 ,,	6 0 ,,
10 0 ,,	6 0 ,,	10 7 ,,	6 7 ,,	10 30 ,,	6 30 ,,
10 30 ,,	6 30 ,,	10 37 ,,	6 37 ,,	11 0 ,,	7 0 ,,
11 0 ,,	7 0 ,,	11 7 ,,	7 7 ,,	11 30 ,,	7 30 ,,
11 30 ,,	7 30 ,,	11 37 ,,	7 37 ,,	12 0 ,,	8 0 ,,
12 0 ,,	8 30 ,,	12 7 p.m.	8 37 ,,	12 30 p.m.	9 0 ,,
12 30 p.m.	9 30 ,,	12 37 ,,	9 37 ,,	1 0 ,,	10 0 ,,
1 0 ,,		1 7 ,,		1 30 ,,	

SUNDAY SAILINGS, Viz:—

From NEW FERRY to LIVERPOOL—1-30 p.m. and half-hourly until 8-30 p.m.

From ROCK FERRY to LIVERPOOL—1-37 p.m. and half-hourly until 8-37 p.m.

From LIVERPOOL to ROCK & NEW FERRY—2-0 p.m. and half-hourly until 8-0, then 9 p.m.

FARE—Twopence between LIVERPOOL & ROCK FERRY or NEW FERRY.

New Ferry Contracts will be available at Rock Ferry and *vice versa*.

RETURN TICKETS 2d. each, may be obtained by passengers using the morning boats (up to and including the 8.30 a.m. from New Ferry and Liverpool and the 8.37 a.m. from Rock Ferry), available to return at any time on day of issue.

July, 1899.   PETER McQUEEN, *Manager*.

The time table published by Birkenhead Corporation at the time of the opening of Rock Ferry pier in 1899.

New Ferry stage only bow on and land and embark passengers by means of a precarious bow gangway. Passengers complained about walking down to the piers only to find that the service was suspended and having to walk back to New Chester Road, often in inclement weather, to seek other means of transport. This problem was partially solved in November 1906 by the placing of special signals comprising two white lights on tramway standards at various points between New Ferry Toll Bar and St. Paul's Road; these were switched on when the ferry service was interrupted for any reason. For these the Ferries

NEW FERRY AND ROCK FERRY. SERVICE.

FOG SIGNALS—NEW CHESTER ROAD.

Notice Boards announcing the sailings of the Steamers, with Fog Signals to denote when on account of fog or for other reasons the Steamers are not sailing, have been placed on the Tramway Poles at four positions, in New Chester Road, viz.:—At the junction of Bedford Road, Rock Lane, Stanley Road and at the old Toll Bar, New Ferry.

Passengers using the Ferries are notified that in future when the Steamers are not sailing on account of fog or for other reasons, a signal showing " **Steamers not Sailing** " will be exhibited at these positions.

At such times **New Ferry and Rock Ferry Contract and Return Ticket Holders will, subject to the observance of the Regulation below but not otherwise, be carried Free by Tram to and from Woodside.**

IMPORTANT REGULATIONS.

Under such circumstances a Contractor or Return Ticket Holder **Going to Liverpool** must on the journey by Tram to Woodside show his Ferry Ticket on demand, and obtain from the Conductor a Special Tram Ticket for which he must pay the prescribed fare, and on giving up such Ticket, and showing his Contract, or giving up Ferry Ticket at the **Contractors' Gate, Woodside Ferry**, to cross by that Ferry to Liverpool the amount paid for tram fare will be refunded, and coming from Liverpool must, **at the Contractors' Gate at Woodside**, show his Ferry Ticket and apply for a Free Tram Ticket.

PROSECUTIONS

On and after the 1st April, 1908, passengers by tram neglecting to obtain tram tickets at Woodside as above will be required to pay the prescribed tram fare for the distance travelled, and failing payment will be proceeded against.

BY ORDER.

An extract from an official handbook giving details of the arrangements for notifying passengers of the suspension of the service from New Ferry and Rock Ferry because of fog, and the ticket arrangements for travel to and from Woodside by tram.

The Birkenhead Corporation steamer **Mersey** *leaving Rock Ferry and with an Eastham steamer behind. The latter called at Rock Ferry to pick up passengers for Eastham (but not for Liverpool) for several years.*

Rock Ferry terminal building in the early years of the 20th century. The shops on the left were demolished about 1919 to make way for a bus turning circle.

Committee was obliged to pay a small acknowledgement rent to the Tramways Committee. Fog tickets could be obtained by contractors enabling them to travel by tram to and from Woodside free of charge.

Because the South End boats were smaller and more economical to run, one was used on the Woodside night service from 1904, 18/-per hour being credited to the South End ferry account. From 27th April 1910, this was reduced to £2-10-0d per night of six hours. Conversely, if a Woodside steamer was used on the South End ferries, the latter account was debited. For the year 1909-10 the charge was £3-5-0d per day.

When it became clear that the losses on the South End ferries were the equivalent of a 3d rate, certain members of the Council agitated for measures to be taken to reduce expenditure. A sub-committee appointed in 1904 recommended no action, accepting in effect that the service was provided as a civic duty. A notice of motion in 1906 failed, but on 9th December 1908 a Special Sub-Committee was appointed to examine the whole question of the finances of the South End ferries. Numbers of passengers carried and losses incurred for the previous nine years since Rock Ferry re-opened were as follows:-

Year ending

31st March	Passengers	Loss £
1900*	1,270,272	3,169
1901	1,560,936	3,594
1902	1,432,837	3,468
1903	1,881,198	3,987
1904	1,778,171	4,768
1905	1,860,273	4,548
1906	1,883,498	4,016
1907	1,891,142	2,600ß
1908	1,995,532	4,591

(Including depreciation but excluding interest on capital)

Notes: * 9 months only.   The proceeds from the sale of *Birkenhead* (the reserve vessel after the sale of *Firefly* on 12th May 1904) were credited to the account in this year.

The sub-committee did their work conscientiously. Three days after their appointment they rose from their beds well before the lark and reported 'We counted 1,046 passengers going into Rock Ferry tunnel station on Saturday 12th December 1908 between 5.0 and 10.0am'. But their report to the Council on 27th January 1909 was against any change being made. They decided that expenditure was well controlled and any curtailment of service would result in a disproportionate loss of traffic. They did not agree with some Council members that the lost traffic would be gained by the tramways and Woodside ferry. They also drew attention to the fact that *Wirral* and *Mersey* were 19 years old and implied that the provision of two new steamers might be a more economical course than making expensive repairs and renewals. The need to renew New Ferry landing stage was also mentioned.

Some interesting figures were quoted. The South ferry steamers averaged 109½ round trips in seven days (616 miles) and 18 round trips on the Woodside night service (another 29¼ miles). The distance between Liverpool, Rock Ferry and New Ferry was 14,850ft. In emphasising the need for repairs to *Mersey* and *Wirral*, it was calculated that in 28½ weeks, the last period that *Mersey* had been in continuous service between dockings for maintenance, the engines had been stopped and started 583,000 times.

The Council accepted the report with only one dissenter and, whilst the losses continued to be a matter of concern to the Council and the ratepayers, no further attempts were made to reduce the service for many years.

The Council appreciated the wisdom of designing smaller purpose-built boats for the South End service and the result was *Storeton*, built by Ailsa in 1910. In length she was almost the equal of the Woodside steamers (142.5ft.) but was much narrower, with a beam of only 32.1ft. The war delayed the delivery of a sister ship until 1925.

The sub-committee had highlighted some of the distortions which arose from preparing separate South End ferry accounts. In the year ending 31st March 1908 the

TO CYCLISTS.

Rides in Cheshire & North Wales.
Beautiful Scenery & Good Roads.

Cyclists should make picturesque **NEW FERRY** their starting point on the Cheshire side of the Mersey.

QUICK SERVICE OF BOATS FROM

Liverpool Landing Stage to New Ferry

Return Fare **5d.** for Cyclists,

Available to return by either New Ferry, Rock Ferry or Woodside Ferry.

Books containing 24 Return Tickets for Cyclists available at either New Ferry Rock Ferry or Woodside Ferry are sold at 8/- per book.

TIME TABLE.

From LIVERPOOL to NEW FERRY :—Week-days, 5-35 a.m., 6-30 a.m.,
    (calling at   7-30 am., and half-hourly till 11 p.m.
   ROCK FERRY)   Sundays, 10-30 a.m. and hourly till
                             1-30 p.m., then half-hourly till
                             10 p.m.

From NEW FERRY to LIVERPOOL : Week-days, 5-15 a.m., 6-5 am., 7
   (calling at ROCK FERRY   a m., 7-25 a.m., and half-hourly till
   7 minutes later).   10-55 p.m. Sundays, 9 55 a.m. and
                         hourly till 12-55 p.m.. then half-

A handbill exhorting cyclists to cross the river by New Ferry dating from early in the century.

South End ferries had been debited with £2,891 for the use of Woodside steamers and credited with £1,111 for use of their boats on the night service. The difference between these sums was, of course, a profit to the Woodside account.

Piers and Stages

Long piers and landing stages, moored in swift-flowing tidal waters, needed both continuous maintenance and constant vigilance. On Good Friday 1904, Rock Ferry stage dragged its anchor and was seriously out of position. Emergency repairs were made on Easter Sunday and, on Friday 15th April, John Gibney and Sons' anchor boat relaid the anchor of the NW mooring and at low water the anchor was bedded into the rock. Almost 30 fathoms of additional chain cable was put next to the anchor, 15 fathoms of which was 2in. chain supplied by Gibneys.

During the summer of 1906, all the iron work on Rock Ferry pier and bridge was cleaned and painted. The ways on the stage upon which the bridge end could move were extended to allow the stage to go further out and to balance up the stage to level without using an iron balance. This was insufficient and small compartments made in the shore ends of some of the pontoons were filled with enough water to get the stage level. In September, the height from water level to the top of the stage was only 5ft. 6in. and there was a scheme to replace a pontoon at Woodside stage and cut the old one in two for use at Rock Ferry to improve buoyancy.

The New Ferry landing stage, which dated back to the beginning of the Macfie era, was in a decrepit state and a decision to renew it was made in 1909. The purchase of a second-hand stage from the defunct Tyne General Ferry Co was considered but that stage was unsuitable and plans for a new one were drawn up. The Commissioners of Woods and Forests were approached about an extension of the lease, which expired in 1945, but they decided that they had no power to grant an extension unless a reconstruction or substantial alteration of the works was contemplated. As there were still almost 37 years to go, this was not pursued. The Conservator of the Mersey approved the arrangements; a proposal to project 6ft. further into the river was not carried out.

The contract for removing the old New Ferry stage, building the new stage and making repairs to the bridge, was secured by the Ailsa Shipbuilding Co for £5,587; the bridge repairs were sub-contracted to John Gibney, Sons & Co Ltd and some finishing work was done by Graysons. The bridge was to be away for one month during which period the service was to be suspended. It was originally intended to close during March 1911 but there were the usual delays and the service was suspended from 3rd April. The bridge was taken away by *Atlas* to Graysons' West Float premises. Ailsa delivered the new stage to Graysons who did some finishing work in Egerton Dock. The old stage, which had been sold for breaking up for £88, was secured at Rock Ferry but had to be scuttled during a gale to prevent it breaking away. The new stage was positioned in mid-May and the bridge replaced on 19th but the latter was resting too low on the stage and the leaf would not fit. After further adjustments, the ferry finally re-opened on 31st May 1911. Glass windscreens had been fitted to the pier in January and the surface was asphalted during the period of closure. The new stage was 24ft. 6in. wide, 8ft. wider than

*New Ferry Pier before the 1914-18 War with a steamer, either **Mersey** or **Wirral** leaving for Liverpool. The ship is **Indefatigable**.*

the old one but the total distance from the shore wall to the outer edge of the stage remained the same at 1,044ft. 6in. Electric light, which had been installed on Rock Ferry pier and stage in April 1911, was first switched on at New Ferry on 14th May 1912, thus completing the modernisation.

The South End ferries settled down to a routine existence but continued to make losses. The finances could be severely affected by bad weather at any of the three Bank Holiday weekends, Easter, Whit and August when, if fine, thousands of extra passengers were carried. It was customary to arrange matters so that no vessel was on survey at any of these times and a third boat would be placed on the South End service. Variations due to the weather are demonstrated by the passenger figures for Easter 1903 (fine) and 1904 (wet):-

	Rock Ferry	New Ferry	Total
1903	15,363	9,008	24,371
1904	13,597	6,493	20,090

The boats were popular with cyclists of which there were large numbers, many of whom were organised into clubs. A reduction in bicycle and passenger fares from 6d to 5d return in 1904 led to a big increase in cycle traffic viz:

	Rock Ferry No. of cycles	£	New Ferry No. of cycles	£
3rd May-5th Aug 1903	5,907	71	24,286	341
1st May-3rd Aug 1904	7,085	78	34,092	399

New Ferry was particularly attractive to cyclists as it enabled the unpopular granite setts along the tramway from Woodside to be totally avoided and landed the riders nearer their destinations. The ferries catered also for those who wished to cycle from home and leave their cycles at the ferry building. A special room was provided at Rock Ferry and this was so overcrowded that in 1913, the manager recommended the provision of more accommodation, but the war intervened and nothing was done until 1924.

The Training Ships

Rock Ferry had special relationships with the training ships *Conway* and *Indefatigable*, moored in the river and their boats had used the slip before the Corporation era. A special steamer was provided for the *Conway* prizegiving on 10th July 1884, embarking and landing passengers at Woodside and Liverpool and this became an annual event. There were many occasions such as prizegivings and displays when special calls were made alongside these wooden walled ships and an extract from the manager's report of 23rd March 1904 indicates how this was done without disrupting the ordinary service.

'On Thursday 17th March 1904, the 6.30pm from Liverpool to New Ferry, after landing all the passengers at Rock Ferry and New Ferry and taking on Liverpool bound passengers at New Ferry, landed a party of visitors at the *Indefatigable*. The 11.0pm boat from Liverpool after landing all at the South End went alongside the *Indefatigable* and took off visitors, landing them at Rock Ferry and Liverpool, before going to Woodside for coal.'

*Boys from the Training Ship, **HMS Conway**, visible in the background, landing at the stairs behind the floating landing stage at Rock Ferry about the turn of the century. Conway was moored in the river off Rock Ferry for 80 years — 1859 to 1939 — and had a long association with the ferries. The bow of the Corporation steamer can just be seen at the stage.*

In November 1913, it was agreed to let a disused ticket office on Rock Ferry stage to the *Conway* at £4 per annum, to enable a telephone to be installed. Facilities were provided for small boats to use the back of the stage and concessionary tickets were issued on the ferry from time to time.

The war years were uneventful, though the improvements in the conditions of labour increased costs and, with them, the losses. Fares were substantially increased from 31st March 1917 and again from 20th September 1920. From 1st April 1917 separate South End accounts were discontinued.

Rock Ferry was closed for approximately a month from midnight on 4th September 1921 whilst repairs were made to the bridge.

In the early hours of 30th January 1922, four of the 14 60ft. spans of New Ferry pier (spans 3, 4, 5, 6 from the river end), were carried away in thick fog by a Dutch coaster *Stad Vlaardingen*. The South End ferry service was cut back to Rock Ferry and, at a special meeting on 1st March, the Committee resolved to reduce the frequency so as to use only one steamer, but the full Council reversed the decision and the two-boat service continued with the frequency stepped up from half-hourly to every 20 minutes. After an initial period of adjustment, these measures resulted in there being virtually no reduction in the number of passengers carried.

Feeling that the damage to the pier was a blessing in disguise, the Ferries Committee decided to explore means of getting out of their statutory obligations under the 1897 Act. On 6th April 1922, the Chairman and Manager had an interview with the Secretary to the Commissioners of Woods and Forests, Mr Evans, regarding the terms and conditions of the lease of Crown Lands upon which the New Ferry Pier was built and to ascertain the attitude the

Crown would take if the Corporation sought relief from its obligations. The representatives submitted the following points for consideration and later confirmed them in writing in the following form:-

(a) That the damage to the structure by the *Stad Vlaardingen* will entail an expenditure of about £15,000 for reconstruction.

(b) That the maximum amount obtainable from the owners of the Dutch vessel, even if the Corporation are successful in fully establishing their claims in the High Court, and exclusive of the costs entailed in contesting the action, will approximate to £7,000.

(c) That our Statutory obligation to maintain a service from New Ferry expires in 1927.

(d) That the Corporation have maintained this service at a considerable loss since their purchase of the Ferry Rights in 1897.

(e) That this annual loss averaged £12,000 until 1918, and owing to the institution of the 8 hours' day, and increases in wages over pre-war rates of payment, now exceeds £20,000 annually.

(f) That the Corporation could only re-build out of revenue—all reserves being exhausted—and this would entail a further heavy burden upon the ratepayers of the borough.

(g) That, since the purchase of this Ferry by the Corporation, travelling facilities in this district have considerably increased by railway, tram and motor bus, and the number of passengers formerly using the Ferry has steadily decreased.

(h) That under these changed circumstances, the Corporation respectfully suggest that the Commissioners should agree to commute the remainder of the Lease, and accept a payment to be agreed upon between the Commissioners and the Corporation in lieu thereof.

(i)   That the Commissioners should also abrogate their rights respecting the maintenance of the Pier, and agree that, under the conditions that have now arisen, the structure should be demolished and the service terminated.

(j)   That we should be obliged if the Commissioners would let the Ferries Committee have their views on the whole matter at an early date, so that a definite statement may be made to the public respecting the future.

Negotiations went on for about two years and it was not until August 1924 that the Council was informed that the Commissioners of Woods and Forests had agreed to accept surrender of the lease of New Ferry to the Corporation on payment of £9,000 and £305 estimated value of rent payable up to expiration of the term, less any amount paid for rent since 1st January 1923. Agents and Surveyor for the Crown were to be paid £105 for out of pocket expenses and cost of plans. In addition the pier had to be removed at the Corporation's expense.

Bebington and Bromborough Council, who had appealed in September 1922 for the re-establishment of the service, wanted to know if the Corporation would be prepared to assign the lease and hand over New Ferry pier and landing stage to any person proposing to re-establish the service, but the Corporation was not interested. A month later they accepted the tender of £405 from Arthur Wilkinson of Liverpool for purchase and removal of pier, bridge and stage. There was later a dispute with Mr Wilkinson, who claimed that material had been removed, and some of the money had to be repaid. The Corporation eventually received £3,739 in settlement of their claim against the owners of the *Stad Vlaardingen*.

In the meantime the Corporation promoted a Bill to extinguish their duty to maintain a service at New Ferry until 1927, and the Birkenhead Corporation (Ferries) Act 1924 passed into law in April of that year. Opposition from Bebington and Bromborough Council and others was finally silenced by the insertion of a clause, offered by the Corporation, to issue a through 3d single ticket between New Ferry Toll Bar and Liverpool Landing Stage, by tramcar or omnibus and Rock Ferry. A bus service between Port Sunlight, Toll Bar and Rock Ferry Pier via New Ferry Toll Bar was envisaged at the time but this never started, the existing service being continued via Dacre Hill. The tickets were first sold on 24th March 1924 and, in practice, passengers walked down Bedford Road from the tram stop in New Chester Road, which was a much shorter walk than from Toll Bar to New Ferry Pier. Although the obligation expired on 22nd September 1927, it was obviously forgotten; almost two years later someone remembered and the 3d through ticket was withdrawn on 31st May 1929.

So ended an empire building adventure which cost the ratepayers of Birkenhead many thousands of pounds.

The Last Days of Rock Ferry

When Birkenhead Corporation introduced its first bus service on 12th July 1919, an event postponed from 1914, one of the declared objectives was to feed Rock Ferry. The route ran from Rock Ferry Pier to Park Station and the ferry's effective hinterland was extended the length of Bedford Road and Bedford Avenue, a district which, for several years to come, had no direct bus or tram service to Woodside.

A second route between the pier and Town Lane, Woodhey started on 4th October 1920 and this was extended to Port Sunlight from 12th March 1921. For many years, Lever Bros. encouraged parties of visitors to tour the Soap Works and the only direct routes from Liverpool were by rail or by Rock Ferry and the connecting bus service. Valuable traffic was obtained from this source and through return tickets were introduced in 1925 at 9d and reduced to 6d in 1928.

In 1924, the Crosville Motor Co was permitted to introduce two rather infrequent bus services from the pier, one to Heswall via Storeton and Barnston and the other to Raby Mere in the summer only. These attracted a little traffic to the ferry.

Some idea of the levels of holiday traffic carried in the 'twenties can be judged by the following statement of passengers carried at Rock Ferry for Easter 1924 and 1925:-

	1924	1925
Good Friday	8,285	10,248
Saturday	7,903	8,297
Sunday	6,536	7,365
Monday	20,642	16,730
	43,366	42,640

In 1925, a new boat *Upton* was built by Cammell Laird & Co for the Rock Ferry service, of similar dimensions to *Storeton* but with four stairways to the upper deck instead of two. *Mersey* was withdrawn and sold for scrap. The pier decking was renewed the following year at a cost of £1,793 but, despite these improvements, the losses mounted, averaging £13,700 per year for the six years 1922-27, and the newly formed Mersey Tunnel Joint Committee, which by that time controlled the ferries' finances (see page 111) clearly favoured closing the service down. In December 1927 the service was curtailed at 10.00pm in winter and the ferries manager was asked to report on the effects of closure. Capt. Langshaw was clearly in favour of retaining it, if only on a seasonal basis. He pointed out that unless the pier were to be demolished, an expensive job, it would have to be staffed and lighted. In the event of a mishap to a Woodside boat, it was the practice to take a boat off Rock Ferry until the spare boat could be got out of dock and during fog, when the Rock Ferry service was suspended, one of the Rock Ferry boats would provide a third boat on the Woodside service to minimise delay to passengers.

Captain Langshaw believed that if Rock Ferry were to be closed, most of the traffic would be lost to the railway.

There was annual contract revenue of £5,000. A third class railway contract from Rock Ferry cost £7-14-9d to James Street or £8-0-9d to Central. By tram and ferry it cost £7-9-0d to the Pier Head—£5-4-0d by tram and £2-5-0d by Woodside ferry. Off peak, passengers could travel by rail from Rock Ferry to Liverpool Central for 6d return compared with 10d by tram, boat and tram on the Liverpool side. Furthermore, the rail journey took only 15 minutes. The Committee accepted Langshaw's view and retained the ferry as 'an asset to the South End'

In 1936 the Borough Treasurer submitted a detailed report on the finances of the ferries but no immediate action was taken. Two years later, three consultants appointed by the Merseyside Co-ordination Committee recommended the closure of the Rock Ferry service 'at the earliest possible moment which legal provisions permit'. There were about 3,000 daily users and heavy seasonal weekend traffic, particularly cyclists, and the general manager favoured the retention of a summer service, but expenditure of £8,000 was needed on the pier and stage and, on 26th April 1939 the Mersey Tunnel Joint Committee passed a resolution to close Rock Ferry and sell

Storeton. Closure was fixed for 30th June, the 40th anniversary of its re-opening under municipal auspices.

Contractors were offered a cash refund or the use of their contracts by bus to Woodside and then on the Woodside ferry. The Ferries Committee agreed to pay the Transport Committee 1d for each passenger carried.

Although no official ceremony was arranged, a large number of Birkenhead councillors and officials boarded *Upton* for the last departure from Liverpool at 10.00pm. Councillors C. McVey and W. H. Egan used the occasion to attack the Tunnel Committee and Liverpool Corporation but, in general, it was a good humoured crowd which witnessed the arrival of the boat at Rock Ferry to the accompaniment of blasts from the sirens of vessels in the river. Finally at 10.20pm, *Upton* left Rock Ferry on the last trip to Liverpool where the crowd waiting on the landing stage sang Auld Lang Syne.

Storeton was sold to the Leith Salvage and Towing Co on 28th May 1940 for £2,375; she had cost £16,407 in 1910. The much newer *Upton* was requisitioned by the Ministry of War Transport and in June 1945, when her return was considered imminent, it was agreed to sell her to

Upton in the later days of the Rock Ferry service in the 1930s.

Rock Ferry about 1931 with Birkenhead Corporation buses — a 1930 Leyland Lion on the Port Sunlight service and a 1928 Leyland Titan, still with its open staircase, on the Moreton route which, by this time, ran through to Bromborough for most of the day, missing out the Pier. There is noticeably less pedestrian traffic than in the earlier view.

the Galway Harbour Commissioners. However by October 1945 the ship had still not been released and the deal fell through. In April 1946 she was sold for £15,000, through C. W. Kellock & Co, to the Southampton, Isle of Wight and South of England Royal Mail Steam Packet Co Ltd for summer excursions, and plied Southampton Water under the same name until broken up at Northam in 1953.

The outbreak of war interrupted what might have been the logical conclusion of the story — the dismantling of the pier as a potential navigational hazard. In October 1939, the Committee came to an agreement with the management committee of *Conway*, who agreed to pay £100 per year to cover landing and embarkation, the use of the slipway and a portion of a shed, and ferriage of personnel between Woodside and Liverpool. The other training ship *Indefatigable* had been moved into Bromborough Dock and it was agreed to charge £15 per year for ferriage or £20 if the ship returned to the river.

In February 1940, J. & A. Lamey Ltd the tug owners, were refused the use of the landing stage and pier, probably to land and embark crews and stores; later the same year the Tunnel Committee considered demolishing the pier for the scrap metal, which was in great demand for melting down for munitions of war. The problem of working in tidal waters and the shortage of skilled labour probably saved the pier from the torch. The following year the Ferries Committee agreed to repair the 'usable footway' suggesting that the pier was being used for some wartime activity. In November 1945, with the war at an end, the Ferries Committee asked the Tunnel Committee what their intentions were regarding the extension of the slipway which would enable the pier to be demolished, but the Tunnel Committee asked who would want to use the slipway and who would pay. It was not anticipated that the training ships would return to the river. Two of the mooring chains were in a bad state and it was agreed that they be overhauled. So Rock Ferry remained intact for the time being.

Between 1946-47 and 1950-51 the 'continuing charges' at Rock Ferry gradually fell from £6,500 to £4,500 pa whilst the annual revenue from landing charges remained about £200.

In November 1951, permission was given for the pier and stage to be used for embarkation of staff employed at Bromborough Tanker moorings and a formal agreement was subsequently made. In 1955 negotiations started between Cammell Laird and Co and the Corporation for the purchase of the pier, a sum of £3,000 being agreed. The pier was to be used in connection with the establishment of a tanker cleaning and degreasing berth, the intention being to lengthen it into deep water. The bridge was removed and in March 1957, almost 18 years after closure, the stage was towed to the nearby beach to be broken up. Since that time, the terminal building has been demolished and the pier, which forms part of the oil terminal, is much modified. The stone slipway is still *in situ*.

Upton as refitted for service on Southampton Water.

6 EASTHAM FERRY

A ferry known as Job's ferry existed at Eastham as long ago as 1509 and the remains of its long abandoned earth jetty can still be discerned about 300 yards north of the Eastham Ferry hotel. It was apparently run by the monks of St. Werburgh, Chester and its principal trade was in farm produce and goods from Chester, North Wales and the South Wirral villages. The ferry probably changed position from time to time as the shifting sandbanks made navigation difficult along this stretch of the Wirral bank of the Mersey. The ferry was sometimes referred to as Carlett Ferry and Carlett Park is still a familiar name in the area today.

In 1707, Nicholas Blundell of Ince Blundell, in his *Diary* records that he made use of the *Eastom* ferry boat to go from Liverpool to Chester and this implies that some sort of land conveyance was available. Before the roads were properly constructed, this short route (ten miles) had advantages over those connecting with the ferries down river.

There are various accounts of sailing boats crossing between Eastham and Garston or Toxteth and it seems likely that the service was flexible, reacting to changing needs. It is certain, however, that until the railway age, the ferry was essentially for produce, passengers being very much a sideline. A regular ferry service was running to Eastham in the 1780s with 'Two very large, commodious and stout boats', leaving the Dry Dock, Liverpool every two hours before high water, for Eastham: 'from whence a stage coach carries passengers, parcels &c. to Chester. Fare by the coach: inside 3/6; outside 1/9'. In 1795, it was announced that 'a very complete decked boat sails from Mrs Urmston's Salthouse Dock Gates, to Eastham where it meets the Chester coach, capable of holding 16 persons. The coach leaves Chester about two hours before high water, with passengers to Liverpool and returns one hour after high water, with passengers from Liverpool to Chester &c. Fare by the boat; First class 1/-; Second class, 6d. Fare by the coach 3/6'. No outside fare is mentioned on this coach and, if it held 16 passengers inside, it must have been a van or omnibus rather than a stage coach. Yet the omnibus is not supposed to have appeared in this country until some 30 years later. Some confirmation of this theory is borne out by the fact that the *Liverpool Guide Book* of 1790 refers to it as a 'double stage coach'. It was evidently an unusual vehicle.

The ferry and the nearby hotel were taken over by Samuel Smith early in the nineteenth century. *Gore's Directory*, 1810 described him as 'master of the Eastham packet' and, in 1816, he placed in service the first steamer to be built at Liverpool. This was the wooden paddle steamer *Princess Charlotte*, launched at Mottershead's

yard at 11.0am on Thursday, 25th July 1816. These early vessels were launched in a completed condition and, according to an advertisement in the *Courier* for 24th July, she was scheduled to enter service on the day after launching:-

'NEW STEAM PACKET TO EASTHAM
'The *Princess Charlotte* Steam Packet will sail from this port on Friday Morning next at Eleven o'Clock and return the same evening; On Saturday Morning she will sail at Eight o'Clock and depart from Eastham at Nine o'Clock. She will sail again from the port at half past Three o'Clock in the Afternoon and return in the Evening. The Packet will sail from Liverpool twice every day at Eight o'Clock in the Morning and at Half Past Three O'Clock in the Afternoon, and will meet the Chester Coach. Places to be taken at Mr. Thomas Dod's, James Street, Liverpool, or at the White Lion, Chester.

Fares to Chester,   3s. Inside
                                         2s. Outside'

The *Princess Charlotte* remained in service for several years and was joined, in 1821, by *Lady Stanley* (61 tons), built by Mottershead and Hayes and engined by Brunton, Birmingham. She was 77ft. long and 17ft. 7in. in breadth. A similar steamer, *Maria*, joined the fleet in 1824 but was replaced by a second vessel of the same name two years later. The latter vessel was built by John Wilson, Chester and is variously described as 60 and 92 tons.

An 1818 Liverpool Directory entry gave details of the coach connections at Eastham:-

'THE PRINCESS CHARLOTTE (STEAM) packet sails to Eastham every morning at 8, and every afternoon at 3 (during Spring, Summer and Autumn months), from the Parade, west side of George's Dock. It meets coaches to Chester, Wrexham and Shrewsbury, every morning at 9, and every afternoon at 4, which are met at Shrewsbury by coaches from Bristol, &c., and all parts of South Wales. During the winter months, the Eastham packet, Joseph Parry, master, sails every day, about two hours before high water, from the same place and is regularly met by a coach from Chester'.

The *Princess Charlotte* was used to tow the sailing ship *Harlequin* out to sea in October 1816, the first example of steam towing on the River Mersey.

Following Smith's death, aged 78, on 19th September 1827, the business was continued by his widow and it

seems that, by this time, the whole route to Chester was controlled by the Smiths as, in 1829, 'Peggy Smith's Conveyance' was running four times a day between Eastham and Chester. Two more ships were added to the fleet, *Sir Thomas Stanley* (100 tons), built entirely of English Oak in 1834 by Thomas Wilson at Birkenhead, with a side lever Fawcett engine, and *William Stanley* (81 tons), built in 1837. The Stanleys were local squires and are commemorated in present-day Eastham by Stanley Lane. There may have been another steamer, *Lady Bulkeley* in 1833-34, of which no details are known. The next generation of Smiths, William and Richard, were still running the ferry and some coaches in the early 1840s and an agreement was signed on 13th December 1841 whereby the Smiths provided feeder services to the railway.

In 1845 or 1846, both hotel and ferry were taken over by Henry Nicholls. *William Stanley* had been disposed of in August 1845 and it is not clear if *Sir Thomas Stanley* remained on the service though she is believed to have been extant as late as 1855. Nicholls bought the 10-year old iron PS *Royal Tar* from J. Henderson and A. McKellar of Glasgow. Built by Tod and McGregor, she was 125ft. long and 16ft. 6in. broad with a net tonnage of 79. Nicholls took her over on 13th May 1846 but in February or March 1847, sold her to William Hilliar. Nicholls also owned the first *Eastham Fairy* of which no details are known. The position is confused as there is evidence of both Nicholls and Hilliar owning ships on the Eastham service but no record of a partnership.

Another Clyde steamer, built by William Denny, Dumbarton and used by Nicholls at Eastham in 1847-49, was the wooden P.S. *Clarence* (70 tons), 92ft. long and 16ft. broad. *Royal Tar* was sold in 1850 for service at Rock Ferry. In 1854 Nicholls acquired *Lochlomond*, a 126ft. iron paddler built in 1845 also by Denny for the Clyde. In 1856 she was registered to Hilliar and, in the same year, Nicholls was fined for overcrowding on *Eastham Fairy* on Good Friday.

As the population of Liverpool increased, Eastham became a popular destination for day trippers. In 1860, William Hilliar was described as the proprietor of Eastham Ferry and boats were advertised to leave for Liverpool at 9.00am, 12 noon, 2.00, 4.00 and 6.00pm on weekdays and at 9.00am, 2.00, 4.00 and 6.00pm on Sundays. By this time there were, of course, no coaches. Hilliar bought two more iron Clyde steamers; in 1858 *Albert* (120 tons), built by R. Napier, Glasgow in 1840 and in 1860 *Toward Castle* (49.57 NRT).

The shifting sandbanks at Eastham were a constant source of difficulty and landing boats were used whenever low tides prevented the ferry steamers getting inshore. An accident to a young lady stepping on board one of the Eastham steamers from the landing boat, reported in the *Liverpool Courier* of 7th April 1847, provides a picture of the hazards of ferry travel at the time. 'She immediately sank but her clothes becoming inflated with air in her descent, she soon rose to the surface and floated down the river for a distance of twenty yards. She was immediately followed by the boat, taken up and conveyed to the hotel where every attention was paid her'. In the 1860s, the provision of a short wooden pier with fixed wooden staircases improved conditions to some extent.

In the early 1860s, operations at Eastham Ferry started to get involved with New Ferry and Rock Ferry, a logical development in view of the limited potential of all three ferries. In 1861, *Eastham Fairy (II)* and *Swiftsure*, Chester-built iron paddlers, 125ft. long and 19.2ft. broad with draught of only 7.7ft., were registered to H. M. Lawrence and Henry Gough. Soon after, Gough became the sole owner and, in 1863 he added *Richmond*, formerly a Loch Lomond steamer named *Prince Albert*. She was 142.2ft. long, 17.1ft. broad and drew only 7ft. All three steamers had a nominal hp of 60. *Richmond* had been built by Denny of Dumbarton in 1850, with engines by Caird and Co. Her naming may have reflected the adoption of the term 'the Richmond of the North' to advertise the amenities of Eastham.

About 1867, Thomas W. Thompson of Eastham became involved with the ferry, possibly as a partner, and

Eastham Ferry from the Hotel

when Gough died in March 1871 the business, together with five steamers, *Eastham Fairy (II)*, *Swiftsure*, *Richmond*, *Sprite* and *Sylph (II)*, passed to Thompson who traded as 'Thompson and Gough'. He developed the hotel, woods and popular zoological gardens and in 1874, commissioned a floating landing stage, connected to the river bank by a very short iron pier and bridge. The ferry operated from Easter to September, hourly from 11.15am to 8.15pm, at a fare of 4d. At Liverpool the steamers used the southern end of George's landing stage, some sources say behind the stage but this has not been confirmed. Liverpool's population increase of the late nineteenth century sustained the popularity of the service. After a lease of Rock Ferry was obtained in 1879, the Eastham steamers called there as well as at New Ferry which had been leased by Gough in 1867. In 1890 Thompson himself built an iron twin screw steamer *Athlete* at Birkenhead with 99 nhp engines by Canada Works. This was 147.7ft. long, 22.8ft. broad and drew 12.1ft, rather a lot for Eastham. Thompson ceased to run Rock and New Ferries about 1887 and seems to have stopped trading at Eastham in 1893. No service was run in 1894-96 and *Athlete* was sold in 1894 and *Wasp*, *Fairy Queen* and *Gipsey Queen* in 1895-97.

New Owners

The hotel, pleasure gardens and ferry passed to Thomas Montgomery, a brewer and William Thomson (sic)—no connection with T. W. Thompson as far as can be ascertained,—described as a valuer of Cook Street, Liverpool. Montgomery resided at Seaview Lodge, Liscard and traded at Victoria Road, Seacombe and Lion Brewery, Chester. These two acquired *Onyx* a a steel paddle steamer formerly the *Norfolk* of the Great Eastern Railway, built by Thomas Ironworks Co. and engined by Young and Son in 1882. With a length of 140ft., beam of 17.5ft. and draught

of only 6.9ft., this 114 ton vessel was particularly suitable for the Eastham service. Her single cylinder oscillating engine developed 50 nhp. In addition, they commissioned two new steel paddle steamers, *Pearl* and *Ruby*, from J. Jones, Liverpool. They were respectively 130ft. and 124ft. long, both with 22ft. beam and 8ft. draught. Gross tonnage was 171 with 2-cylinder compound diagonal engines of 80 nhp. *Eagle*, a 219.5ft.-long iron paddler of 1864, was used for about a year in 1898-99.

Meanwhile a new company, the Eastham Ferry, Pleasure Gardens and Hotel Co Ltd, was registered on 24th July 1897 to take over the various activities as a going concern, implying that the ferry had been re-opened earlier in the 1897 season. Nominal capital of £50,000 was made up of 5,000 £5 7% preference shares and 25,000 £1 ordinary shares., The Memorandum of Association set out a bewildering array of activities—'.... ferry proprietors, owners or proprietors of Pleasure Gardens and a hotel; Restaurant, Café, Tavern, Beer House, Refreshment Room and Lodging House Keepers, Manufacturers of Aerated Mineral and Artificial Waters, Coach, Cab and Carriage Proprietors, Jobmasters and Farriers, Dairymen, Hairdressers, Chemists, Proprietors of Baths, Reading, Writing and Newspaper Rooms and Libraries. To lay out on the lands acquired or controlled ... and to construct, alter, make or work tramways and telegraph lines'. Under an agreement of 26th July 1897, the leasehold ferry, Eastham Hotel, 'woody hereditaments and premises', the three vessels and a new electric lighting plant were transferred to the company for £60,000. The purchase was completed on 1st November and back-dated to 4th June, which was probably the date of resumption of the ferry. The hotel lease ran for 50 years from 1st June 1897 and it was tied to Thomas Montgomery and his successors. The boats were valued at £18,000. Montgomery and Thomson had seats

Ruby moored at Eastham ferry. The general design resembled that of the Birkenhead steamers though the gangway door spacing was more in line with Wallasey practice. Note the disembarking passengers climbing the steeply inclined bridge and one of the sandbanks which made navigation hazardous on this part of the river.

Sapphire passing the Albert Dock warehouses en route from Liverpool to Eastham in the last days of the ferry. The double-ended design and the absence of masts were notable features.

An aerial view of Eastham landing stage with the hotel and, to its left, the Jubilee Arch.

The landing stage and bridge at Eastham

on the board, the other directors being E. J. Bird of Abergele, E. T. Hargreaves of Borough, S. E. and Peter J. Feeny of 67 Lord Street, Liverpool. A 'Jubilee' arch, built on the lines of the Arc de Triomphe to celebrate the Queen's Jubilee, formed an impressive entrance to the Pleasure Gardens.

The company added a third steamer *Sapphire*, similar to the other two but longer (140ft.), broader (24.1ft.) and registering 233 tons gross. All three vessels, which were capable of 15 knots, had rakeless funnels and identical bow and stern, but were not double ended as their appearance suggested. Funnels were at first buff with a black top; apparently this was changed for a time to blue, white and red but latterly became blue with a black top.

On 18th November 1902, a company was formed to lay down a tramway from New Ferry and Eastham Ferry to Chester and both the ferry company and Montgomery as an individual, took shares. However, massive opposition from the railways and the County Council defeated the scheme in Parliament.

The Edwardian years were the heyday of Eastham Ferry but the traffic was mainly at weekends and Bank Holidays and the midweek traffic was very scanty. Through bookings were available from Liverpool Overhead Railway stations at very low rates. The ferry was popular with cyclists, as it cut the pedalling distance to Chester or North Wales by about five miles each way. However the company was inclined to be selective when bicycles were likely to take up too much room on board to the exclusion of passengers, as is borne out by this account from the *Birkenhead News* of 7th August 1901:-

'The Eastham Ferry Co. on Bank Holiday did a roaring trade. So busy were they in fact that cyclists instead of obtaining the benefit usually conferred upon them by the company were unable to get their bikes conveyed across the river either for love or money.'

For the 1901 season, the boats called at Rock Ferry to embark passengers for Eastham, a proportion of the fare going to Birkenhead Corporation. It is not clear if this continued every year as, when the arrangement was renewed in 1911, the manager used the words 'as they did in 1901' suggesting that they had not done so since then.

From early times, on the busiest holidays a boat was hired from Birkenhead who would bring the spare South End steamer out of dock for the purpose. On Good Friday 1869 a fine of £15 was imposed on the Commissioners' steamer *Queen* for overloading while on charter to

Eastham; in 1904 *Firefly* was hired from 12 noon on Easter Monday for £15 and *Birkenhead* for August Bank Holiday for £30. The rate continued unchanged up to 1912 but £40 was demanded for Whit Monday 1913.

In 1909, tenders were optimistically invited for a new vessel but in that year, the company defaulted on their massive mortgage of £25,000 and Sidney Stanley Dawson, chartered accountant, of 51 North John Street, Liverpool was appointed receiver and manager. Statements of account prepared during more than three years of receivership show that, taking one year with another, the ferry was profitable but losses were incurred on the hotel and other activities. Ferry receipts and expenses were as follows:-

	Receipts £	Expenditure £	Profit (Loss) £
1910	4,546	4,236	310
1911	5,420	4,129	1,291
1912	4,220	4,436	(216)
	14,186	12,801	1,385

But the whole undertaking had to be considered as one, as the ferry was the only practical way of reaching the hotel and other amenities except on foot or by cycle.

A new company, the New Liverpool, Eastham Ferry and Hotel Co Ltd took over the business from 10th October 1913 and had barely started trading when World War I closed down the ferry. *Onyx* had been disposed of some time before 1912 and the three newer steamers were requisitioned for war service as minesweepers. On their return in 1919, the owners prefixed the vessels' names with 'Royal' in a similar manner to Wallasey Corporation's *Iris* and *Daffodil* which took part in the Battle of Zeebrugge. However the honour was unauthorised and the prefix was removed after about six weeks.

The immediate post-war fare was 9d single, 1/2d return but, by 1928, it had fallen to 7d single, 1/- return. Through railway excursion bookings were available from various stations throughout Lancashire including those on the Liverpool Overhead Railway.

In the 1920s, Eastham declined in popularity as a tripper resort, becoming run down and unsuitable for family outings. The growth of motor traffic offered alternative venues and the ferry attracted fewer and fewer passengers. The boats ran for the last time in the 1929 summer season and were broken up soon after. They were the last ferry paddle steamers on the river. In March 1934, Bebington Council tried to persuade Birkenhead Corporation to re-open the ferry but too much money was being lost on Rock Ferry for there to be any interest in another ferry at the south end. The pier and bridge were dismantled and the stage towed away by Lamey tugs for breaking that same year. The Jubilee Arch was condemned as unsafe and demolished.

No trace has been found of the winding-up of the company and it may still exist under another name as a property or catering concern. Only the short stone stub of the pier and some wrought iron at the entrance to the hotel gardens remain as a reminder of this once popular pleasure ferry.

7 THE LUGGAGE BOATS

Up to the 1940s, most people on Merseyside knew that a 'luggage boat' was a unique broad-beamed vessel used for conveying vehicular traffic across the river. The origin of the term is obscure; it was certainly current in 1851 when *Kingfisher*, then in use on Monks Ferry, was somewhat disparagingly described in that fashion. But until the provision of floating roadways on both sides of the river, the conveyance of vehicles across the river was difficult and, in the days when luggage and goods were unloaded, ferried across the river and reloaded on the other side, 'luggage boat' was a suitably descriptive term.

In the early days, the conveyance of goods across the Mersey was of greater importance than the conveyance of passengers. This was reflected in the rating of ferry property as being part of a freight-orientated undertaking, thereby obtaining certain rebates. This continued until 1956 when the privilege was withdrawn with expensive consequences to the ferries undertaking.

The rapid expansion of the town and its industrialisation in the mid-nineteenth century increased the volume of goods crossing the river very considerably. Agricultural produce from Cheshire traditionally carried by Eastham and New ferries and, to a lesser extent, Rock Ferry, tended to be diverted to rail after 1840 and was, therefore, handled at Monks Ferry. During the lease by Willoughbys, Tranmere Ferry enjoyed a large volume of goods traffic including traffic for the Wallasey townships which, before the building of the bridges across the Great Float, had to go by road round the west end of the Pool. Willoughbys employed three carts on this traffic until Wallasey Ferries introduced their own goods service about 1862.

The Commissioners fixed certain charges on 19th July 1842 of which the following are examples:-

Carriage with two horses, family, servants and luggage		10/-
Ditto without servants and luggage		8/-
Geese per score		6d
Pocket of hops		6d
Cheese	each	1d
Calves, pigs and sheep	each	1d

The conveyance of a carriage would have entailed the unharnessing of the horses and the separate loading of animals and vehicle. Naturally carriages were taken across the river only in exceptional circumstances.

In 1846 two 'flats' (unpowered barges) were being used for goods traffic at Woodside. Two such craft, named *Railway* and *Transmit* were disposed of in the 1850s. Revenue from goods and parcels from 1840 to 1845 was as follows:-

	£	% increase year on year
1840	282	
1841	342	21
1842	448	31
1843	1,054	35
1844	1,387	32
1845	1,947	40

The growth of freight traffic soon necessitated its separation from passengers and, for many years, older passenger steamers were converted for goods and livestock traffic. In the days before deck cabins, the work of conversion was nominal and contemporary reports make it clear that vessels were transferred on occasions from one activity to the other.

In November 1851, a sub-committee recommended that the goods traffic be sub-contracted if possible, the lessee finding his own boats. Price's trustees would agree only to a non-exclusive licence, not a lease, and it was on this basis that negotiations were carried out with the railway company in 1852. However the deal was dependent upon the latter taking back Monks Ferry and no agreement could be reached.

It was agreed that goods traffic should be handled only from the slipway on the south side of the Woodside jetty and in 1855 this slipway was altered to improve access for vehicles by easing the gradient. Steps were put in about half way down and an 'L' shaped road constructed on the south side joining the slipway immediately below these steps.

By 1854 the Ferry Committee had authorised the engagement of a separate goods manager and specific cartage contractors were being appointed to collect and deliver goods to and from Woodside and Monks Ferry slips. On one occasion in 1855, the Commissioners invited tenders for this work and it is not clear how matters were arranged as they had no powers to charge for handling or carting goods until 1891. The 'modus operandi' of the goods manager is also obscure, as certain reports suggest that, for a short time at least in the mid-1850s, contractors were prepared to pay for the right to handle the goods traffic.

In July 1855 Daniel Corkhill replaced Thomas Jones as cartage contractor for collection and delivery and, the following month, Corkhill complained of being 'much interrupted' by Mr Jones and his men who defied 'the parties in authority' at Monks Ferry and refused to leave the slip. They had taken forcible possession of goods consigned to him for cartage. This suggests that the carters tendered for the right of access to the slipways and collected cartage charges COD from the consignees. A policeman was assigned to the slip to keep order amongst them.

In 1855 a Mr Beggs was variously described as the goods manager or the goods clerk. In August 1855, Beggs and Corkhill were in dispute and Beggs was instructed to 'obey the ferry manager'. It was resolved that all goods, for which no direct written order was produced, be taken by Corkhill before the carts of those having written orders be admitted through the ferry gates. The following month the manager told the Committee that he had seen Corkhill and Beggs with reference to arranging for working the goods traffic together but found it impracticable. Mr Corkhill would give £25 per week in advance for the privilege of carrying on the goods traffic on his own account, if he could use the luggage boat and Monks Ferry slip, and this was accepted. Beggs was told to confine himself in future to his duties at the parcel gate and office at Woodside ferry. One can speculate that Beggs was being bribed by carters to direct goods their way, to the detriment of Corkhill. A contract was drawn up by the Law Clerk in October and it is not known what happened to Corkhill as, on 2nd November, Beggs offered to take over the goods traffic and was dismissed as Commissioners' Goods Clerk 'at the end of year of his engagement'. The traffic was let to Beggs for a period from 5th November 1855 to 24th April 1856, subject to the same terms as the agreement with Corkhill. On 11th April he was reported as being in arrears with his payments and was given a week's notice. A month later he was described in a report as the former goods manager.

As far as is known, there were no further attempts to sub-contract the goods traffic which was increasing at a steady rate to produce revenue of £2,329 in 1857-58.

MDHB Intervention

Following the unification of the port with the founding of the Mersey Docks and Harbour Board on 1st January 1858, attention was paid to the improvement of facilities for handling cross-river traffic. An Act of 1858 enabled the Board to acquire a portion of the foreshore, beaching ground and ferry slip at Woodside from the Birkenhead Commissioners and this led to the construction of the Woodside floating landing stage of which 300ft. at the south end was reserved for the use of the Birkenhead ferries. In the meantime, at Liverpool, goods traffic was now handled at the north end of the new Prince's Landing stage, opened on 1st September 1857. However, for six hours during each tide, the service was confined to handled goods as the gradient was too steep to be negotiated by horses or vehicles of any kind. A hut which had been erected on Prince's stage was removed in August 1858 and this act may mark acceptance of the principle that tolls should not be collected on the Lancashire side of the river. The Mersey Docks (Ferry Accommodation) Act 1860 empowered the MDHB to erect floating bridges at Liverpool and Woodside. The MDHB sought means of recovering at least some part of the very great expenditure involved from the users and, to avoid subjecting the public to the nuisance of two transactions, one for the use of the

floating bridges and the other for ferriage, an agreement was made with the Birkenhead Commissioners whereby 25% of the gross receipts from the carriage of goods other than passengers' luggage would be paid over to the Board. However this levy was abated to a considerable extent pending completion of the contemplated works and only 5% was paid over from 1st January 1864.

In 1860, the Commissioners surrendered their monopoly rights to the carriage of goods between Liverpool and Birkenhead by agreeing to goods being lightered between docks on either side of the river.

The new landing stage at Woodside (see page 32) was brought into use in 1862 and, pending installation of the floating roadway, the goods traffic was allowed to use the north bridge and pass over the MDHB portion of the stage. As at Liverpool, the gradient was too steep to be tackled by wheeled traffic for several hours each day.

It is on record that in each of the years 1863 and 1864 fewer than 25,000 horse drawn carts visited Woodside stage; in addition there were 3,207 handcarts in 1863 and 3,998 in 1864. Of the horse drawn carts, only 2% crossed the river, an average of fewer than two per day. This is not surprising in view of the high tolls, about 13/- for an omnibus, 5/- for a cab and 1/- for a handcart. The total revenue from carriage of vehicles in 1862 was £163-8-6d. Total revenue from goods and vehicles in fiscal 1862-63 was £2,713, a 24.3% increase on 1859-60. More detailed figures for the 1860s appear below.

VEHICLES CROSSING THE RIVER BY WOODSIDE FERRY

	Calendar Years		
	1862	1865	1866
Omnibuses	9	2	1
Carriages	17	26	21
Phaetons	32	55	40
Cabs	27	18	4
Gigs	40	72	80
Loaded Carts	276	739	1,026
Empty Carts	215	61	63
Handcarts	837	985	832
TOTAL	1,453	1,958	2,067

Source: Ferry Manager's Memorandum Book.

The conveyance of carriages was often stimulated by special events, such as Hoylake Races, at that time held in April and October.

Work on the Woodside floating roadway commenced in 1865 and it was apparently brought into service early in 1868 though the most exhaustive enquiries have failed to reveal the exact date. The MDHB levy was then increased to 8⅓%. During the construction period, several sub-committees considered the implications of embarkation facilities free from tidal restraints but there was really no change until the Liverpool floating roadway was able to provide comparable facilities on the Lancashire shore. Indeed the revenue in each year 1868-71 was less than that of ten years earlier. A goods shed and clerk's office was built on the stage and the MDHB section was fenced off.

There were many schemes for getting vehicles and goods across the River Mersey. The shipping interests opposed all the bridges because of headroom and the potential dangers of the intermediate piers, especially in fog.

There were many schemes for getting vehicles and goods across the River Mersey. The shipping interests opposed all the bridges because of headroom and the potential dangers of the intermediate piers, especially in fog.

The floating roadways at Woodside and Liverpool were of similar construction, the former being 677ft. long and the latter 560ft. Sections of roadway were flexibly joined and floated on enormous iron pontoons of which there were nine at Woodside and seven at Liverpool. The wheel track ways of the twin roadways were laid with steel plates to reduce wheel resistance with girders to prevent wheels straying, whilst the part between each wheel track was paved with rough wooden blocks to assist the horses' hooves to get a firm grip. Planked footways were provided at each side. The Liverpool floating roadway came into service with the new landing stage on 27th July 1874 but was rendered inoperative on the following day due to the destruction of the stage by fire. During the ensuing year, no vehicles were able to cross the river, as the Prince's landing stage facilities were used as emergency berths for the passenger ferries. Revenue dropped from £4,021 in 1873-74 to £2,607 in 1874-75 and a loss of £720 was incurred. From the restoration of full facilities in 1876, the Board claimed the full 25% of the gross receipts and revenue rose to a record £4,594 in 1876-77 and continued to increase almost every year. From September 1876 charges for vehicles and goods were reduced, reflecting the better utilisation of men and vessels. The old converted luggage boats were hard pressed to cope with the traffic and long queues frequently lined the floating roadways and spilled over into the streets. It was obvious that a considerable expansion of facilities was necessary.

Chain Ferries Proposed

The idea of purpose-built luggage boats had been suggested as long ago as 1862 when George Harrison, Chairman of the Ferry Committee, had prepared a long report on steamer design. Although his ideas on passenger steamers had largely been accepted (see page 37), no action had been taken on luggage boats as conversion of old passenger boats was considered to be a cost-effective means of extending the economic life of the vessels. Harrison's concept of a luggage boat was a vessel not less than 150ft. or more than 180ft. long, with 30-35ft. beam and drawing 8ft. with 100 tons payload. It should be able to steer from both ends to assist manoeuvrability. In 1866 the Dock Board Engineer, G. Fosbery Lyster, proposed a system of chain ferries from Liverpool to both Woodside and Seacombe. The vessels were to be circular and built to carry both vehicles and passengers; they were to be steam-powered pontoons which hauled themselves along a pair of chains on the principle developed by Rendel and which can still be seen at Torpoint, Dartmouth, Cowes, Poole Harbour and elsewhere. The example of the Portsmouth-Gosport 'Floating Bridge', a chain ferry which had worked successfully for 30 years was cited; there were others which had worked even longer. However, the much longer passage and greater tidal range of the Mersey presented difficulties. The greatest obstacle was the practice of ships being anchored by pilots in the track of the ferries. This was

RIVER MERSEY APPROACHES AND FERRY.

DESIGNED BY MR. G. F. LYSTER. ENGINEER TO THE MERSEY DOCK BOARD.

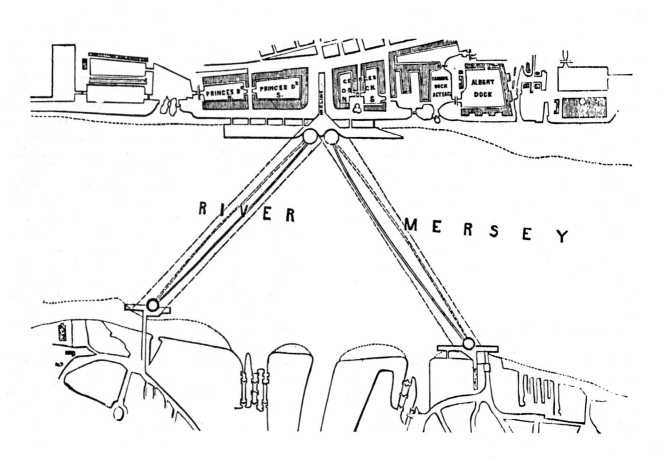

G. F. Lyster, the Dock Board Engineer designed this 1866 scheme for chain ferries, catering for both passengers and vehicles on the same vessels, to both Woodside and Seacombe. The resemblance to many train ferries will be noticed. The map includes some planned changes to the dock system which were never carried out such as the division of Georges and Princes Docks into north and south sections.

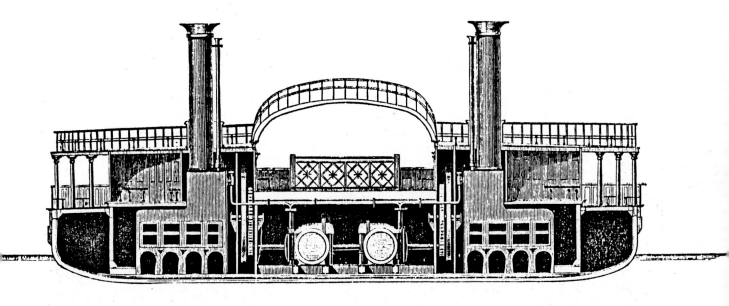

Cross-section of the proposed chain ferry of 1866

a real hazard for years, especially in fog, and the cause of bitter complaint. But at least a free vessel could dodge around, whereas the chain ferries were tied to a track which could vary, say 40 yards up or downstream with the flow. Lyster rightly foresaw another snag, which was the threat to the chains posed by anchors dragging along the river bed. He proposed to lay down guard chains on either side of the haulage chains. The pilots were not impressed by anything which interfered with their freedom of action when in charge of a vessel, as was shown by their attitude to the electric telegraph cable which the Dock Board laid across the river. It was repeatedly hauled up on the flukes of ships' anchors, whereupon the pilot would simply take an axe to it, putting a quick end to communications. With so much shipping at anchor in the river the chains would have been constantly threatened but the idea was otherwise technically sound.

It is not known if Harrison was influenced in any way by the design of *Newport*, an iron paddler built in 1853 by Fenton and Smeaton of Perth. It had been inspected in 1859 and purchased by the Commissioners from the Scottish Central Railway Co about 1860. Little is known of this vessel except that it had a gross tonnage of 163 and was bought specifically as a 'baggage vessel'. It had a short career as it caught fire in 1864 and was sold to T. C. Gibson, Liverpool.

Increased Traffic

The installation of floating roadways on both sides of the river stimulated vehicular traffic between Liverpool and Birkenhead and Birkenhead Corporation was soon faced with the same kind of problems experienced with the passenger traffic in 1863 — the need to match the vessels to the improved landing facilities. This led to the design of the first purpose-built luggage boat. *Oxton* revolutionised the conveyance of vehicles and set a standard for vehicular ferries on the Mersey for the next half-century. She cut the traffic queues to such an extent that less than three weeks after she went into service the Committee was proposing to withdraw two of the old luggage boats, leaving the traffic to be handled by Oxton alone. The same meeting resolved that the service should start at 6.00am instead of 7.00am and that all horse-drawn wheeled traffic embarking or disembarking from the new vessel without the assistance of ferry staff should be allowed a reduction of 50% in charges. Tariffs for certain types of vehicles and goods had already been reduced on 1st February 1879 and this second round of decreases came into force during October. A comparison of the reductions in tolls for vehicles and goods between 1876 and 1880 will be found in Appendix 5. A decision was taken in November 1879 to order a second luggage boat with a few slight modifications suggested by the manager. The order for *Bebington* went to W. Allsup & Co of Preston in January 1880. The existing service was further accelerated by placing a clerk on board the vessels and cutting out the collection of tolls from vehicles disembarking at Woodside. The Committee was worried about what would happen if *Oxton* had to be taken off the service for any reason and asked the manager to advise on what would need to be done to convert *Queen* and *Liverpool* for carrying on the goods traffic temporarily but it is doubtful if any work was done on these vessels.

One of the last passenger boats to be converted for goods service was *Cheshire* of 1863 and an undated memorandum believed to have been made in the 1870s, sets out the cost of operating her as a luggage boat working from 8.00am to 6.00pm for one year.

*The first **Oxton**, built in 1879, was specially designed to speed up the handling of vehicular traffic, revolutionised by her introduction. Note the facility for horse-drawn carts to board and alight simultaneously via the two gangways on each side as well as the assortment of 'handled goods' which caused so many problems before the days of pallets and containers. She is seen at Woodside early in the twentieth century.*

	£
Wages, coal and stores	1,660
Proportion of salaries, allowances and sundries	200
Wages of clerk and porters	200
Repairs 5% on £10,000	500
Interest on capital (5% on loan) (	
Depreciation 5% (	1,000
	3,560

The MDHB agreed to a proposal to increase the maximum vehicle weight, (1 ton per wheel, maximum 4 tons) by 50% and, in the light of the financial results, tariffs were again reduced in October 1880. The cart with two horses which paid 8/- in 1876 now crossed the river for 1/9d. *Bebington* which initially did not come up to specification, entered service in November 1880 and, within three months, the Committee was agitating for a third vessel but this time the full Council decided to wait until the two new boats had fully settled in. They also needed the borrowing powers of the 1881 Bill, not then passed. It was not until two years later, on 28th February 1883, that the order for *Tranmere* was placed with W. A.

Stevens, Canada Works, Birkenhead, and the vessel entered service the following year.

Experiments were made with running late vehicle boats. The first lasted for the month of January 1882 being dropped due to lack of support. In October 1882 it was agreed to run a late boat to convey the carriages of patrons of the Hallé concerts and this became a regular practice.

These improvements discouraged any action being taken on a scheme of dubious feasability which nevertheless was authorised by Parliament in 1880.

The Subway Scheme

In 1880, 11 eminent men promoted a private Bill to construct a tunnel for pedestrians and road traffic between Birkenhead and Liverpool. The promoters were W. L. Gladstone, John and William Laird, William Jackson, Christopher Bushell, William Blain, G. B. Gow, D. Duncan, J. H. Hind, C. G. Mott and J. A. Tobin. The Liverpool and Birkenhead Subway Act received the Royal Assent on 6th August 1880. The main entrances were to have been in Canning Street, Birkenhead, 25yds. west of the corner of Taylor Street and, in Liverpool, 25yds. west of the James

Street/Back Goree junction. There was also to have been a branch tunnel from Hamilton Square joining the main tunnel 40yds. south of the Argyle Street/Cleveland Street corner.

Capital of £500,000 in £10 shares was authorised and Liverpool and Birkenhead Corporations and the Mersey Docks and Harbour Board were each empowered to purchase shares to the value of £125,000 in the Liverpool and Birkenhead Subway Co leaving 25% of the equity to private investors. The Birkenhead Corporation Act 1881 gave Birkenhead permission to borrow money for this purpose.

The principal tolls were to be 1d for foot passengers, 1/- for each omnibus, coach, chariot, phaeton (with 2 horses and including occupants); 9d for a gig or carriage (one horse and occupants) and a whole range of tolls for other vehicles. Double tolls were to be charged between 12 midnight and 5.00am.

The ruling gradient was to have been respectively 1 in 25.75 and 1 in 26 on the Liverpool and Birkenhead sides. The subway was to have been built in the form of an iron tube with a 19ft. wide road and 19ft. headroom in the centre. The lower section of the tunnel would have been used for drainage, utilising hydraulic pumps. Amending Acts were obtained in 1885, 1888 and 1889 and the final scheme, which was dropped in 1890, provided for a near level tunnel with lifts at the foot of James Street, Liverpool and at Canning Street, Birkenhead. The passing of the Act coincided with the commencement of trial borings for the railway tunnel and the commissioning of a second purpose-built luggage boat by Birkenhead Corporation. A high-level bridge scheme was proposed in 1898 but all such schemes were opposed by the Admiralty and merchant shipping interests and nothing more was done.

Handled Goods

Whilst the greater part of the goods traffic was carried across in vehicles, parcels and many other items were delivered by consignees to the landing stages for individual carriage across the river. Light parcels and newspapers went by passenger boat but most unaccompanied goods used the luggage boats. During the 1880s this traffic, along with the vehicular traffic, increased enormously and caused the Corporation some embarrassment. Somewhat cramped warehouses were provided on both sides of the river and goods clerks were employed. Lower tariffs had been authorised by the Birkenhead Corporation Act 1881 but the expenses of handling these goods could not be legally recovered. Furthermore the Corporation was statutorily prevented from collecting tolls on the Liverpool side of the river.

In July 1884, the Corporation flew a kite by proposing to cease carrying handled goods and this immediately brought forth howls of anguish from organised commerce. A deputation was received and no immediate action was taken. A sub-committee, considering various economy measures in view of the loss of passengers to the Mersey Railway, pointed out that handled goods which in 1886 brought in almost 10% of the goods revenue (£1,187 out of £11,974), slowed down the service to the extent that a 20-minute frequency was the best possible. By eliminating

Another bridge scheme was announced in 1898. Steep gradients were beyond the capability of horse power but the alternative was long approach roads resulting in prohibitively costly property demolition. This scheme favoured hydraulic lifts of which an example had been installed at Seacombe goods ferry in 1879.

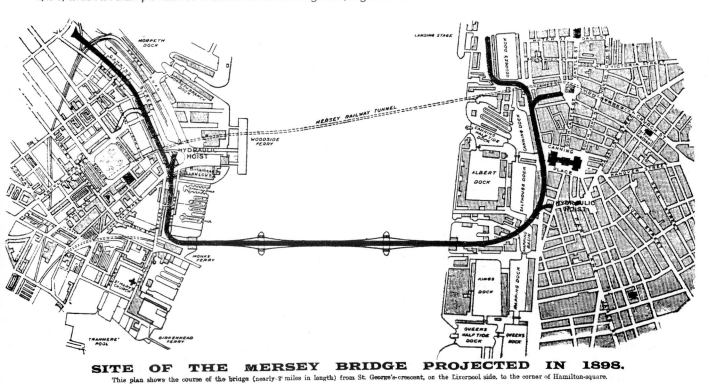

SITE OF THE MERSEY BRIDGE PROJECTED IN 1898.

This plan shows the course of the bridge (nearly 2¼ miles in length) from St. George's-crescent, on the Liverpool side, to the corner of Hamilton-square.

them, the same vessels could provide a 15-minute frequency and £4,000 per annum could be saved on the ferry service as a whole (see Chapter 3). The matter was constantly under review and it was finally accepted that the traffic could not be discontinued and the solution lay in obtaining statutory powers to charge for handling.

A graphic account of the handling of this traffic is to be found in the evidence of Capt. R. E. Pinhey, the ferries manager, before the Select Committee examining the Birkenhead Corporation Bill in 1891 in which *inter alia* powers were sought to charge for services rendered in addition to ferriage.

'The Corporation are in a peculiar position, as they profess to be Ferry Owners only and not Common Carriers or Warehousemen and yet at the same time they have to perform services and accept responsibilities which would attach to Common Carriers and Warehousemen.

For example goods are brought to a warehouse on the Liverpool stage consigned to persons in Birkenhead. The Corporation have to keep a staff at this warehouse who receive goods and give receipts and the persons who bring the goods down assisted by the Corporation's Porter and Boatmen if necessary place these goods on board the steamer. The Goods are then conveyed across the River and there being no person on the stage to receive these Goods they are landed by the Boats crew and put on the stage at Birkenhead. If the Consignee is waiting the arrival of the boat he of course takes away the Goods himself but if he is not as is most likely the case the Goods are put into a warehouse that the Corporation own on the stage and unless, in the exceptional case of being called for they are taken by Carters who ply for hire on the stage and are delivered in certain circles to their destination the Carter charging according to distance when he also collects the Ferriage.

The Corporation men very frequently have to give assistance in embarking and disembarking vehicles or articles or goods which it is contended would render them liable as Common Carriers and very frequently the Corporation pay damages for injury to goods which if they were simply Ferry Owners they could disclaim but the fact of being obliged to handle goods and to perform services in respect of these various articles it is contended would render them liable. The space available to the Corporation in conducting their goods traffic is so small that they have no opportunity and means of warehousing goods to any very large extent for any lengthy period. It is therefore absolutely necessary that the goods must be discharged and delivered without loss of time otherwise the traffic would become immediately blocked and great inconvenience and difficulty would ensue and sometimes does ensue as the traffic is a perpetual stream.

The Carter on delivering goods is sometimes refused payment and it has been held in the Law Courts that he is unable to recover for such delivery inasmuch as there is no privity of Contract between himself and the consignee. He therefore takes the risk, and if Carters were not found who would be willing to undertake this risk of payment the traffic must become blocked.

The Corporation consider that they ought to be entitled to charge something, however small, in respect of the services which are rendered by their Employees in addition to the Ferry toll and they are quite prepared and desire to undertake to become Common Carriers and Warehousemen. They also desire to be in a position to engage or retain the services of carts or to authorise Carters to deliver and to collect goods and to be in a legally qualified position to receive payment therefor.'

One of the aims of the 1891 Bill was to obtain some relief from payment of the 25% toll to the MDHB. The Corporation's case was that they had been obliged to spend £30,129 on the provision of new boats as a result of which the traffic expanded but the profits declined as the law of diminishing returns took effect. The MDHB's percentage, being based on turnover, increased every year. A clause in the Bill sought to limit payment to £1,500 per year but this was withdrawn before the Select Committee, a limit of £3,500 being accepted; this was slightly less than the £3,780 paid over in 1890. An agreement was made for five years from 25th March 1891 and thereafter until termination by either party by six months' notice. It was eventually terminated by the Dock Board from 30th July 1904 by which time £3,500 represented only about 14% of the ferry tolls. The amount demanded by the MDHB was £4,500 which was about 19% of the 1904 receipts and therefore well below the £5,800 which the Board could have demanded on the basis of 25%. The Corporation rather greedily attempted to tie the payment to an obligation on the part of the Dock Board to dredge the river at George's Landing Stage to a greater depth and threatened to go to Parliament to get the necessary powers to force them to do this work. In a report dated 5th October 1904, the manager strongly recommended that this line of action be abandoned pointing out that the MDHB's demands were eminently reasonable and, as the Board was already spending large sums on dredging, it was unlikely that Parliament would be sympathetic. The wisdom of this argument was recognised by the Council and the new agreement, dated 13th February 1905, set a £4,000 limit for two years and then £4,500 for five years, the Corporation promising not to go to Parliament about dredging during the currency of the Agreement, which remained in force until 1921.

Increased Sailings

In the earlier years, vehicular traffic could be handled adequately by a half-hourly service between 8.00am and 6.00pm, requiring two boats but, as traffic increased, it became necessary to start earlier in the morning and continue later into the evening. With fast, purpose-built boats, loading and unloading was accelerated and it was just possible to run a half-hourly service with one boat and a 20-minute service with two. By the late 1890s, the service started at 6.30am and ran half-hourly until 9.30am then every 20 minutes until 5.30pm and half-hourly until 8.30pm. In practice, boats could be ordered in advance outside these hours and this was often done in connection with the meat trade and other perishable market traffic. In March 1904, the manager reported that there were many occasions when vehicles were shut out of the half-hourly sailings and recommended that the 20-minute service be extended to run between 8.00am and 6.30pm. Practical difficulties seem to have prevented this being fully implemented immediately though the 20-minute service was continued until 6.30pm. *Bebington* and *Tranmere* had new gangways fitted in 1904 because of increased weight, the old ones being taken into Woodside ferry yard to make foundations for new cranes. There was normally no Sunday service but special work was undertaken by prior arrangement. On 2nd July 1904 *Bebington* made two trips in the morning to convey the Lancashire Artillery and their gun carriages back to Liverpool and on the following Sunday Bostock and Wombwell's Menagerie was conveyed, thirty shillings being charged for 35 horses to cross and return the next week.

When traffic was heavy, it formed long queues up the floating roadways on both sides of the river and sometimes congested the streets. At Liverpool the floating roadway was shared with the Seacombe traffic so the congestion was worse and there were complaints from the police. The manager emphasised the gravity of the situation in a further report to the Committee in January 1905. If a boat was out of service, there were serious problems and the traffic was badly disrupted when a steam-powered gangway was out of order for two days. For every four months on the ferry, each of the three boats was in dock for two months for surveys, boiler cleaning and general repairs. As the traffic continued to increase every year, the solution lay in the provision of a fourth boat so that an increased service could be operated, and the Council ordered a steel vessel of similar design and dimensions, originally intended to be named Liverpool but eventually commissioned in 1907 as *Prenton*. She was built at Preston by Caledonian Shipbuilding Co. and drew slightly more

Birkenhead Corporation Ferries
LUGGAGE SERVICE.

A SPECIAL

LATE STEAMER

Will run on the

21st, 22nd, and 23rd Dec.,

Leaving WOODSIDE at 7-50 p.m.

AND

Leaving LIVERPOOL at 8-10 p.m.

PETER McQUEEN,
Ferries Manager.

20th Dec., 1905.

A 1905 handbill announcing a 'late' sailing prior to Christmas. Some years later, the service ran all night.

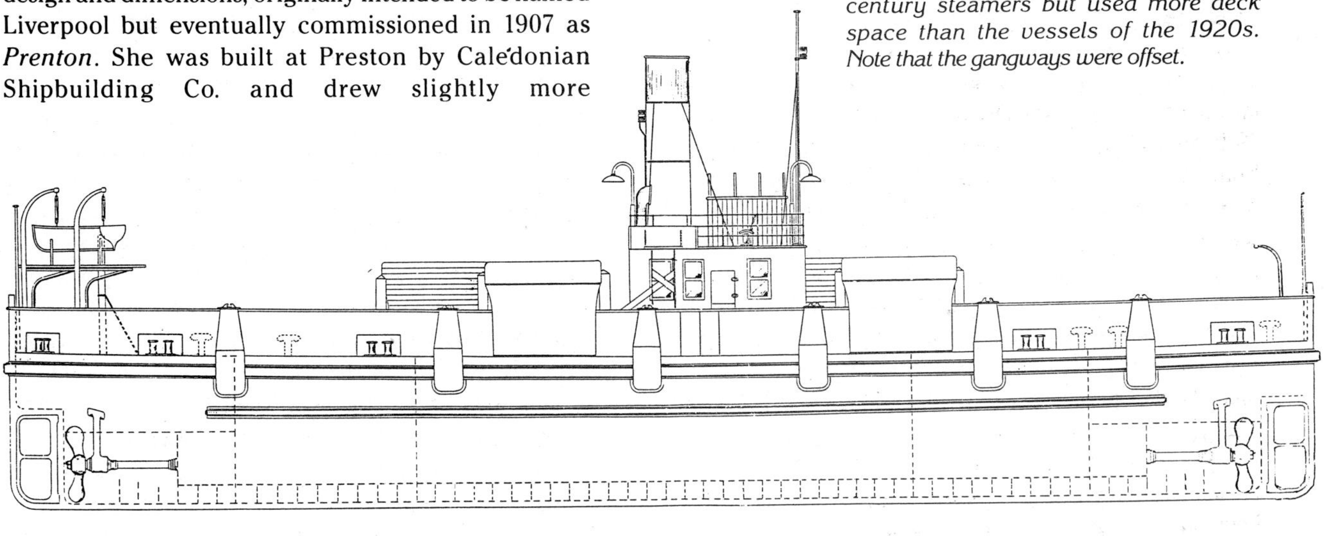

A general arrangement drawing of Prenton, put into service in 1907 after having been returned to her builders and renamed from Liverpool. The bridge was smaller than those of the nineteenth century steamers but used more deck space than the vessels of the 1920s. Note that the gangways were offset.

The luggage berth at Liverpool in the early years of the century with one of the vessels of the 1880s flanked by two Wallasey steamers, the New Brighton passenger boat on the left and the Seacombe goods boat astern. A three-boat service is in operation and another Woodside luggage boat is standing off, waiting for the berth to clear.

water than the older boats. The latter had all been reboilered between 1893 and 1898 and *Oxton* had had new engines fitted in 1897. It is on record that she was grounded on the bank beneath the Time Gun north of the Morpeth channel for examination in May 1905 and subsequently refloated and taken into dock for repairs. Because *Prenton* was needed to replace the older steamers when under repair, the 15-minute service was not introduced until August 1908. This required three steamers, two of which could load and unload simultaneously at each side of the river while the other crossed, the berths being more or less permanently occupied. In 1908, a regular Sunday service was introduced but this was discontinued for the winter from 29th November, being re-introduced on 11th April 1909 from 10.00am to 10.00pm, at double tolls It was the growth of motor traffic which created this demand in the summer season. By this time, the advertised weekday service was being run between 6.00am and 8.50pm but special demands were being made outside these hours. In August 1912 the manager reported that during a two week period, eight special early morning trips had been made for the meat trade and four late trips for the Great Western Railway.

In September it was agreed to extend the service to run between 5.30am and 10.35pm. Prior to this the boats had been manned with single crews who spent 105½ hours on

board in seven days though the nominal working hours were 64½. The new arrangements provided for double crews manning the steamers round the clock. Deckhands' hours were reduced to 58 plus time at the mooring buoys off Woodside. The extra cost was £493-11-6d per annum, less a saving of £43 in overtime. Coaling was done during the night hours and extra trips, which were now much reduced, could be provided within normal working time. A special sailing at 11.10pm was put on for theatre patrons for the winter of 1912-13 but it was withdrawn in March 1913 after the manager had told the Committee that only one or two cars and sometimes none at all used the facility.

When the luggage boats were not running, cars were carried on the passenger steamers. After all passengers had boarded, the car would be carefully driven over the forward gangway and parked in the smoking saloon. On 1st March 1913 there was a serious accident when a car belonging to J. Blake & Co Ltd mysteriously started, demolished the gangway door of *Woodside* and plunged into the river taking two passengers with it. The driver drowned. The carriage of cars on the passenger boats was immediately banned, extra trips by the luggage boats being authorised on demand. In May 1913 this was amended to allow cars to be carried on the passenger steamers between 12 midnight and 5.00am (8.00am Sundays). A scale of charges was published for special luggage boat trips as follows:-

Between 10.35 and 11.00pm

Between 11.00pm and 12 midnight

Between 12 midnight and 5.00am

for one car 7/6d, two cars can share the charge. More than two cars 3/-each. double the above charges. on the passenger boat 10/- each or if special luggage boat needed for cars too large for the passenger boat £2.

There were also special charges for early Sunday trips. New regulations for carrying cars on the passenger steamers were made as follows:-

'None of the passengers, except the driver, are to be allowed to be in the car while the car is passing to or from the boat, and the driver must also alight when the car has got to its proper place on the boat and the engines (sic) of the car have been stopped. The driver must not re-enter the car nor start the engine until the gangways are down and all the other passengers have disembarked. The petrol and oil tanks must not be refilled while the car is on the boat. Motor cars using the passenger steamers must not exceed 6ft. 3in. in height and 5ft. 5in. in breadth over all.'

The Cattle Trade

Ireland was a major source of cattle for the English meat trade and the Mersey was in competition with Holyhead, Fishguard and other ports. The Welsh ports had the advantage of a short sea passage which caused less upset and loss of weight to the animals but Liverpool and Birkenhead were closer to the huge consumer population of industrial South Lancashire and the North Midlands. In addition, the Mersey enjoyed a substantial transatlantic cattle trade with both North and South America. In the days before refrigeration, the animals had to be slaughtered as close to the market as possible whereas nowadays, they can be slaughtered close to home and transported to their destinations as frozen carcases.

Hundreds of thousands of live animals were transported across the Irish Sea annually and the LNW railway, B&I and other lines maintained special fleets of purpose-built cattle boats equipped to handle the traffic as expeditiously as possible. The Woodside lairages and abattoir were built in Shore Road on reclaimed land in 1879 and there was direct connection with the Dock Board (north) end of the Woodside landing stage. The Wallasey lairage, situated between the Alfred channel and Pump Road, was demolished many years ago. On 15th May 1876 an additional stage, 352ft. long, built by Brassey's Canada Works, was placed in position between the Low Water Basin and the Morpeth Channel about ¼ mile north of Woodside. This stage, originally called the South Reserve Landing Stage, was soon misnamed the Wallasey Landing Stage and was intended for use by railway traffic (see Chapter 3). It was connected to the wall by bridges salvaged from the Low Water Basin landing stage. A special wooden walkway was constructed from the river

The Liverpool goods berth about 1912. Scaffolding is still in position on the towers of the Liver Building and the Cunard Building is yet to be erected. Wallasey and Birkenhead vehicle boats are berthed and the stern of a New Brighton boat is just visible.

The Wallasey Landing Stage (Cattle stage) was little photographed but this aerial view taken in the 'twenties shows how close is was to Woodside, where the luggage boat can be seen. Between the two stages is the Morpeth Channel.

wall above the stage to both lairages and to the head of the north bridge at Woodside.

High boarded sides prevented the animals from seeing anywhere but straight ahead. The walkway gained elevation, passed the Time Gun and then turned to follow the Morpeth Channel which it crossed by means of its own hydraulically-powered double swing bridge, before descending gradually and entering the lairages from the rear. The thunder of hooves and the plaintive lowing as the terrified animals stampeded the length of this wooden corridor is well remembered many decades later. The remains of this cattle walk were still in position in 1988.

Cattle and other animals had been ferried across the Mersey from time immemorial and, as goods traffic increased, parts of the vessels had to be set aside for live animal traffic at certain times. Many men made a hard living as skilled drovers, self-employed and competing within a declining activity as more and more cattle were

conveyed by rail. Until quite late in the nineteenth century it was quite acceptable for animals to be herded through town and city streets for quite long distances; for example livestock was driven from Liverpool landing stage to the Cheshire Lines' Wavertree Road (later Wavertree and Edge Hill) goods depot. Some of the animals railed from Liverpool had first paid a brief visit to Birkenhead. The number of livestock using the luggage boats fluctuated considerably over the years from 5,158 in 1879-80 to 70,751 in 1882-83 but little more than half that number (36,050) in the following year. However, in 1913 the luggage boats started to play a much bigger part as, following an outbreak of foot and mouth disease in Ireland, it was decided to make Birkenhead the sole port of entry for Irish cattle so that control measures could be concentrated in one place.

The advantage of landing livestock destined for Liverpool on the Birkenhead side of the river was that, by using Woodside or the misnamed Wallasey goods stage, the Irish vessel did not need to enter a dock, not only reducing costs but enabling a quick turnround to be made. Whilst 'lairage' became almost synonymous with slaughterhouse in the minds of many older Birkonians, its true meaning is a place for cattle to lie and, in fact, a large part of the premises was set aside as an animal transit camp. After the trauma of a sea crossing and the stampede along the walkway, the animals needed to be fed, watered and calmed down and after disembarkation they would rest in the lairage for 10 hours or more.

Calls at Wallasey Stage

Irish cattle started using the goods boats on a regular organised basis on Friday 31st January 1913 and by Monday night, 10th February, 2,301 cattle, 95 pigs and 162 sheep had been carried for £43-14-6d, a 33⅓% rebate having been granted at the request of the MDHB. The cattle drovers objected to paying double tolls on Sundays and said they would bring their weekday traffic if the Sunday tolls were reduced. It is not clear what alternative means were available to them, but the Sunday tolls were rebated by 50% from about 16th February and a month later, reduced to the weekday rate. From 26th February 1913, it was agreed to berth luggage boats at Wallasey stage thus enabling animals to be driven back along the walkway and assembled into economic herds. The simpler solution of using the north end of Woodside stage was ruled out by the Dock Board Act of 1858 which reserved it for use by shipping from beyond the port. The Ferries Committee agreed to charge the ordinary rate if not less than 150 beasts were embarked; special trips on Sundays cost £5-5-0d and £4-0-0d on weekdays before 7.30am or after 8.30pm. It was agreed that animals would be loaded expeditiously so as to disrupt the normal service as little as possible but it was obvious that an additional call could not be made without incurring some delay. It took time to tie up and cast off and the lowering and raising of a steam-powered gangway could not be speeded up. The manager's report of 12th November 1913 summed up the situation very succinctly:-

'The vehicle and goods steamers have suffered the usual delays almost daily due to calls made at Wallasey stage, vehicles breaking down and heavy traffic. The number of calls made at Wallasey stage since the last regular meeting number 234 and livestock carried as follows:-

11,890 cattle, 22,449 sheep, 2,482 pigs, 788 calves, a total of 275,180 since service started on 31st January 1913'.

The MDHB was making a determined effort to attract the Irish livestock traffic permanently and met the Ferries management in September 1913 with a view to reducing the tolls further. The MDHB wanted to be able to quote an inclusive rate to unload, drive them to the lairage, tie them up for 10 hours, drive them to railway truck or ferry boat and load them into road vehicles at the Liverpool landing stage and was prepared to do the work below cost to induce traffic to use the port. The Corporation agreed to charge special rates for through-booked livestock — a 50% rebate for cattle (3d instead of 6d), 5/- per 100 instead of 7/6d for sheep and 11/1d per 100 instead of 16/8d for calves.

Two months later, the MDHB invited the Ferries Committee to consider reducing the tolls on dead meat. Of the Irish livestock landed at Birkenhead in 1913, 53% was railed from Birkenhead, 33⅓% went to Liverpool (two-thirds being railed and one third sent to Stanley Cattle Market or Liverpool Abattoir) and 14% were killed in Birkenhead. The Board wished to attract more of the meat trade and increase the killings at Birkenhead Abattoir. There were problems with Liverpool Abattoir and a possibility that public killings there would be suspended. Existing dead meat from Birkenhead Abattoir was mainly handled by two cartage firms, Cornfield's and Alderson's. In 1912-13 Cornfield's gross ferry traffic was £889 and he enjoyed 10% discount on the first £500 and 12½% above £500 — a mean of 11.1%. Alderson's gross traffic was £753, with the same discount rates, a mean of 10.02%.

A sub-committee appointed to consider the request was torn between the need to appease the MDHB, from whom they wished to obtain better all round facilities, and a desire to reduce rebates in the wake of increased wages and materials costs. The manager correctly predicted that if the Board's policy succeeded, there would be a considerable reduction in the 11% of the traffic crossing the river alive to Stanley Cattle Market and the Abattoir and gave the Committee a report on the comparative economics of carrying dead and live meat as follows:-

'A lorry carries 20 sides equal to 10 beasts and pays 2/- less 11%   1s.9½d
and comes back loaded with other stuff and in some cases empty but it pays us another   1s.9½d.

Total toll paid   3s.7d

10 cattle crossing at 4d each pay   3s.4d

Again 100 sheep carcases go on one lorry   1s.9½d one way
Returning   1s.9½d
    3s.7d

For 100 sheep walking across we get   5s.0d

On balance it appeared that it was preferable to carry the animals live but it was conceded that if Birkenhead would benefit, it was economically sound to give the same discounts to meat whether dead or on the hoof. The manager favoured the giving of a discount of 33⅓% to a loaded vehicle and half tolls less 25% to an empty vehicle going for Irish meat, a double journey discount of 48% compared with the GWR's 54% discount in similar circumstances. The Committee was favourably disposed to this but the MDHB subsequently shelved the proposal.

One of the problems associated with carrying live animals in large numbers was cleaning up the mess they made. At the outset, the Liverpool Health authorities were a little difficult. With so much horse drawn traffic the problem was ever-present and it was not too difficult to intensify the cleansing procedure. A not inconsiderable proportion of deckhands' time was taken up with hosing down, disinfecting and scrubbing the decks.

The outbreak of war disrupted the flow of Irish livestock and after the war, political events and the growth of refrigeration gradually changed the patterns of trade. However, livestock remained an important constituent of cross-river traffic for many more years and calls continued to be made at the Wallasey stage, certainly until 1939 and possibly up to 1941, when the service ceased. A one-week census in May 1925 recorded 3,805 cattle being carried. Numbers declined annually from 195,000 in 1928 to 10,600 in 1938-39 (of which 6,500 were embarked at Wallasey stage). By that time, all sheep and pigs were carried through the tunnel in lorries and in 1940-41 only 1,955 beasts used the ferry.

Motor Traffic

It has already been mentioned that the popularity of the private motor car in the Edwardian years brought the ferries new traffic, particularly on Sundays; in November 1913 it was reported that the Sunday motor car steamer continued to be profitable, averaging £14-16-1d over four Sundays. By 1912, commercial motor traffic was also having an impact. The Great Western Railway, with a major goods station in Birkenhead but only receiving depots and no rails in Liverpool, was now firmly established as the Birkenhead vehicular ferry's largest customer. From September to December 1909, the GWR had tried to stimulate its passenger traffic to and from the Midlands and London by operating a motor bus service between Liverpool hotels (and private homes by arrangement) and Birkenhead Woodside station. The ferry management obligingly gave the railway bus priority of embarkation, a special position on the vessel and first-off status.

Horse-drawn and motor traffic extends for the full length of the Liverpool floating roadway in June 1925. Note the solid tyres and the absence of mudguards on the leading Thornycroft lorry.

Some idea of the volume of railway goods traffic handled can be judged by reference to the December 1912 figures, when their vehicles made 4,465 crossings of which 4.3% were made by motor vehicle. A horse lorry paid 1/4d whilst a motor lorry paid 1/8d. This distinction was maintained over the years despite the fact that the motor lorry utilised the deck space more efficiently. Possibly it was a subtle application of the principle of charging what the traffic would bear. The motor vehicle's progress was eclipsed by commandeering by the military and fuel shortages during the 1914-18 war but numbers increased rapidly from 1919. When the Committee decided to discontinue the Sunday service as an economy measure from 30th March 1919, it was obliged to rescind its resolution following pressure from a deputation representing the Motor Trade Association, RAC, the Commercial Motor Users' Association, Auto Cycle Union, Liverpool Motor Club, the North West Automobile Association and the British Carriage Workers Institute. The service was retained with a 50% surcharge.

Discounts

The granting of rebates or discounts to volume customers was an important facet of the goods ferry's charging system. A discount was granted to a Mr John Robinson, who conveyed oil across the river, in 1889. The reason for the Corporation's generosity is obscure but, by 1913, when it was 37½% on a 2/- vehicle and 40% on a 2/6d vehicle, the Committee reviewed it and cancelled it from 1st February 1914. The general rule during the first decade of the 20th century was 5% if the yearly total exceeded £100: 7½%—£200; 10% on the first £500 and 12½% on the excess.

From 1st May 1905 the GWR negotiated a special rate of 15% if the total was less than £800, 20% between £800 and £1,000 and 25% if the total exceeded £1,000. From the same date, two parcels carriers, Liverpool Parcel

Delivery and Globe Express, were granted 25% if they reach £250 or more. With expanding traffic, the GWR negotiated an even better rate of 33⅓% on traffic of £2,500 from 20th January 1909. For the year ending 31st May 1911 the GWR account totalled £4,983 less 33⅓% equals £3,322.

Whilst the total figures seem low by present day standards, it should be remembered that £250 represented 3,000 crossings by a light van or almost 10 per working day. The availability of low cross-river rates enabled traders on both sides of the river to compete with each other throughout the whole of Merseyside. The GWR competed successfully with the LNW, CLC and Midland Railways for London traffic despite having to carry all its goods across the river and, in the process, provided a better service to Birkenhead customers and gave considerable employment to Birkenhead people. In 1915, wartime conditions reduced traffic and increased costs and a deficit of £2,000 on the ferry undertaking was anticipated. It was decided to discontinue all rebates and discounts on freight accounts from 31st March 1915 but no doubt the Great Western was excepted as their traffic was virtually indispensable to the ferries undertaking. Whilst Morpeth Dock goods station was nearer to Woodside than to Seacombe, it was not too inconveniently placed in relation to the latter ferry and one can speculate that the GWR used this as a bargaining point but Seacombe had no floating roadway until 1926, handling the traffic by means of a bridge at high tide and a hydraulic lift when low water made the gradient too steep. A report in *Modern Transport* for 12th May 1928 quotes GW ferry traffic as being 1,004 tons, conveyed in 300 vehicles, in one recent busy day. Clearly such volumes were worth retaining at substantial discounts. After the passing of the 'Derating' Act in 1929, the saving to the undertaking was passed on to users by means of rebates. 12½% was allowed to monthly account holders and purchasers of prepaid freight tickets and 25% on milk and cattle traffic. On 1st October 1931, under

THE PROBLEM OF THE AGES.

*A cartoon which appeared in the **Birkenhead News** of 26th November 1921 when ferry congestion was getting a great deal of publicity.*

THE MERSEY LUGGAGE FERRY IN THE YEAR 1

THE MERSEY LUGGAGE FERRY IN THE YEAR 1921

DIFFERENT DAYS, BUT THE SAME OLD COMPLAINT.

Tunnel Committee directives, these rates became 10% and 20% respectively.

Woodside, despite its floating roadway, was not totally free of problems caused by the Mersey's 32ft. tidal range. In the days of horse haulage, heavily laden drays had difficulty in climbing the floating roadway at low tide and could be stalled if forced to stop for traffic at the foot of Hamilton Street. A few firms, of which Joseph Perrin and Sons was one, supplemented their other activities by supplying pull-up horses which were attached to the front of the team. A standard rate was charged to the top of the floating roadway and more if required to continue up the gradient of Hamilton Street or Chester Street to the Town Hall. The former was usually selected as the gradient was easier. In 1911, the ferry manager was trying to persuade the pull-up horse owners to stand their horses on the south side of the goods stage. Perrins' horses were standing on the Dock Board stage and often had difficulty getting through the traffic to assist the 'up' carts. Laden carts often came down the floating roadway virtually out of control, pulling up on the level stage or driving straight on to the gangway. Pull-up horses, being attached to the nearside shaft were also using the wooden footway which became slippery in wet weather and there were only light chains between the horse and the water. The ferries staff were constantly urging the horse attendants to keep off the footways but with mixed success.

At Liverpool, only railway horses were available as pull-up horses and there was a GW stable on Prince's Landing Stage. Horses were made available to all from about 1920 but it is unlikely that these were railway horses; a local contractor probably provided them, as at Woodside.

Landing Stage Improvements

During the Edwardian years, it became more and more apparent that the cross-river facilities for both passengers and goods were becoming increasingly overtaxed. The Agreement between Wallasey, Birkenhead and the MDHB in 1911, providing for an additional passenger bridge at George's Landing stage (see page 00) eased pedestrian congestion but the vexed question of delays to vehicular traffic and the nuisance to other traffic in the vicinity of the floating roadways on both sides of the river remained.

A sub-committee of the Ferries Committee was appointed early in 1914 to explore means of increasing the facilities for vehicular traffic and there were some talks with the Dock Board aimed at obtaining a double berth at Woodside and more room for vehicle movement. The Committee twice resolved to purchase an additional luggage boat, to be named *Noctorum* but the war prevented it. Consideration was also given to installing a goods lift at Woodside, possibly with the idea of removing handled goods from the stage and enabling vehicles collecting and delivering those goods to avoid the congestion on the floating roadway and the stage. A receiving and delivery office could have been built at street level at the head of the lift shaft.

In January 1914, following a report by their tramways manager, C. W. Mallins, on a £3 million subway scheme, Liverpool City Council proposed that all the neighbouring towns should confer with a view to setting up a joint rate fund to improve cross-river travel by means of a bridge or tunnel. The outbreak of war in August 1914 prevented any progress being made but, despite wartime conditions, talks with the Dock Board were resumed in November

The purpose of this aerial view seems to have been to illustrate the progress of the new Liverpool Pier Head layout, completed in March 1921, with three tramway loops. One Birkenhead vessel (almost out of the picture) has left the stage whilst another, rather lightly loaded, approaches. A Wallasey boat is moored at the stage. This picture pre-dates the extension of the stage, which permitted an additional berth for the luggage boats.

1915, with a view to obtaining two goods berths on both sides of the river. As Birkenhead had three boats on the service and Wallasey had only one on the Seacombe service, it was agreed that Birkenhead could use the Seacombe berth at Liverpool when it was not required by the Wallasey boat, but progress at Woodside was stymied when the Admiralty commandeered 400ft. of the Woodside cattle stage. Nevertheless, plans for alterations to Woodside stage, drawn up by the ferries manager, were approved by the Dock Board engineer but shelved for the duration of the war. In the course of a series of meetings, the Dock Board promised to provide double berths on both sides of the river whenever the Corporation was in a position to run a four-boat service.

Prices rose steeply towards the end of the war and, in April 1918, the MDHB gave notice to Birkenhead Corporation, terminating the 1905 agreement which had fixed the ceiling on the toll for use of the floating roadways at £4,500. Birkenhead felt that any increase should be dependent upon improved facilities and, after some discussion, the 1905 agreement remained in force for the time being. The end of the war in November 1918 was followed by increased port activity and, as the use of the Birkenhead quays intensified there was further pressure on the inadequate cross-river facilities. In March 1919, the eight-hour working day was implemented and congestion

on the goods ferry became even worse as traffic previously spread over 12-15 hours, was being concentrated into a much shorter time. Long queues of vehicles formed on both sides of the river and at Liverpool, where the traffic for Woodside and Seacombe ferries and deliveries to cross channel steamers and liners at Prince's stage all used the floating roadway, it was not unusual for a double line of waiting traffic to extend back down St. Nicholas Place and southwards across the Pier Head frontage. Ferry congestion became a major issue on Merseyside, with extensive press coverage and the events that put an end to it are set out in Chapter 9.

8 THE HALCYON YEARS

The turn of the century found the Birkenhead Corporation ferries undertaking in a prosperous condition and in virtually undisputed control of the ferry passages between Liverpool and Birkenhead. Tranmere ferry was on its last legs and the seasonal pleasure ferry to Eastham was no threat. There was no competition with the Wallasey Council ferries to the north which served different districts. The acquisition of the South End ferries in 1897-99 proved to be a financial burden but one which, by cross-subsidisation, the undertaking as a whole was able to sustain for forty years. Population and industry were expanding and patronage of the ferries increased year by year. The only threat was the Mersey Railway but the ferries' market share had been increasing annually since the low point of 1890.

The steamers commissioned in the last decade of the nineteenth century proved to be transitional in design and all had relatively short lives on the Woodside passage. The superiority of the twin-screw steamer over the paddler was self-evident, but *Mersey* and *Wirral* of 1890 proved to be too small for the Woodside service and were soon relegated to the South End ferries. *Cheshire* of 1889 was sold to T. W. Ward Ltd in 1903, becoming a tender for the Great Western Railway at Plymouth until she was wrecked in 1913. The Committee's extraordinary aberration, PS *Birkenhead* of 1894, was sold in 1907 and became the White Star tender *Gallic*. The replacements were *Lancashire* and *Claughton* of 1899 and *Bidston* and *Woodside* of 1903, powerful twin-screw steamers with passenger certificates for about 1,600 passengers, all of which gave some 30 years of satisfactory service.

The elimination of paddle boxes enabled gangway layout to be simplified and passenger flow improved. The standard arrangement provided two wide gangways for the main deck, counter-weighted and with limited swivelling capability, and a smaller gangway giving direct access to the promenade deck, mounted on a platform at the head of a staircase. The high-level gangways at Liverpool were the subject of an agreement with the Dock Board in November 1882. All the gangways had a rope secured to the underside. The deckhands could grasp the ropes of the main gangways and pull them down on to the deck assisted by a push from the stage hands. The promenade deck gangway was used only at peak hours. An officer would descend from the bridge, slide back a section of railing, reach for the rope with a grappling iron and pull the light gangway down. This gangway was used only for traffic in the ruling direction and at Liverpool, homegoing workers would be embarking at promenade deck level whilst others were still disembarking from the main deck. 1,000 or more passengers would be embarked or disembarked in the three minutes lie-over permitted by the two-boat 10-minute service which operated from 8.00am to 8.00pm, reducing then to every fifteen minutes and finally to hourly between 12.30am and 4.30am when one of the smaller South End boats usually took over the service for reasons of economy. From 1897 to 1903, a three-boat 7-8 minute service was operated on summer Saturdays, but was found to be excessive and thereafter this timetable was run only on three days a year, Easter Monday, Whit Monday and August Bank Holiday, if fine. At such times there would be five or six passenger boats in service — three on Woodside, two on the South End and sometimes one on charter to Eastham.

The electrification of the Birkenhead Tramways in 1901-02 brought a big increase in ferry passengers. The Corporation underestimated the increase in tramway traffic and had to order more cars; the popularity of the new mode derived from its relatively high speed, frequency, cleanliness and the low level of fares. Journeys between the ferry and the suburbs became more acceptable, particularly by ladies, and additional travel was generated; more businessmen found it possible to go home to lunch which had been impracticable with the slow, expensive horse cars.

An earlier electrification project was the replacement of gas lamps at Woodside by electric lights on which the manager reported in February 1897. The ferry buildings, offices, approach etc. were lit by 142 gas lamps with (to use contemporary jargon) 'a total candle power of 260 16-candles'; the annual consumption of gas totalled £390. The electrification scheme proposed improved lighting for the floating roadway and stages and 150 lamps with a capacity of '360 16-candle power lamps' were envisaged.

In the days before the general use of electricity, cables had to be specially provided and the cost of a supply from the Borough Electric Works would have been prohibitive at about 6d a unit — £1,140 per year. This problem was overcome by installing two 30hp steam engines each coupled direct to two dynamos with an output of 300 16-candle power lights at 100v and storage cells for twelve hours current. The equipment was integrated with the power supply for the Ferries Yard where there was a 19-year-old low pressure (35lb to the sq.in.) boiler. This was replaced by two high pressure boilers (120lb per sq.in.). The power for the saw and other equipment in the ferry workshop was improved and about £100 per year saved compared with gas. However, the use of electricity as a source of power was stimulated by the success of the tramways and, by 1903, the ferries had gone over to mains supply and were the biggest user in the town after the tramways.

Woodside ferry approach in 1901 and again in 1925. The six-track tramway layout was unusual and the massive centre pole supported the overhead for all six. Note the single deck car in the earlier view as used on the New Ferry route because of a low railway bridge in Chester Street. The inadequacy of these cars assisted both the South Ferries and the Mersey Railway to gain traffic. One of the few surviving horse buses withdrawn in 1903, is seen on the right. Trams still dominate the scene in the later picture but the Corporation Leyland Leviathan double decker has already replaced the Claughton Road trams and Crosville 'contractors' buses' have captured the Heswall traffic from rail. The railway station is seen on the right.

Railway Competition

Between 1892 and 1902, the Birkenhead ferries' share of the cross-river traffic increased from 40.8% to 68.4%, though traffic overall had increased by 22%. The ferries management recognised that the ability to provide a town centre to town centre facility potentially gave the railway a powerful advantage over the ferry. The prime cause of the railway's loss of favour was the air pollution in the stations and tunnels but the high-handed arrogant attitude of the directors and an erratic service had been contributing factors. The Mersey Railway had obtained Parliamentary powers to electrify its lines in 1896 but there was no money available. A year later it was virtually bankrupt and only the intervention of George Westinghouse, who was looking for a railway electrification demonstration project in Britain, saved the line. Further statutory powers were obtained in 1900 and

Birkenhead Corporation now had some cause for concern at the likely effect on the ferries as, given a clean atmosphere, the railway was likely to win back the lost passengers and more besides.

In late 1902, when electrification was proceeding apace, the committee considered various measures for safeguarding the ferry traffic. Adjustments to the tariff were considered and mostly rejected though the re-introduction of a 1d workmen's return between 5.00am and 8.00am was recommended. One theory was that an almost continuous service of boats would attract traffic and an experiment was carried out between 8.00am and 8.00pm on Saturday 20th December 1902 when a six-minute service was provided by *Lancashire*, *Cheshire* and *Birkenhead*. The weather was fine and conditions were generally favourable. All three steamers used more than the usual amount of coal—about one ton between them—and over 26,000 passengers were carried, but these could easily

The passenger bridge at Woodside in course of reglazing in 1904.

have been carried on the normal two-boat service. The cost of a regular daily three-boat service was put at £6,650 per year and another boat would have been needed in the long run. 1,600 additional ordinary fare paying passengers a day each way would have been needed to break even. The committee rejected the idea but recommended continuing the 10-minute service until 10.00pm instead of 8.00pm. The potential capacity of a three-boat service was eventually adequately demonstrated on 19th August 1911, during a strike of Mersey Railway employees, when 45,000 passengers were carried on Woodside ferry.

The provision of a covered walkway between the railway station and the ferry turnstiles was also recommended once more but nothing was ever done. Porters were employed to carry passengers' luggage between the ferry pay gates and the boats on the Cheshire side and to and from the Pier Head on the Liverpool side. This continued for about 15 months, the manager reporting in March 1904 'that the free porterage for luggage at Woodside is not much appreciated by passengers ...'. During the previous two weeks the greatest number of packages carried had been 24.

Electric service on the Mersey Railway commenced on 3rd May 1903. The tunnels and stations were thoroughly cleansed of soot and grime and, with plenty of whitewash and electric lights along the entire line, the atmosphere was completely changed. A poster campaign and modest fare reductions for third class season tickets probably had more effect than increases in speed, though these were substantial. The journey from Birkenhead Park to Liverpool Central took only eight minutes compared with 11 by steam, while Rock Ferry came down from 15 to 11 minutes. There was an enormous increase in the number of trains, with a three-minute frequency on the under-river section of line, six-minutes on each route. Contemporary commentators rightly described this as an unnecessarily frequent service but it was influenced by a guarantee from British Westinghouse that the cost of power should not exceed 6⅓d per train mile. There was thus an incentive to run as many trains as possible in order to spread the overhead costs. 1902 had been a particularly bad year for the railway, only 5.6 million passengers being carried. In 1903, with eight months of electrification, they rose to 7.2 million and increased year by year until they reached 15.0 million in 1912. In that year the market shares of the respective modes were very close to those of 1892 — 59.6% by rail and 40.0% by the ferries but the total passengers carried across the river had increased by about 75% in those 20 years and ferry passengers at 10.2 million in 1912 were almost double those of 1892.

Railway competition encouraged co-operation between the ferries and the tramways though the two committees had several disagreements in the early years of the century. The Ferries Committee, having been

BIRKENHEAD CORPORATION

Ferries and Electric Tramways

Fresh Air & Beautiful Scenery.

Cheap Through Return Tickets

FOR

FERRY and TRAM

FOR THE JOURNEY FROM

LIVERPOOL LANDING STAGE

TO

CLAUGHTON VILLAGE

On the Oxton and Claughton Circle Route,

Are issued each SATURDAY and SUNDAY after 1 p.m. at the WOODSIDE FERRY TURNSTILES at a charge of - - - **4D. EACH.**

BEST AND NEAREST ROUTE FOR

Bidston Hill and Woods, which are open to the public free.

Flaybrick Hill.

Squire Vyner's Rhododendron Gardens.

The Pass of Thermopylæ, and

Oxton Common (Wirral Ladies' Golf Links).

SPECIAL FOR PARTIES.—Parties of not less than 20 may obtain these cheap Return Tickets for use at any time during the week by giving previous notice to the Ferries Manager, Woodside, Birkenhead.

By Order.

WOODSIDE FERRY, 27th March, 1907.

WILLMER BROS. & CO., LTD.

Full co-ordination of municipal ferry, tram and bus services was not achieved until 1928, but the first through tickets, designed to attract Liverpool people to visit Bidston Hill, were introduced in 1907, as advertised by this handbill.

established in 1842, regarded itself as a kind of Senior Service and was inclined to treat the upstart Tramways Committee with contempt, especially when the latter criticised the running of the ferry service which they did on more than one occasion. Some councillors seemed to have difficulty in comprehending that a six-minute tramway service could not be co-ordinated exactly with a 10-minute boat service and there were several special sub-committees set up to examine aspects of co-ordination. Through tram and ferry return tickets were introduced over certain sections from 1st July 1905 and there were many bulk concessionary tickets issued for travel to Bidston Hill. There was, however, no universal scheme of through fares until 1st April 1928. The electrification of the Mersey Railway made no difference to the policy of the LNW and GW railways who continued to offer their passengers a free choice of travel to Liverpool Central Low Level via Rock

LICENSED PORTERS' CHARGES
At Woodside Ferry, Birkenhead.

For every hat box, valise, bundle of shawls, carpet bag, gun case, or other separate small package, that is to say a package weighing less than ten pounds carried from any of the Woodside steamers to outside the paygates within the Ferry approaches, and from outside the paygates within the Ferry approaches, to any of the Woodside steamers ... ... 1d.

If carried any distance less than a quarter of a mile and not exceeding half a mile including landing ... ... 2d.

Half a mile, and not exceeding one mile ... ... 3d.

For every additional quarter of a mile ... ... 1d.

For every box, portmanteau, trunk, or other large package, that is to say a package weighing ten pounds, or more than ten pounds, carried from any of the Woodside steamers to outside the pay-gates, within the Ferry approaches, or from outside the Pay-gates within the Ferry approaches, to any of the Woodside Steamers.

For every such large package carried less than a quarter of a mile ... ... 3d.

Not exceeding half a mile ... ... 6d.

For every additional half mile ... ... 3d.

If two or more porters are necessary to carry any package each porter shall be entitled to be paid on the same scale.

For every half hour, or any part thereof, during which a porter is employed by the person hiring him ... ... 3d.

And for every half mile beyond the boundary of the borough, one third more than the fares aforesaid

Provided that the foregoing fares shall include the renumeration for the services of the porter in carrying any package or articles on board a Ferry steamer or in removing any package or article therefrom.

Excerpt from the bye-laws fixing porters' charges at Woodside. Licensed porters with distinctive cap and red armband with brassard were once a familiar part of the cross-river scene.

Ferry and the Mersey Railway or to Liverpool Landing Stage via Woodside ferry.

Holiday Traffic

Railway competition had little effect on holiday traffic because the ferry crossing was part of the outing. In the early years of the century, Liverpool people crossed the river in their thousands to join railway excursions from Woodside to Chester, North Wales and the Deeside villages. Horse drawn waggonettes also undertook excursions into the Wirral countryside. Thousands travelled by tram to Claughton Village, walking thence up Upton Road to Bidston Hill; others took the Prenton car and walked to Woodchurch. Rock Ferry and New Ferry were riverside resorts in their own right.

Other revenue earning activities were special charters and cruises. In the past, there had been royal occasions too; *Claughton* was placed at the disposal of the Prince and Princess of Wales on 8th September 1881 when they opened Liverpool's North Docks and the same vessel, suitably decorated and equipped for the occasion, took Queen Victoria for a river cruise during the celebrations marking the opening of the Liverpool Exhibition in 1886. *Claughton* also undertook a special charter from Manchester to Liverpool on 2nd January 1894, the day following the official opening of the Manchester Ship Canal. On the way, she managed to collide with the Wallasey steamer *Water Lily*. Special services of a different kind were rendered on 17th October 1898 to various flats which were swamped when Morpeth Dock Gates broke open; salvage claims were later made by the Corporation.

In 1900-01 there was talk of extending the ferry services on the Cheshire side of the river in conjunction with Wallasey Council. These ideas came up from time to time but nothing ever came of them. There was insufficient sustained demand for a Woodside-Seacombe or Woodside-New Brighton service and, while the general physical layout of the Wallasey steamers was similar to that of Birkenhead, the dimensions were different so that the gangways did not fit. Agreement could not be reached on a joint night service where, by using only one gangway, these difficulties could have been overcome. Occasionally, specially chartered Wallasey steamers would embark railway excursion passengers for New Brighton at the goods berth and Birkenhead Corporation would be entitled to the statutory 1d toll for the use of the stage. The sail was an attractive part of the excursion.

The Shropshire Union Canal Co chartered *Lancashire* for a trip from Liverpool to Ellesmere Port on 10th May 1899 for £30. On another occasion *Woodside* went up the Manchester Ship Canal to Latchford, embarked members of the Warrington Conservative Association for Seacombe and New Brighton the next morning and returned to Latchford at 11.00pm. When King Edward VII visited Liverpool to lay the foundation stone of the Anglican Cathedral in July 1904, special trips were made from Woodside to view the Royal Yacht, anchored in the river, at close quarters at 6d for adults and 2d for children.

Cycle Traffic

Another important source of revenue was the cyclist and only a part of this was holiday traffic. The emergence of the 'safety bicycle' in the last two decades of the nineteenth century had led to cycling becoming very popular, both as a workaday means of transport and a form of recreation. Numerous clubs were formed and cyclists became a powerful lobby.

Ferries revenue from cyclists fell into three categories:-

1. **Workers travelling with cycle**. These people cycled to the ferry, took their cycles on board and cycled to their work on the other side of the river. Special combined passenger-with-cycle fares and contracts were eventually provided.

2. **Workers travelling without cycle**. These people cycled to the ferry and stored their machines there, continuing their journeys as ordinary passengers.

The pattern of cycle traffic — April to October 1938.

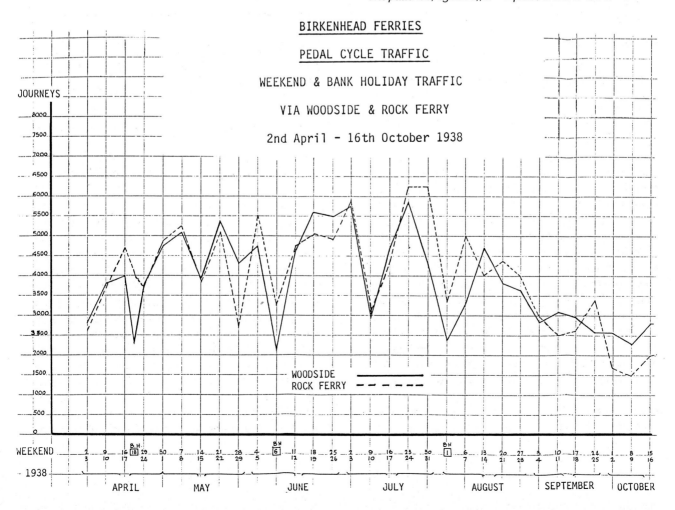

Churton, built in 1921, introduced the new generation of luggage boats with the compact central layout. Note the navigation lights mounted on slender towers each side of the vessel and the rope fenders, expensive items to some extent superseded by superannuated tractor tyres in the post-war era

3. **Recreational cyclists**. These people usually travelled from Liverpool to Birkenhead on Sundays, sometimes in groups of 40-50 and returned the same evening.

Conditions for leaving 'tricycles, bicycles and similar vehicles' at Woodside Ferry were first laid down in 1894 and the practice grew to such an extent that additional storage had to be provided two years later. A 4d bicycle and passenger return ticket, available for the outward journey between 4.30 and 8.30am, was introduced from 1st April 1903 for those who wanted to take their bicycles with them. The normal bicycle and passenger return was 6d but, in the same month the National Cyclists' Union and other clubs petitioned the Corporation for bulk concessions. It was agreed to issue batches of 50 tickets at 5d each, but within a month, the minimum had been reduced from 50 to 12. From May 1904, the 5d return was made available to everyone and at all three ferries, not just Woodside. As explained elsewhere, the South End ferries were popular with cyclists, as they enabled the granite setts and tram lines along New Chester Road to be avoided. The Corporation's gesture was probably one of expediency rather than generosity, as it enabled the load to be spread among the three ferries.

The 5d return resulted in an increase of 16.5% in cyclist traffic at Woodside and this traffic was of considerable importance for half a century or more. In the years immediately before and after World War II, the cycling clubs were numerous and well organised. There were tandems for couples and sidecars for children and Woodside was a popular meeting place for the riders. Small advertisements in the *Liverpool Echo* and *Evening Express* would announce the destination and departure time of the Sunday run and, in many cases, the assembly point would be Woodside.

At very busy periods, cyclists in large numbers were a potential nuisance as protruding pedals were apt to encourage claims for laddered stockings and other damage and there were occasions when their numbers had to be limited on any particular sailing or they were directed to the luggage boat. Cyclists were required to wait until all other passengers had disembarked and they usually co-operated. At certain busy times, cycle tickets were sold on Liverpool landing stage, a rare exception to the practice of accepting ferry tolls only on the Cheshire side of the river. About three times as many cyclists were carried in summer than in winter.

Alterations and improvements were made to the cycle rooms at both Woodside and Rock Ferry between the wars.

Prior to the opening of the Mersey Tunnel in 1934, about 900,000 cyclists per annum were carried. The tunnel took some traffic, but was never popular with cyclists due to the traffic conditions. In 1951-52, only 121,000 cyclists used the tunnel and changes in social habits brought the post-1945 ferry total down to about 475,000 per year. In the post-war boom period of 1946 consideration was given to converting the luggage boat Oxton to carry cycles and other light vehicles but the idea was not pursued and the growth of car ownership finally reduced bicycle traffic to negligible proportions. A sign of things to come had been the provision in 1929 of a ferry car park on the land between the ferry approach and the floating roadway and the issue of monthly tickets at 15/-.

Working Arrangements

The crew of a Birkenhead passenger steamer consisted of nine men, the master and mate, one engineer, one engine room rating, three seamen and two firemen. The pecking order of the officers was Woodside passenger, Woodside goods, and South End, each category having its separate pay scale. From September 1912, in common with many other occupations, crew working hours were reduced. Some vessels were manned or partially manned round the clock even if not in service as there was cleaning, coaling and clearing out of ashes to be done during the night. Users of the night ferry service in years gone by will recall areas of the decks being roped off whilst seamen on their hands and knees scrubbed the timbers white. The slatted wooden seats were periodically polished. Coaling was done at Woodside and there were a number of mooring buoys adjacent to the stage, secured for many years by blocks of concrete but later by anchors, under the control of the Dock Board but permanently allocated to the ferries department. During the night hours, vessels would be moved between the buoys and the stage as their turn came for coaling. For many years, coal was conveyed to the landing stage in flats which loaded at one of several coal berths on the Mersey dock system. A memorandum, believed to date from 1864, describing the method of unloading is illustrated. 'The bank' was the railway land adjoining the ferry yard on the south side of Woodside where reserves were held. Coal cost between 8/9d and 9/6d per ton at this time; 10,000 tons were consumed in 1863-64 but this increased with the arrival of the new steamers to 14,000 tons in 1867-68 falling to 11,000 in 1870-71 as economy measures were applied.

Following the coal and railway strikes in 1911, an action was brought by Ardeola Steamship Co Ltd against one Clinton (principal of the Star Lighterage Co) and Birkenhead Corporation for conversion of coal removed from Coburg Dock by the Corporation, by arrangement with Clinton. It seems that this coal was legally the property of the Ardeola Co but was diverted to Woodside to keep the ferries going during the strike. Eventually the matter was settled out of court. Latterly coal was carted from Abbey Street sidings, stockpiled on ferries land

between Woodside railway station and the river wall and behind the hoarding on the north side of the ferry approach. It was bagged, and carted up Rose Brae from the former site and down the floating roadway to the stage. This was originally a horse hauled operation but, in 1929 the Corporation purchased an International tractor which accelerated the operation. The sacks of coal were tipped by hand through an opening in the main deck, normally covered by a steel grating about the size of a normal manhole cover. Ashes were bagged on board and stacked on the goods stage for removal by contractor; Henry H. Crutchley had the contract in 1921 and was asked to reduce the contract price because carters' wages had fallen. He refused, saying that the ashes exceeded the agreed 4-5 tons per day by 30cwt. Nevertheless, the contract price was reduced by 12/- per month. As each steamer consumed 4-5 tons of coal per day, and six or seven vessels required coal overnight, the whole operation was costly and, in retrospect, it is surprising that some form of mechanisation was not devised, particularly as coal-fired vessels were used at Woodside until 1960.

Coal economy was considered to be of great importance and, apart from containing operating costs, there was the question of controlling smoke emission as some environmental control legislation dated from early times. In fact, as early as February 1851, the Commissioners' Parliamentary Committee had recommended opposition to clauses in the Liverpool New Sanitary Bill requiring consumption of smoke on board steamboats on the river, condemning them as 'arbitrary'. The Smoke Bonus Fund had been established by 1912, the Corporation paying in fixed sums every month. Smoke fines were paid out of this fund, and whatever remained was distributed to the employees concerned on an agreed basis. There was only one smoke fine in 1912 and £17-0-2d was shared by 32 men who received 14/-, 13/- or 10/3d according to rating. By 1924 non-collision bonuses had been introduced for officers. The no smoke bonuses in that year, when there were no fines, totalled £368-9-0d whilst captains and mates received £241-2-6d in non-collision bonuses. The scheme was taken seriously and, in 1925, the manager recommended that two captains lose two years' bonus each, following a collision between Churton and Lancashire. The Committee reduced the punishment to one year. Although it was possible to travel on the ferry for many years without experiencing a collision, there were a great many of them, mostly minor, reported in official records. The need to maintain a tight schedule across a busy waterway required keen observation, sound judgement and forward planning to avoid having to heave to or reduce speed in mid-stream, to give way to an impudent tug or a string of barges. The dangers of other vessels colliding with the piers and landing stages, particularly in fog, were ever-present. The Woodside stage was struck twice within a month in 1928. On 26th January Jennie, a coaster, struck the southern end of the stage and became wedged underneath, causing damage of £15,000, whilst on 22nd February, another vessel, Kent, struck the stage causing considerable damage. The extensive repairs carried out lengthened the life of the stage significantly.

In August 1911 the manager, Capt. Peter McQueen resigned due to ill-health and was given the customary token appointment of Consulting Engineer at £250. The job was filled by the internal promotion of F. S. Legge, chief clerk and cashier, on a scale of £400 increasing to £600 pa. Less than three years later, certain irregularities were detected in the running of the department and both the manager and the chief clerk/cashier, Briscoe, were asked to send in their resignations, though they were permitted to remain *in situ* in acting capacities. Both men were demoted to clerical positions in the Borough Treasurer's department and Capt. W. E. Langshaw, assistant superintendent of Alexandra (Newport and South Wales) Docks and Railway Co was appointed manager at £400-£500 p.a. in July 1914.

The 1914-18 War and its Aftermath

The first World War, despite the absence of the widespread air attacks of the second conflict, presented many problems particularly of staff and material shortages and not least, an unprecedented increase in passengers carried. Wallasey Corporation had two boats, *Iris* and *Daffodil*, requisitioned by the Admiralty and they took part in the assault on the Mole at Zeebrugge. Despite her unsuitable gangway spacing, *Lancashire* was frequently chartered by Wallasey in 1917-18 to fill the gap but she also was requisitioned in 1918, leaving Birkenhead without a spare vessel. Costs rose sharply in an inflationary spiral and, for a time, the extra revenue generated by the increased tempo of the port and other industries, was sufficient to take care of the additional costs. Free travel was granted to servicemen in uniform, a generous gesture which the War Office formally acknowledged. As the war progressed, the Ferries Committee was taking measures to discourage casual traffic or, alternatively, to make it more expensive. Tram and ferry book tickets were abolished in 1916 and other through tickets with the tramways followed suit in 1918.

In the post-war inflationary period, costs rose so rapidly that a fares increase became essential. The ordinary fare at Woodside was increased from 1d to 1½d on 1st January 1919 and to 2d on 1st May 1920. This was the statutory maximum laid down by the 1881 Act and application had to be made to the government for additional powers. Two Provisional Orders of 1920 and 1922 authorised maximum fares of 3d (day), 9d (night) and contract rates of £3-7-6d, £2-5-0d and £1-10-0d for 12, 6 and 3 months respectively, subject to the proviso that the amount of the authorised fares for the prescribed categories, as existing immediately before the enactment of 1920, should be exceeded only with the consent of the Minister of Transport. By letter dated 15th March 1921, the Minister authorised increases to 2½d (day), 9d (night) and £2-12-0d, £1-9-0d and 16/- for 12, 6 and 3-monthly contracts and these rates were put into force from 1st February 1922. The impact of the increases on workers was alleviated to some extent by the introduction of workmen's returns on 20th September 1920 and falls in prices made it unnecessary to charge the new statutory maximum.

By 1917-18, passengers carried at Woodside reached 11.2 million compared with 7.9 million in 1911-12. Traffic peaked at Woodside at 13.6 million in 1919-20 but the greatest number of passengers carried in one day was on Whit Monday 1918, when 92,789 passengers (excluding contract holders), used Woodside, more than twice the number carried during the Mersey Railway strike in 1911. From 1920-21, traffic started to decline as the post-war boom fizzled out and by 1922-23, passengers carried at Woodside were 10.7 million, a fall of 21.5% in four years.

From 1922 prices stabilised and then started to fall. Cost of living pay increases had been given in the form of a war bonus which left the basic wage structure unchanged. When costs started to fall, the war bonus was gradually eliminated. A circular has survived informing men engaged on ship repair work that their gross wages would be reduced in four equal instalments on 3rd and 24th January, 14th February and 7th March 1923, the amounts varying from nothing for those receiving 37/6d per week to 10/- for those on 52/6d or more.

The 1920s

The most important event of the years between the wars which affected the ferries was the decision to build the first Mersey road tunnel. This is described in Chapter 9 as it is bound up with the story of the goods ferry. The Mersey Tunnel Act 1925 and subsequent legislation gave the ferries undertaking some financial security against the competition which the tunnel would undoubtedly cause but it seems unlikely that this security influenced capital expenditure decisions in the 1920s. Indeed, most of the unemployment was rife and Merseyside was one of the worst sufferers. A year or so earlier, the employment exchanges were issuing free ferry tickets to enable job seekers to cross the river, and the Committee issued 1d return tickets on production of unemployment cards, to enable further trips to be made. The job creation was well to the fore in the decision to have four new steamers built, two passenger and two goods, and the extent of deflation can be judged by the total cost — £220,000 — which was less than the Corporation had paid for two goods steamers in 1921. The order was given to Cammell Laird & Co, the first time the local yard had had a Birkenhead ferry order for many years. The Unemployment Grants Committee agreed to pay half the interest payments for 15 years.

The Corporation wanted to name the new passenger steamers *Cheshire* and *Wirral* but these traditional names were already in use on other vessels. The Committee then chose *Hooton* but that too, was disallowed and they had to settle for *Upton* and *Hinderton*. *Upton* was a small boat for Rock Ferry, replacing *Mersey* which was withdrawn at the end of October 1925. *Hinderton* was a full size boat for Woodside and took up service on 30th December 1925. These were the first Birkenhead steamers to have promenade decks extending over the full width of the hull.

The International tractor purchased by Birkenhead Corporation to haul coal to the landing stage. Note the transverse front spring, beam axle and solid tyres and the two trailers adapted from horse-drawn carts.

An aerial view of Woodside dating from the 1920s. Behind the ferries workshop on the left is the arched roof of Woodside railway station while several trams occupy the six terminal tracks on the ferry approach. Above is the Woodside Hotel which, before mid-19th century land reclamation, stood on the river bank. There is plenty of traffic on the floating roadway; all the buildings to its right are occupied by the meat trade. The cattle walk can be seen starting from the head of the north bridge and following the river wall to the Morpeth Channel, just out of the picture to the right. The tall chimney belongs to the Mersey Railway pumping station and the square tower houses the hydraulic equipment for the lifts at the railway's Hamilton Square station. The ships are in Morpeth Branch Dock above which is the Cheshire Lines goods station.

Intensified Railway Competition

The ordinary fare at Woodside was reduced to 2d on 1st October 1924, but was never to fall further. During the post-war inflation period, there had been a gentleman's agreement with the Mersey Railway that the fare from Hamilton Square to James Street should be ½d more than the ferry fare. This time the railway did not follow suit but, early in 1925 introduced a 6d return ticket from all Birkenhead stations to Liverpool after 10.00am and in 1926, lengthened the hours of availability on Wednesdays, Saturdays and Sundays. Large numbers of availability on Wednesdays, Saturdays and Sundays. Large numbers of off-peak passenmgers were induced to forsake the ferries for the railway. From 13th December 1925, the ferries introduced weekly contracts at 1/3d from Woodside and 1/9d from Rock Ferry and a 4d return on the latter. As cheap railway fares continued to be issued, the Corporation brought in a full range of tram or bus and ferry tickets on all routes from 1st April 1928 at 5d, 6d, 8d, and 10d and, when bus routes were extended, following an agreement with Crosville Motor Services Ltd in 1930, further fares up to 1/4, reaching as far as Heswall, were made available, the facility being offered also on certain Crosville routes. Crosville wanted to extend the availability of these tickets to routes. Crosville wanted to extend the availability of these tickets to Ellesmere Port but the Ferries Committee opposed it as they received only 2½d per ticket, irrespective of the length of the bus journey and the revenue from a through rail ticket was slightly more. From 1st July 1928, cheap rate scholars' contracts, hitherto available only for 12 months, were issued for three and six months also. Ferry and railway competition continued unabated to the undoubted advantage of the passengers but the low through fare also generated off-peak and wekend traffic for the ferries, tramways and buses. In October 1935, the Mersey Railway went so far as to object to the renewal of bus service licences before the Traffic Commissioners, with a view to having the through fares cancelled.

The layout of Woodside landing stage in the mid-1930s and arrangement of the twenty pontoons which supported the Corporation end.

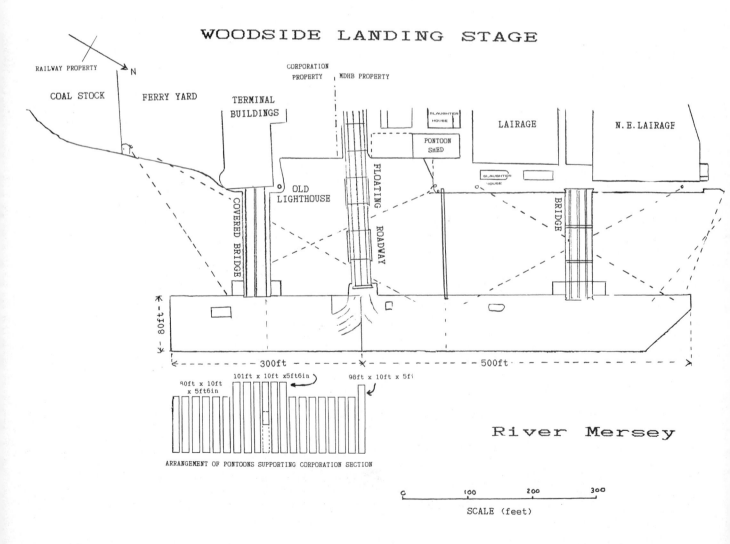

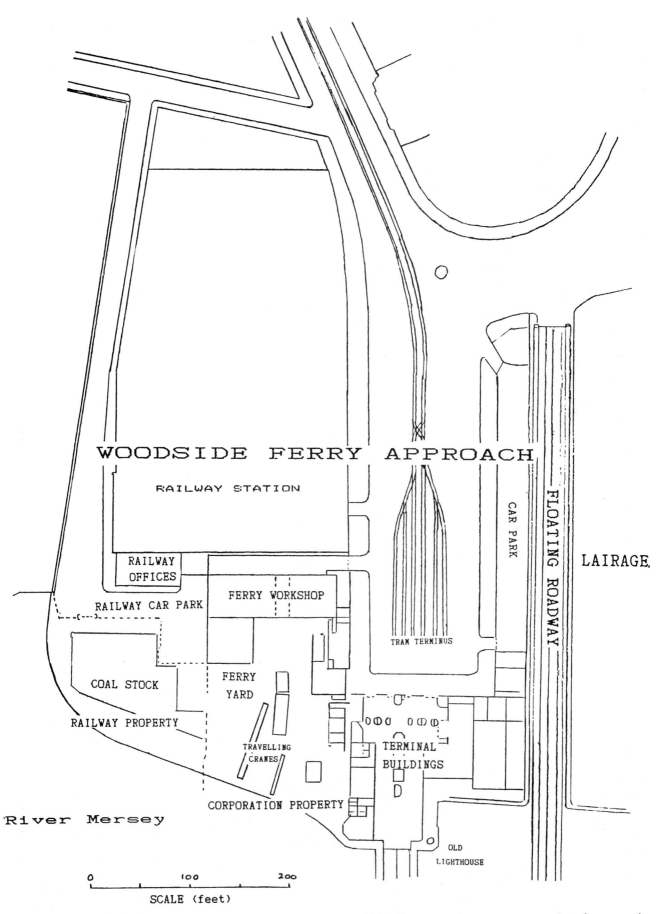

WOODSIDE FERRY APPROACH

RAILWAY STATION

RAILWAY OFFICES

RAILWAY CAR PARK

FERRY WORKSHOP

TRAM TERMINUS

CAR PARK

FLOATING ROADWAY

LAIRAGE.

COAL STOCK

FERRY YARD

RAILWAY PROPERTY

TRAVELLING CRANES

TERMINAL BUILDINGS

CORPORATION PROPERTY

River Mersey

OLD LIGHTHOUSE

0   100   200

SCALE (feet)

The extensive shore facilities at Woodside as they were in the mid-1930s. Heavy components were craned up from vessels moored against the river wall at high tide into the ferry workshops 'on the bank'. The railway station was a major terminus with through trains to London (Paddington) via Shrewsbury and Birmingham, to South Wales on the Great Western and to North Wales on the LMS.

In terms of passengers carried, 1926-27 was Woodside's most prosperous year, 14,093,136 passengers using the ferry, 900,000 more than in the previous year, 13 million was exceeded in the three succeeding years and again in 1933-34. The year 1926-27 was also the best year for the ferries undertaking as a whole as the 2.8 million passengers using Rock Ferry brought the total passengers carried to 16,902. Rock Ferry's zenith, however, was in 1924-25 with with 2,917,652 passengers. Passenger counts in the 'thirties were in excess of 11 million every year but the air raids of 1941 resulted in a low of 7,930,416 in 1941-42.

The Road Tunnel

As described in Chapter 9, the impact of the opening of the Mersey road tunnel on 18th July 1934 was borne by the goods service, as all vehicular traffic except horse drawn carts and vehicles carrying dangerous goods transferred to the tunnel. However, a proportion of passenger traffic was now being carried in private cars and revenue gradually declined. Small parcels and newspapers had always been carried on the passenger boats and this traffic continued. Numerous staff were transferred from the ferries to the Mersey Tunnel and the refreshment kiosk which formerly stood on the goods stage was transferred to the passenger stage at the same rent of £40 per year.

It was inevitable that demands should be made for the running of bus services through the tunnel but the local authorities on the Cheshire side of the river did not wish to compete with their own ferry services. Crosville made the first move by applying to the Traffic Commissioners to extend their Loggerheads-Mold-Woodside service to Liverpool and, at the hearing in December 1934, this was strongly opposed by the Joint Committee and Liverpool and Birkenhead Corporations. In May 1935, at a meeting attended by Representatives of Liverpool, Birkenhead, Bootle and Wallasey Corporations, the municipal operators decided to apply for licences to run buses from various districts of Liverpool to places in Wirral; if the municipal applications were refused, all company proposals were to be opposed. Liverpool's transport manager advised that as the tunnel toll for a bus was 5/- and 2d for each passenger, the return fare from Liverpool to Birkenhead by bus would need to be 1/4d compared with 4d by ferry and 6d by rail. A similar conclusion was reached by the Birkenhead manager and the local authorities decided that tunnel bus services were economically impracticable. The Loggerheads application was refused but the Crosville and Ribble companies then applied to run an hourly service between Southport and Chester, which was strongly resisted and finally refused on appeal to the Minister of Transport. Only the long distance coach services between Liverpool and London, North Wales and South West England, which had used the luggage boats, were licensed to use the tunnel.

The Merseyside Co-ordination Committee spent many

George's Landing Stage in the early nineteen-thirties after the reallocation of berths. In the foreground are two Birkenhead luggage boats, with a variety of vehicles aboard, and, successively, the New Brighton, Seacombe and Woodside passenger steamers.

THE LANDING STAGE, LIVERPOOL.

hours talking about tunnel buses and cross-river facilities and, in 1938 they appointed three independent consultants, A. Collins, an expert on municipal finance, Frank Pick (Vice-Chairman of the London Passenger Transport Board) and A. R. Fearnley (general manager of Sheffield Transport Dept). Fearnley had been manager of the Birkenhead tramways in 1900-04. They made their report in March 1939, recommending the closure of Rock Ferry, the introduction of a trial tunnel bus service and the merger of the Birkenhead and Wallasey transport undertakings. As described in Chapter 5, the Tunnel Committee lost no time in arranging for the closure of Rock Ferry but the outbreak of war in September 1939 prevented any further steps being taken.

More traffic was lost by the ferries when the Wirral lines of the LMS Railway were electrified from 14th March 1938 and through trains commenced operating over the Mersey Railway from West Kirby and New Brighton to Liverpool.

Mr R. S. Cowan, engineer and susperintendent of the ferries, replaced Capt. Langshaw as general manager on the latter's on 1st March 1937. There was no discernable change in the operation of the ferries, which continued to carry a substantial but gradually reducing traffic. In 1939 the Tunnel Committee agreed to expenditure of £2,000 on improvements to the booking hall and floating stage at Woodside to facilitate passenger flow, the main change being the widening of the contractors' gates.

The root cause of the problem was the replacement of trams by buses which was completed in 1937. The 'keep right' rule on the passenger bridge was convenient for crowds of railway passengers making their way from the station to the ferry boats and for disembarking passengers boarding trams in the middle of the Ferry Approach. But, by 1939, the majority of passengers used buses which arrived on the north side and departed from the south side, thus causing conflicting flows. This was particularly serious when large numbers of impatient shipyard workers wee hurrying to cross to Liverpool at the same time that returning passengers were making for the buses and there were several cases of people being knocked down. The collectors on the contractors' gates were quite unable to control the crowds and no doubt many passengers evaded payment of fare. The declaration of war prevented the work going ahead and the original report was resubmitted to the Committee in 1945. However the full scheme was never carried out.

The 1939-45 War

The outbreak of war on 3rd September 1939 had little initial impact on the ferry. The following notice appeared:-

NOTICE TO PUBLIC
Woodside Ferry
AIR RAID PRECAUTIONS

Passengers are hereby informed that on an air raid warning being sounded the Ferries Steamers on passage or moored at the stages at Birkenhead or Liverpool will immediately take up position in mid-river and remain there until after the 'all-clear' signal has been given.

In such circumstances, the passengers are requested to fit their gas masks and remain quiet until the steamers are able to return to their appropriate stage.

4.9.39.   R. S. COWAN. General Manager.

In practice, the masters usually tried to get the workers home.

To save fuel, bus services were reduced in frequency and the Woodside ferry passenger service was operated every quarter hour instead of 10 minutes. Saloon and navigation lights were dimmed and masked in accordance with the blackout regulations and boats were painted grey all over immediately after a daylight air raid on 31st August 1940; evening traffic declined dramatically because people stayed at home. Merseyside experienced its first aid raid in July 1940, the attacks being of greatest intensity in December 1940, March and May 1941. There were many occasions when vessels were showered with incendiary bombs and rocked by near misses and, in May 1941, *Claughton* had her saloon blasted by a bomb in mid-river. On the same night, the upper works of *Bidston* were damaged by large pieces of concrete which were blasted from the Pier Head as she lay at Liverpool landing stage. The Woodside service was maintained whenever possible, the only occasions when it was suspended being after enemy aircraft dropped mines in the river. On these occasions, an emergency bus service was run through the tunnel but most people made for the railway and the buses were little used. There were no air raids after January 1942 and lighting restrictions were eased later that year. The 10-minute frequency was restored between 7.00am and 8.00am, 9.30am and 10.00am and 6.00am and 7.00pm from 11th June 1944 and funnels were repainted in their normal colours.

Hinderton had her red funnel restored to do some river cruising earlier in the war. A commentary script dated 1942 for a cruise on the Manchester Ship Canal has come to light but it is not certain that this actually took place. In March 1942, the 'Holidays at Home Committee' asked the Corporation to arrange ferry cruises as part of it programme and the Government agreed to allocate additional coal. There is a record of the vessel leaving the luggage boat berth at Woodside at 6.30pm on Saturday 25th July 1942, crossing to Liverpool to pick up more passengers (probably at the old Rock Ferry berth) then to the river mouth, upstream to Eastham and back to Woodside for 8.30pm. Cruises were run on a few days in 1943 and 1944 and on four days a week during the peak summer holiday season in 1945. In that year it had been intended to apply for a catering licence but no staff could be obtained. Cruises ran between 16th June and 12th August 1946, carrying an average of 500 passengers compared with 750 in 1942, but they incurred a loss and were not resumed in subsequent years.

9 THE FIRST ROAD TUNNEL AND THE DEMISE OF THE GOODS FERRY.

Early in 1920, a Cross-River Traffic Committee was formed by Liverpool, Birkenhead, Bootle and Wallasey Corporations and the Dock Board and the newly appointed Minister of Transport, Sir Eric Geddes, attended the Committee's first meeting on 11th February 1920. A technical sub-committee comprising Capt. Mace, the Dock Board Water Bailliff, Capts. Langshaw and Fry, the ferries managers of Birkenhead and Wallasey with Mr Charles Livingstone, a Dock Board official as chairman, was charged with reporting upon possible solutions to the very serious congestion at the goods ferry approaches on both sides of the river. The sub-committee reported within six weeks, recommending the provision of two goods berths on each side of the river, adaptation of the Liverpool floating roadway to take four lanes of traffic (a practical impossibility), more pull-up horses and the relocation of some of the huts on Prince's stage to assist vehicle movement. Langshaw dissented, submitting a minority report advocating the lengthening of George's stage and the provision of a second floating roadway from Mann Island, for the exclusive use of the Woodside boats. He claimed that this would solve the problem for 40 years and also minimise the risk of collisions by eliminating the need for the Birkenhead goods boats to cross the tracks of the Wallasey passenger boats.

The Traffic Committee agreed broadly with the majority report as a palliative measure but there was growing realisation that the vehicular ferry services, as they then existed, were outmoded and more radical action was really needed. In June 1920, another joint body, the Merseyside Parliamentary Committee, sent a deputation to London to see the Minister of Transport. The delegates included the chairman, deputy chairman and manager of the Birkenhead ferries and members of trade organisations. Meanwhile, Birkenhead ordered two new goods boats and Wallasey ordered one, and agreement in principle was reached with the Dock Board on the second goods berth at Woodside. The 1860 Act gave Birkenhead the right to use only 300ft. of the Woodside stage, ie two berths, one for passengers and one for vehicles and it was necessary to appropriate 150ft. of the cattle stage. This required major alterations to the stage, general strengthening, improvement of buoyancy and repositioning of bollards etc.

The MDHB told the Corporation at a meeting on 30th September 1920 that the work would cost £20,000 and the Corporation would have to pay 12½% per annum for 20 years, including insurance, depreciation and repairs. After 10 years, the Dock Board would consider reducing the percentage. The Dock Board quickly followed this up with

their assessment of the changes necessary to solve the problems at Liverpool. This involved extension of George's stage by almost 50ft., moving all the passenger berths further to the south and establishing a new goods berth on the site of the New Brighton berth, which was then at the foot of the floating roadway. This solution had been put forward by Alfred Chandler, General Manager and Secretary of the Dock Board in 1915, but the provision of double berths on the Birkenhead side had been frustrated by the Admiralty commandeering 400ft. of the Woodside cattle stage.

The full financial implications were not finalised, but Birkenhead Corporation was alarmed at the potential financial burden for solving a problem which they felt was not strictly domestic, as a proportion of the traffic was merely passing through the district and had business neither in Liverpool nor Birkenhead. There followed various meetings and correspondence in the course of which the MDHB again terminated the 1905 agreement, and in January 1921 the Birkenhead Town Clerk was instructed to write to the Minister of Transport once more 'in regard generally to the state of the facilities dealing with ferry traffic between Birkenhead and Liverpool and the Minister....... be requested to interest himself in the matter with a view to steps being taken to deal with the difficulties existing at the present time'.

Alterations to Woodside Stage

Work on the second berth at Woodside went ahead and was completed a few days before the signing of the formal Agreement on 25th February 1921. The existing goods stage was redecked and some alterations made to the passenger berth. The following month, there was general agreement on the Liverpool alterations, which were tied up with the renewal of the toll agreement which now expired on 6th July 1921. The Corporation was to pay a maximum of £7,000 per annum for 10 years with the usual six months' notice thereafter, but the cost of the landing stage alterations and extension was to be borne by the Dock Board. A new supplemental agreement, dated 7th July 1921, redefined all the ferry berths at Liverpool (see Appendix 6). The new goods berth was to be at the foot of the floating roadway, all passenger berths being moved one position to the south. The most southerly berth was to be shared by the Corporation's New Ferry/Rock Ferry boats and the seasonal Eastham ferry, with provision for use, if necessary, of the angled berth at the south-east of the stage. Corporation steamers had priority over Eastham steamers. It is of interest to note that provision was made

A fine view of **Churton** of 1921 at Liverpool Landing Stage with motor traffic tightly packed. One van of Lewis's and two belonging to Coopers can be identified. The latter was a northern Fortnum and Mason's, situated at the corner of Church Street and Paradise Street, Liverpool. Note the rope fenders protecting the timber 'rubber' which encircled the vessel, and the Wallasey vehicular steamer with flying bridge in the background.

(Below) Order on the Liverpool landing stage about 1925 with a boat load of mainly motor and steam traffic marshalled ready to board the boat. The first of a pair of open chars-á-banc, possibly Crosville Leylands, is already embarking. Note the economical grouping of the bridge and funnel whereas the 1921 Wallasey boat approaching the stage keeps the deck clear by fitting a full width navigation bridge.

for the berth to be used also by vessels employed by the LNW and GW railway companies for carrying railway passengers. The railways still had this right even though it had not been used since 1878.

The technical sub-committee's report had advocated better traffic control arrangements on the floating roadways as a means of reducing some of the congestion and new regulations were promulgated in February 1921. Semaphore signals were installed part-way down the floating roadways to regulate downward traffic and marshalling areas were defined on Prince's stage so that a boat load of vehicles was already clear of the roadway and ready to embark. These measures helped, but traffic was increasing at such a rate that no overall improvement was discernable. In 1914, 448,478 vehicles had been carried by the Woodside goods boats of which about 80% had been

horse drawn. In 1919 the number of vehicles had fallen by 37% to 284,768 but 60% were motor vehicles carrying heavier loads or pulling trailers, and they tended to concentrate because of the shorter working day. In 1920, the number was up 38% to 392,365 and in 1921 to 422,883. Mechanically propelled vehicles had a much greater range than horse drawn carts, and goods which had previously come by rail were now travelling by road and often needed transport across the river.

A road tunnel was now being freely discussed but it is interesting to reflect on the various alternative schemes that were put forward in the local press and elsewhere. Arthur Maginnis, a consulting civil and marine engineer, favoured scrapping the Mersey Railway so that the tunnel could be used for road traffic thus solving the problem in about two years instead of the 5-7 years estimated for the

Road traffic lined up on the floating roadway at Woodside. Note the wooden footwalks each side. On the left is the lairage.

construction of a new tunnel. Professor S. Wright Perrott, head of the Department of Engineering at Liverpool University, advocated a tunnel tube laid on the river bed. A Mr T. L. Dodds suggested a light car ferry between the South End of Liverpool and Rock Ferry, to replace the passenger service and cartage contractor Henry H. Crutchley thought that with two new boats, all would be well for 10 years if a third track could be provided on the Liverpool floating roadway. However, influential opinion was in favour of a tunnel. Sir William B. Forwood, KBE, a man of enormous influence in Liverpool, lived at Bromborough Hall and therefore had frequent personal experience of crossing the river. He favoured twin tunnels under MDHB control. Sir Archibald Salvidge, leader of the Liverpool City Council, was another strong tunnel supporter and he was destined to play the major role in the events which followed.

The Birkenhead Town Clerk's letter sent in January 1921 was instrumental in starting the train of events which led to the construction of the first Mersey road tunnel. In 1921, the Merseyside Municipal Co-ordination Committee, comprising six members from each of the Corporations of Liverpool, Birkenhead, Bootle and Wallasey was established 'to confer .... on the best way of co-ordinating municipal transport and other necessary services and improving cross-river facilities by bridge, tunnel or otherwise, with power for eminent engineers to investigate and report'. Sir Archibald Salvidge was appointed chairman and Sir Maurice Fitzmaurice, Mr (later Sir) Basil Mott (who, a quarter century or so earlier, had been responsible for the construction of several of London's tube railway tunnels) and Mr John A. Brodie (Liverpool City Engineer) were retained to make the report.

Tunnel Plans

There had been many schemes for bridges and tunnels over the years, all of the former having been turned down on grounds of cost and/or interference with shipping. The 1880 subway scheme, the only one apart from the Mersey Railway, to receive Parliamentary approval, is described in Chapter 7. The consultants supported their recommendations with statistics showing that the population residing within a 10-mile radius of Liverpool Town Hall had increased over 20 years at an average rate of 11,000 per annum to 1.2 million. Cross-river passengers by ferry and railway had increased between the same years (1901-21) from 33 million to 62 million while vehicles using the Birkenhead and Wallasey goods ferries had risen in number from 380,000 to 640,000. Once more a bridge was ruled out because of the cost, estimated at £10.5 million, headroom of 185ft. needed at high tide, length of span (2,200ft.) and steep gradients at both sides to avoid extensive property demolition. A tunnel with four 9ft. traffic lanes was recommended; it was to consist of a cast iron tube lined with concrete. Beneath the main carriageway, located just below the diameter of the tube, there was to be a separate tunnel with a double track tramway. Originally the entrances on the Cheshire side were to have been near Woodside and Seacombe ferries but the plans were changed more than once and final agreement was reached on a four lane entrance at Grange Street and a two lane entrance in Corporation Road. Because of lack of accord on several points, Wallasey dropped out of the scheme altogether.

The first Mersey Tunnel Act received the Royal Assent on 7th August 1925 and work started in the following December. The tunnel was controlled by the 17-member Mersey Tunnel Joint Committee (MTJC), composed of ten from Liverpool City Council and seven from Birkenhead Town Council. There were a number of important provisions in the Act affecting the Birkenhead ferries which gave the MTJC powers to take over financial control of them for a period of 21 years from the date of opening of the tunnel. Under the provisions of a further Act of 1933, the Corporation could, not later than 18th January 1955, serve notice on the MTJC requiring them to continue financial support for a further 21 years in which event the MTJC might, on giving six months' notice, require the

Corporation to alter, modify or discontinue the ferry service. If the Corporation was unwilling to comply with this requirement, the ferries would revert to the Corporation which would become financially fully responsible for them.

Authority was also given for the Minister of Transport to authorise ferry fare increases above the statutory maxima fixed in 1920 and 1922 during the post-war inflationary period.

The tramway scheme was quite logical in the context of the public transport network on Merseyside at that time. A high proportion of ferry passengers reached Liverpool Pier Head, Woodside and Seacombe by tram, so what more logical than to use that mode to take them all the way and perhaps even abolish the ferries altogether. But there was no enthusiasm for the tramway scheme in Birkenhead or Wallasey. Both towns had already started motor bus services and, in fact, the first tram route on Merseyside to succumb to the motor bus, Birkenhead's Claughton Road route, did so within three weeks of the passing of the Act. The tramway case was ill-prepared and the revenue and passenger projections were easily debunked. The Mersey Railway secured protection from tunnel bus services within an eight mile radius of Birkenhead Town Hall based on minimum fares.

New Luggage Boats

The first of the new goods boats, *Barnston*, entered service on 19th October 1921, followed by *Churton* a few weeks later. These boats were faster and roomier than their predecessors and motor lorries with trailers could manoeuvre on deck. The Dock Board had always maintained that the floating roadways were adequate and, to a degree, they were right, as there would have been very little congestion if traffic could have been kept constantly on the move. The Liverpool berths were altered during 1922 and the ability to load and unload boats simultaneously on both sides of the river made an enormous difference. A suggestion made in 1924 to abolish the footways on the Liverpool floating roadway to accommodate two tracks up and one down was dismissed as impracticable as new pontoons would have been needed to support the added weight. The doubling of the frequency of the Seacombe goods service undoubtedly diverted some traffic from Woodside but the full benefits were not realised until 1926, when a three-track floating roadway was installed at Seacombe.

The Birkenhead ferry manager was not formally authorised to run a four-boat service until 31st March 1924 but it seems likely that it ran before then.

The post-war pattern of vehicular traffic was now established and, whilst motor traffic was increasing all the time, horse drawn lorries continued to play a significant role for a few more years. Season tickets for motor cars had been introduced at the end of 1924 at £2, £5, £9 and £16 for one, three, six and 12 months; they were available for more than one car of the same owner. The four-boat service was to become a summer phenomenon when the normal commercial traffic was augmented by additional motor cars and charabancs. There were not too many of the latter as the ferry tolls were a deterrent to Liverpool excursion operators running trips to North Wales.

There is a case on record where ferry staff removed and retained an acetylene headlamp from a charabanc belonging to the New Brighton Motor Coach Co Ltd, apparently as security for non-payment of tolls. The inconvenience of being without the lamp for two or three weeks was not suffered entirely in vain as the incident caused the Ferries Committee to review the tolls. The rates of 4/6d up to 14 passengers and 7/6d over 14 passengers were changed, retaining the lower rate but adding an intermediate charge of 5/6d for up to 20 passengers and 7/6d over that number. The Corporation was often sympathetic to special applications. In September 1927, the rate for petrol and milk tankers (3/6d) was revised to 3/6d loaded and 2/6d empty and the double toll for goods on Sundays and holidays was reduced to 50% above the weekday rate in February 1928. The establishment of regular time-tabled motor coach services from 1928 onwards, brought new traffic to the ferry as several of the competing operators on the London services started in Liverpool and crossed by ferry to Woodside or Seacombe. The North Wales services were added in 1930 together with seasonal routes to the West of England.

Before the Mersey Tunnel Act was passed in 1925, Birkenhead Corporation had already ordered two more goods steamers, *Bebington* and *Oxton*, enabling the 40-year old vessels to be withdrawn. An hourly night goods service started in December 1923 at tolls 50% above the day rates. In its later years, the vehicular service was efficient and very profitable. As more motor vehicles took to the roads there was a marked increase in summer traffic and more than a million vehicles crossed the river via Woodside in 1930.

By 1927, the road tracks of the floating roadway at Woodside were in urgent need of renewal and talks took place with the Dock Board on how best to do this with the minimum of disruption to traffic. It was decided to do the work during February 1928, arrangements having been made for the Woodside goods steamers to operate to and from Seacombe on payment to Wallasey Corporation of 10% of the gross tolls. There had been a similar arrangement on 28th-30th June 1924 during minor repairs. However a delay in getting the necessary materials caused a postponement, the roadway being closed for one weekend while temporary repairs were effected. It was impractical to close during the summer and the diversion to Seacombe eventually took place between midnight on 23rd January and 10.00am on 16th February 1929.

The likely effect of the opening of the Mersey Tunnel was the subject of discussion by the Birkenhead Town Council and the ferries committee from 1928 onwards and sub-committees were appointed to consider various aspects. A ferries sub-committee met the Birkenhead representatives on the MTJC on 16th April 1929 to consider the financial and future management policy to be adopted. A detailed financial report was available and it was resolved to recommend that the MTJC should be

Woodside stage propped up by a camel following a collision with a coaster in January 1929. The lower view shows the wreckage of the coaster. Note the photographer wearing plus-fours.

asked to take over the goods ferry under Section 63 of the Act and that two new boats should be ordered for the Woodside passenger service, irrespective of the future of the ferries. Meetings went on until January 1931 when it was resolved to give the goods service to the MTJC but keep the passenger service. The latter decision seems to have been based on sentimental rather than good commercial grounds as the goods ferry was by far the more profitable of the two. However, on 22nd July 1931 the MTJC decided to take over responsibility for the whole of the Birkenhead ferries undertaking which would continue to be operated on their behalf by Birkenhead Corporation.

The 10-year agreement with the MDHB on the use of the floating roadways expired on 6th July 1931 and the Board gave notice to terminate it as from 6th January 1932. Counsel's opinion was sought on the true legal position and this was to the effect that the MDHB was entitled to 25% only in respect of tolls paid by the classes of vehicle listed in the 1860 Act. These naturally did not include motor vehicles and the Town Clerk was instructed to write to the Board and tell them that henceforth no tolls would be paid in respect of mechanically propelled vehicles. This attitude was, of course, outrageous as the Corporation had willingly paid on such vehicles since they started to use the ferry. Furthermore, the £7,000 per annum paid to the MDHB for the use of the floating roadways and landing stages was a bargain as 25% of the gross receipts for 1931 would have exceeded £30,000. The MDHB pointed out that the 1860 Act also stipulated that mechanically propelled vehicles could use the floating roadways only with the Board's consent which could be withheld or separately charged for. In the end, the parties had to sit down and talk and it was agreed to allow the 1921 agreement to remain in force until the effect of the tunnel opening could be assessed. When consultants tried to do this in 1932 they found it impossible as the Tunnel Committee had not fixed its tolls and there was no means of estimating how much traffic would transfer from the ferries.

A comprehensive 24-hour census taken on Grand National Day, Friday 18th March 1932 (see appendix 7) shows that of 3,384 vehicles carried both ways, 45.27% were motor cars (obviously inflated because of the day's

event), 43.76% were commercial vehicles and only 2.25% were horse drawn. 66 vehicles were carried between midnight and 6.00am.

The Tunnel Opens

The full impact on the goods ferry of the opening of the road tunnel was grossly underestimated. The Tunnel Committee approved their own tolls only on 11th July 1934, one week before the tunnel was opened and only on 16th July, two days before the ceremonial opening by the King and Queen, were the Tunnel Committee's proposals for ferry tolls placed before the Ferries Committee. Even so, some further amendments were necessary. Tolls for motor vehicles were generally the same as those for using the tunnel and in certain cases represented a reduction compared with the previous tolls. The only vehicles prohibited from using the tunnel were handcarts, horse drawn vehicles and motors carrying explosive or inflammable materials of which there was a long list. The Great Western Railway still used horse drawn vehicles extensively for their cross-river traffic. Consultants suggested the use of 'some truck system' for taking horse drawn vehicles through the tunnel on mechanically propelled conveyances so that the goods boats could be withdrawn.

The Final Years

The Birkenhead Ferries Committee optimistically continued a two-boat 15-minute goods service and, even though it was apparent on the first day that this was excessive, nine months elapsed, until 23rd April 1935, before it was reduced to a half-hourly one-boat service operating between 6.00am and 10.00pm. Many of the ferries staff transferred to the Tunnel. Weekly receipts on the goods ferry fell from £2,500 to £290 and by October 1934 were down to £260. On the last Sunday before the tunnel opening, receipts were £495; on the Sunday after, £27 and the Sunday after that £14.

Discussions on the MDHB tolls were resumed in October 1934, the Town Clerk having previously written 'We are without means of financing the Dock Board out of this ruined undertaking'.

The losses were, of course, being borne by the Tunnel, but the Corporation was still bemoaning the loss of rate contributions of over £10,000 per year from the goods ferry. The MDHB said that the sensible solution was to close Woodside and let the remaining vehicular traffic go to Seacombe but civic pride would not allow this. The 1921 Agreement was allowed to continue in force but the £7,000 ceiling was irrelevant, as never again would revenue reach a level requiring as much as that to be paid. MDHB receipts from this source from tunnel opening to closure of the ferry were about £13,000.

The Committee still owned five goods steamers. The 27-year old *Prenton* was quickly sold in October 1934 through ships' brokers C. W. Kellock and Co for £760, less 5% commission, to Robert Smith and Sons for scrap and was broken up on New Ferry shore. It is known that its mast was

A close-up of the passenger gangways at Woodside as viewed from the stern of a departing steamer. There were three main gangways and a promenade deck gangway. The 'spare' gangway to the north was for emergency use. The broad beam of the luggage boat **Barnston** *is clearly visible.*

fitted to the Lamey tug *Troon*. On 5th July 1935, the Corporation made an Agreement with the Isle of Wight Ferry Co Ltd which proposed to establish a new car ferry between a point near Lymington and Yarmouth. The Agreement gave the company an option to purchase *Bebington* and *Oxton* within one year for £25,000, £2,500 being paid to the Corporation as deposit and a further £2,000 payable in monthly instalments, in respect of dock dues, watching, maintenance and other services. The scheme was delayed as the company found that it needed statutory powers to proceed and the option was several times extended, eventually to 31st May 1937. A few days before the expiry date the company, which was running out of money, asked for a new option on the older *Barnston* and *Churton* and this was granted until 30th September at £8,000 each, subject to a deposit of £2,000 and payment of actual out-of-pocket expenses. The £2,500 paid in terms of the earlier agreement was transferred and the option was extended until 31st December 1937. Finally in February 1938, the Corporation lost patience and told the manager to advertise the older vessels for sale. In January 1939 the offer of T. W. Ward Ltd for £3,900 was accepted provided they were broken up for scrap and the materials were not shipped abroad. The Joint Committee deferred confirmation and *Barnston* and *Churton* finally went to Dutch owners in February 1939.

These events kept these vessels in the Mersey much longer than would otherwise have been the case. *Bebington* and *Oxton* maintained the service alternately as traffic declined with motors progressively taking over from horses, a process which was temporarily reversed with the introduction of petrol rationing when war broke out in September 1939. However, in the financial year 1940-41 the 6,629 horse-drawn carts carried were only 18.9% of all four-wheeled traffic.

The last peacetime years of the luggage boats were uneventful. The Corporation seems to have assumed liability for 'pull-up' horses and tried unsuccessfully to recover £536-13-5d, the cost of this service, for the period 18th July 1934 to 31st March 1936, from the Dock Board tolls. As the toll was based on gross receipts the Corporation had no hope of winning and, later in 1936, the service of pull-up horses was reduced to save £74-2-0d per year. Talks with Wallasey aimed at co-ordinating the goods service, perhaps by means of a triangular service, came to nothing and there were financial reports and economy drives undertaken at the behest of the Tunnel Committee. A further serious blow was the loss of the GWR traffic to Seacombe in 1937. Wallasey Corporation made a 10-year Agreement with the railway company who perhaps felt that they had more security by using a ferry which was not under the control of the Tunnel Committee.

The vessels and stage escaped damage during the air raids of 1940-41 but the service was on several occasions suspended for short periods during raids and when enemy mines had been dropped in the river.

In March 1941, *Oxton* was requisitioned by the Ministry of Shipping for work under the control of the Dock Board. Two large derricks were erected on the deck and she was used to unload military aircraft, manufactured in the

AREA LINKED BY FERRY TO LIVERPOOL

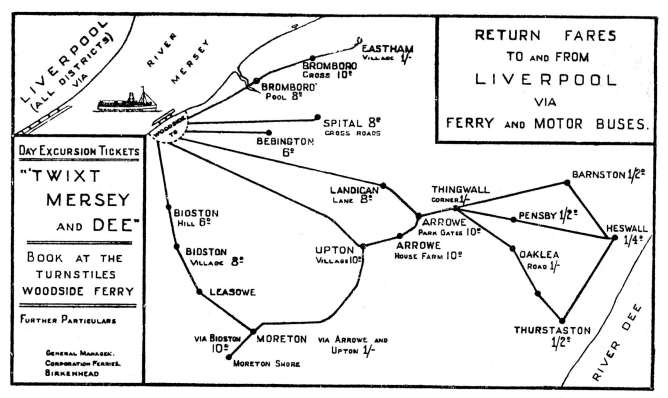

A coloured reproduction of this diagram adorned the Woodside berth at Liverpool for many years. The same fares were in force for over 20 years from 1930.

Bidston of 1933 leaving Woodside for Liverpool about 1938. The funnel of the luggage boat, whose master is apparently no longer interested in the 'no smoke' bonus, can also be seen.

Bidston of 1933 leaving Liverpool landing stage in immediate pre-war days in company with the Wallasey steamer **Royal Iris II** and (lower) approaching Woodside on 23rd November 1957. The vessel is little altered except for the removal of the awning frame and the fitting of a mainmast to satisfy new regulations.

United States, from ships and land them at the landing stage for onward movement by road to a Government factory at Speke, where they were finished off and finally assembled. A charter party was drawn up and ferrymen continued to man her. Birkenhead was now left with one boat and an agreement was made with Wallasey Corporation for the hire of one of their three boats, *Liscard*, *Leasowe* and *Perch Rock*, in the event of *Bebington* going for survey. That was on 16th July 1941 but only two days later, there was an emergency meeting of the Committee to consider the situation arising from the requisition of

Bebington by the Ministry of War Transport for similar duties. Eventually one of the Wallasey boats was also requisitioned for use as a crane and between them, the three vessels put ashore 11,000 aircraft.

End of the Goods Service

The Woodside goods service ceased abruptly and it seems that Wallasey Corporation was not inclined to be too co-operative, seeing an opportunity to boost revenue for their own loss-making goods service which was not supported

Hinderton, dressed overall and her red funnel restored, on cruise work during the 1939-45 war. She is embarking passengers between the passenger and goods berths at Woodside, using a portable gangway.

A poster issued in 1944 advertising 'Holidays at Home' cruises for which Hinderton was repainted from its wartime grey. Note the 'V for Victory' symbolism.

MERSEYSIDE HOLIDAYS AT HOME, 1944

Commencing May 28th   Last Sailings August 13th

FARE 1/6

WEDNESDAYS and THURSDAYS

2.30 p.m. from Woodside Stage

2.50 p.m. from Liverpool Stage

SUNDAYS and BANK HOLIDAYS

2.30 p.m. and 5.30 p.m. from Woodside Stage

2.50 p.m. and 5.50 p.m. from Liverpool Stage

BOOK alongside Steamer

CHILDREN must be accompanied by Adults

TICKETS may be obtained in advance by applying at the FERRY OFFICES, Woodside, Birkenhead

R. S. COWAN - - General Manager

by tunnel revenue. On 21st July 1941, the day the service ceased, there was a meeting of representatives of the Ministry of War Transport, Mersey Tunnel Joint Committee, the Dock Board, Birkenhead and Wallasey Corporations, after which the Town Clerk was told to request the Ministry to transfer temporarily to Birkenhead one of the Wallasey goods boats or some other suitable vessel so that the goods service could be restarted.

The result was a conference convened by the Regional Port Director on 8th September at which the broader view was taken that one goods service across the Mersey was sufficient in the then existing circumstances. This was endorsed by the Minister of War Transport three months later, 'subject to Birkenhead Corporation being at liberty to re-establish the goods service on their own terms as and when the opportunity presented itself and that the present arrangement was entirely without prejudice to Birkenhead's Charter or the Mersey Tunnel Acts'. The closure of the Woodside vehicular service led to the early retirement of seven long service employees and the disrating of several others. Horse drawn and dangerous goods traffic transferred to Seacombe without serious inconvenience. Even with this unexpected bonus, the Seacombe service incurred a heavy loss and a Bill was promoted to discontinue it in 1944. It finally closed when

the GWR agreement expired on 31st March 1947.

The hire of the luggage boats as cranes brought in revenue of £12,624 per year and the goods ferry account showed a profit in the final years when no traffic was being carried. In 1945, the MDHB considered buying *Oxton* and *Bebington* for their own use upon their release from Government service but eventually decided that their

Birkenhead luggage boat on war service, transferring military aircraft from USA ashore for final assembly. The aircraft were taken by lorries to Speke. It was the requisitioning of vessels for this duty that brought Birkenhead's luggage service to an end, though already in decline because of the tunnel.

permanent conversion would be too expensive. *Oxton* was derequisitioned on 1st April 1946 and consultants Casebourne and Turner reported to Birkenhead Corporation on a plan to convert her to carry passengers, bicycles and light vehicles. Nothing came of this unlikely scheme. *Bebington* was released about September 1946 and agreement reached on compensation due to the Corporation in January 1947. The cranes were removed in the summer of 1947 and the vessels advertised for sale. Alas, there were no takers and both went for scrap at £2,100 each in February 1949.

The importance of the goods ferry to the economic well-being of the Birkenhead ferries over the years was fundamental. In the years following the opening of the Mersey Railway the proportion of revenue derived from its traffic increased from 24% to 44% in five years. In the early years of the twentieth century, after railway electrification took its toll of ferry passenger traffic, the luggage boats' share of revenue increased year by year until, in 1913 it reached 53.6%. Once more, during the slump years the goods service kept the undertaking afloat until, in the last full year before the tunnel opened, it generated 61.8% of total revenue. Except in odd years such as those in the

1870s after the burning of George's Landing Stage, it was always profitable.

Despite the passage of time, memories of the luggage boats linger. The thunder of hooves and jingle of harness as horses and empty carts careered down the sloping roadway at low tide, the stench of horses mixed with the oily aroma of the steam wagons; the staccato clang and gentle chuff of the donkey engines as the gangways were raised and lowered; the cries of the carters with their flat caps and sack aprons as they strained to sooth their excited horses; the honk of bulb-horns and straw and chaff blowing in the breeze. But the most vivid memory is the crab-like but nevertheless stately precision of the red and black funnelled vessels, crossing and recrossing the swift flowing tide under the unerring guidance of the skilful masters aloft in their polished wood wheelhouses.

Within 25 years of their passing, the traffic queues built up once more but this time, not on the floating roadways but in the central streets of Liverpool and Birkenhead as the 1934 tunnel reached its capacity. Flyovers and another tunnel were needed to cater for the demands of the insatiable motor vehicle.

10 THE POST-WAR YEARS 1946-90

The transition from war to peace was a gradual process spread over several years. Limited lighting had been restored in 1944 and traffic in 1943-44 was 14% above the low point of 1941-42. Continued fuel rationing and many other restrictions in the immediate post-war years were a constant irritant but there was a pent-up demand for pleasure travel and all public transport operators experienced a boom, particularly in the summer months. Passengers exceeded 11 million in 1947-48, 1948-49 and 1949-50 but the post-war high of 11,400,795 in 1948-49 was still 9.5% below 1938-39. The ferries were able to absorb this extra load at little or no additional operating cost. Increased costs of wages, fuel and materials had raised expenditure by 94% compared with 1938-39 and, if the debt on the ferry had not been paid off, the increase would have been 146%. The Woodside passenger service, which had made a small profit of £970 in 1938-39, was set to lose £50,000 annually.

A sub-committee appointed to examine means of reducing losses had recommended modest fares increases and withdrawal of the night service in December 1948. As will be seen, there were statutory obstacles to abandoning the night boats but fares were increased from 1st April 1949, the delay being necessary to give the railway time to adjust the many through fares and for the Licensing Authority for Public Service Vehicles to approve higher bus and ferry through fares. The ordinary fare increased from 2d to 2½d, the first rise for almost 25 years, and contract rates increased proportionately. A weekly contract cost 1/8d (instead of 1/3d) for unlimited travel and there were still concessionary rates for the wives of six and 12-monthly contractors. Thus a man and his wife could enjoy unlimited day time travel between Liverpool and Woodside for £4-2-0d per annum, a rate of a little over 1d a trip for daily travellers. The ferries took the whole of the 2d increase on bus and ferry tickets and this facility waned in popularity year by year. In 1947-48, 32% of ferry passengers used these tickets, producing 26% of the revenue but by 1951-52 these proportions had declined to 16% of passengers contributing 17% of revenue.

Through traffic to and from rail had been falling for decades. From 252,000 in the first year (1878-79) it had risen to 396,000 in 1880-81. It peaked at around 450,000 passengers in 1903-04 and by 1915 it had fallen to 234,000. Post-war traffic declined annually from 131,000 in 1947-48 to 60,000 in 1951-52, producing a paltry £309; by 1964-65, after which separate figures were not published, the annual revenue was £50. This trend reflected a gradual decline in the importance of the railways as passenger carriers and a greater use of the Mersey Railway, which had been nationalised along with

the main line railways on 1st January 1948. It was only natural that railway management should promote the use of their own facilities. The 1949 fares increase was softened by the full restoration of the 10-minute service but there was a reversion to a 15-minute frequency in September 1950, except during morning, lunchtime and evening peak periods.

By 1951-52, 65.15% of passengers paid tolls (45.53% adult ordinary, 13.68% workmen and 5.94% children), accounting for 70.15% of the revenue. Contractors had increased from 9.66% of passengers in 1947-48 to 17.87% in 1951-52; in terms of trips made this was an increase from 1,170,000 to 1,750,000. Some of the additional passengers apparently found it cheaper to buy a contract rather than a bus and ferry ticket. One of the ferries' problems was the great fluctuation in traffic throughout the year and throughout the day. Figures for 1946-47 show that 13.74% of annual passenger traffic was carried in August and only 4.12% in February.

Whilst the Birkenhead ratepayers were sheltered from the ferry losses by the Tunnel Committee, the latter kept up constant pressure on the Ferries Committee to seek out economies. The members were acutely aware of the advantages enjoyed by the railway in bad weather. There were still bad fogs in the 'fifties as full-scale clean air legislation was yet to come. A foggy day meant 20% loss of revenue.

The Radar System

Wallasey Corporation made history in 1947 by installing a radar system at Seacombe which enabled virtually normal services to be maintained in the densest of fogs; it was claimed as the first commercial adaptation of this wartime invention. Radar was still in its infancy and there were many practical difficulties to be overcome. Wallasey found that none of the shore-based instruments were suitable and installed a Cossor ship's instrument in a control room located beneath the elegant clock tower which had been built at Seacombe in 1932. A scanner was mounted on top of the tower, high enough to avoid all adjacent obstacles and a stand-by generator was purchased in case of power failure. Vessels were equipped with radio telephones and received verbal advice from the land-based operators.

Birkenhead made a close study of the system and there was a demonstration on board *Claughton* on 11th February 1948, using the Seacombe control and, later that year, the two authorities came to an agreement whereby Wallasey provided radar guidance to Birkenhead for £600 per annum. *Hinderton, Claughton, Thurstaston* and

A replica of the Wallasey Ferries Cossor radar station at Seacombe which provided guidance services for both Seacombe and Woodside ferries for many years.

Bidston were equipped with radio telephones in October 1948. The system worked perfectly but, in a typical demonstration of the Birkenhead Ferries Committee's antipathy to anything Wallaseyan, an investigation was made into installing an independent system in 1951. The manager set out the facts very fairly. There was no suitable tower at Woodside, no skilled operatives, the Post Office would oppose a separate radio wavelength and a host of other objections. The Cossor installation at Seacombe gave good service until 1971 when it was replaced by more modern equipment integrated with the Merseyside PTE's communications network.

When the post-war travel boom started to decline in 1950, economies were sought to reduce the ferries' losses. Wallasey, with no Tunnel Committee support, was much more concerned than Birkenhead and, in 1950 they worked out a scheme whereby Wallasey steamers would work a triangular Seacombe-Woodside-Liverpool-Seacombe service between either 8.00pm or 12.30am and 5.00am from October to March, claiming potential economies for both services. There was a joint meeting with Birkenhead and Wallasey Committee members on 16th August 1950 followed by a manager's report in which it was claimed that Birkenhead would, in fact, not benefit at all. At the time there were eight crews employed—three for each of two steamers, one to cover days off and the last

relieving to reduce the working hours from 48 to 44 with two days in dock.

The normal shifts changed at 7.00am, 3.00pm and 11.00pm and an 8.00pm shut down, whilst nominally reducing the number of crews by two, introduced many rostering problems. However the main objection was the potential increase in maintenance costs. To quote from Mr. Cowan's report:-

'Considering all these points, if our steamers discontinue sailing after 8 p.m. during the six winter months, i.e., October to March inclusive, I estimate a saving of £1,378 in wages and £1,000 in fuel, of which 50% would go to Wallasey.

I have been very loath to suggest an alteration in the operation of our night service as from past experience I have proved constant steaming reduces maintenance costs and adds considerably to the lives of our steamers.

During my early years in your service we fitted new boilers to boats, patched shells, renewed furnaces, tube plates and tubes, in fact we were continually carrying out repairs and renewals to the boilers of the fleet, but since 1920 all this has been cut out, and the maintenance costs reduced considerably; if this proposed arrangement of sailings is adopted it will not be possible to keep the repair costs down, in fact the whole of the advantage will be with Wallasey.'

He went on to compare Wallasey's average general repair and maintenance expenditure of £34,812 for 1948-49 with Birkenhead's £10,898 or £5,802 per Wallasey steamer against £2,724 for Birkenhead and predicted expenditure of £5,000 per steamer if vessels were laid off for long periods each night during the winter months, the worst part of the year.

Policy Decisions

In 1951, the Town Clerk advised the Council that it was essential to make a policy decision on the future of the ferries, bearing in mind the mounting losses and the option which had to be exercised on 18th July 1955. Before that date the Council had to decide whether to continue to accept Tunnel Committee management for a further 21 years or resume municipal control with a consequent loss of revenue support. If there were to be any radical change in the status of the ferries, Parliamentary powers would be required, so early decisions were necessary.

A joint report was compiled by the Town Clerk, Borough Treasurer, Ferries Manager and Transport Manager with some input from the Borough Architect. Every aspect of the ferries undertaking was examined in great detail and numerous alternative strategies to increase revenue or reduce costs were examined. The superiority of the Mersey Railway as to speed and accessibility was recognised.

Possible economy measures examined included the reduction of crews by one deckhand and one fireman (subject to successful negotiations with trade unions); operation of a 20-minute service with one boat after 7.00pm and on Sundays for seven months of the year; abandonment of the night service and abandonment of the whole winter service. There were advantages and disadvantages for each proposal but none would achieve savings sufficient to eliminate the deficit of £50,000 per annum.

The report showed remarkable prescience as to the future course of events:-

'It may well be that the Ferries are becoming less and less an integral part of the Merseyside system of communications and tending to become an amenity.'

This view was not officially accepted by the politicians until 1977. To support this statement the report drew on antipodean experience.

'Ferries appear to be unable to compete with modern forms of transport and this is borne out by events in Australia. In 1914 Sydney Ferries had 42 boats and carried 25 million passengers per annum and in 1928 they had nearly 50 boats and carried 50 million passengers p.⅞a. Their final fleet of 16 boats carried about 7⅓ million passengers and in consequence the undertaking had to close'.

Tunnel Buses

The question of running buses through the tunnel was examined in great detail and it was accepted that if the night service or the winter service were to be abandoned, there would be a moral obligation to provide some alternative means of travelling between Liverpool and Birkenhead, at least during the hours when the Mersey Railway was not running ie 11.15pm to 6.00am. The railway could not run on a 24-hour basis as maintenance work was done at night. Whilst the 1871 Agreement required the concurrence of the Railway Executive to withdrawal of the night service until 1955, that body had previously expressed willingness to discuss the matter. While there was the possibility of relatively substantial numbers of railway excursion passengers occasionally presenting themselves for passage, the substitution of a bus service presented difficulties and this was still felt to be a problem at the time the report was written. The economics of buses were calculated on the basis of the existing legislation and toll structure whereby the Tunnel Committee would charge tolls of 5/- a trip for each bus and 2d for each passenger, making it necessary to charge a fare of at least 1/- but the costs were worked out on the basis of a route between Lime Street Station and Charing Cross which would be more convenient to the public and there was plenty of time to cover the extra distance. By this time, peak hour tunnel traffic congestion had already become a nuisance and 'tidal flow' had commenced with three lanes of traffic in the ruling direction and only one the other way. The physical limitations of the Queensway tunnel would have prevented bus services operating during such times; the tunnel is circular in cross-section and there is insufficient headroom for double deckers in the nearside lanes or the branch tunnels. The relatively low-capacity single deckers of that time would have been quite uneconomic.

Problems at Woodside

The final section of the report was devoted to the dreadful condition of the 80-year old terminal building, passenger bridge and landing stage. The foundations of the wooden booking hall and offices had collapsed because of uneven settlement in the area of the old stone pier, the timber piles having rotted away. The wooden buildings had fared rather better than the more solidly constructed office and workshop as their light construction had made them more sympathetic to the continuous settlement that had taken place. The report went on:-

'The general amenity, waiting rooms and lavatories are poor and reminiscent of the Victorian Railway era. The offices which appear to have grown up piecemeal are outdated functionally, designed originally to cope with heavy volume of goods traffic, they now occupy at least twice the area necessary. The workshops which are capable of dealing with almost any contingency .... are no longer called upon to carry out this large amount of work for which they were originally designed. The number of boats has decreased, as has, therefore, the maintenance, the quay cannot apparently withstand the load of hoisting the pontoons ashore and therefore they cannot be repaired in the workshops.'

Consulting engineers, Wilton and Bell, had estimated the cost of repairs to the passenger bridge at £23,200 whilst replacement would cost £35,000. Some attention was needed to the stage, though major work had been done in 1928 after it was rammed by a coaster. The report concluded that:-

'if the ferries were to continue to operate, the whole Woodside complex was in need of renewal.
'.... the lack of amenity and the inconvenience of the facilities offers very little incentive to use the Ferry except under very ideal conditions. Yet Woodside is the focus of all the transport organisations of the County Borough. It is the bus terminus, the the steam railway terminus, the Ferry terminus, there is an electric train station close by and it has car parking facilities at the end of some of the main traffic routes from the Wirral.'

Whilst agreeing with these sentiments, the Council had only to turn its eyes towards Seacombe, where Wallasey Corporation had renewed the ferry terminal in 1930-33 at great expense but their financial problems were as serious if not worse than at Woodside. In the event, a great deal of money was to be wasted in patching up over the next 30 years before a bold decision was taken to renew — at a cost unimaginable in 1952.

The Council concluded that the only course of action open to them was to negotiate with the Tunnel Committee. In brief, Birkenhead Corporation gave notice to the Mersey Tunnel Joint Committee that it wished them to continue to support the ferries after 18th July 1955. The Tunnel Committee duly required the ferries to discontinue the night service and to raise fares and abolish certain concessions. Financial responsibility for the replacing night bus service was assumed by the Tunnel Committee. The Agreement was confirmed by the Mersey Tunnel Act 1955. The tunnel financial support arrangements were finally revised following the decision to construct a second road tunnel between Liverpool and Wallasey. The Mersey Tunnel (Liverpool/Wallasey) etc Act, 1965 limited the Tunnel Committee's period of support to 40 years from the opening of the first tunnel and contributions ceased on 17th July 1974.

Higher Fares

From 1st August 1955, the ordinary fare was increased from 2½d to 4d and weekly and monthly contracts went up from 1/8d to 2/- and from 5/10d to 7/- All contracts for periods in excess of one month were abolished as they expired, thus simplifying administrative work. There was no further increase in the ordinary fare until after the ferries had passed into the ownership of Merseyside Passenger Transport Executive in 1969.

As an economy measure, the Transport and Ferries Committees were combined in 1955 as the Municipal Transport Committee under the former bus general manager, G. A. Cherry, a course of action facilitated by the retirement of the ferries general manager, R. S. Cowan.

It was agreed that the night bus service would be provided for alternate three-month periods by Birkenhead and Liverpool Corporation buses on hire to the Mersey Tunnel Joint Committee and that fares of 1/- between midnight and 4.00am and 6d thereafter were to be collected at tunnel toll booths. The night ferry service operated for the last time on 13th May 1956 and at 12.10am on 14th, the first bus, provided by Birkenhead Corporation, left the Tunnel Entrance, Birkenhead for Liverpool, returning 10 minutes later. On the first night 97 passengers were carried to Liverpool and 102 from Liverpool. The saving to the ferries was estimated to be £4,000 per year, less than 7% of the annual loss.

The Corporation was now confronted with two problems — a rapidly ageing, obsolescent fleet and a landing stage which was over 90 years old and, if the facts were faced, in need of total renewal. The fortunes of the ferries were affected by constantly increasing car ownership, causing steadily falling traffic and the general decline of the port with a consequent shortage of funds at the disposal of the Mersey Docks and Harbour Board.

The closure of the Woodside floating roadway from 14th February 1955 on the grounds that it was not worth repairing the decking, and its removal in 1958, after a new boom had been placed in position, caused serious problems. Since the closure of the goods service in 1941, the roadway had been used by cyclists and vehicles delivering coal to the stage and removing ashes. Not only ferry steamers were coaled at Woodside but also some tugs made use of the facilities. The difficulties caused by the cutting of vehicle access to the stage were overcome by the purchase of two pedestrian controlled battery electric trucks on which the coal was transported down the passenger bridge during the night and the ashes removed on the return trips. The coal was stockpiled as before on the land behind the ferry offices. This operation was by no means straightforward as, when the tide was low and the bridge angle very steep, the trucks tended to run away and there were several cases of accidents narrowly averted. These difficulties added weight to the argument in favour of the renewal of the ferry fleet but it was not until 1958 that the Tunnel Committee agreed that new boats be ordered as described in chapter 11. Coaling was finally eliminated in 1962 and an oil pipeline was carried to the stage via the passenger bridge.

The determination of Birkenhead to find fault with any suggestions put forward by Wallasey concerning the ferries, was once more demonstrated in 1957 when the chairman of Wallasey Ferries Committee, Ald. J. P. Ashton, aware that Birkenhead was about to renew a substantial portion of its fleet, put forward the perfectly reasonable suggestion that the two undertakings should investigate the feasability of eliminating the duplication of stand-by boats and using vessels from either fleet to replace vessels out of service for survey or repair. The main problem was the different gangway spacings, Wallasey's main deck gangways being 44ft. apart whilst Birkenhead's were 50ft. The question had come up in earlier years but had never been pursued because of the cost of the structural alterations necessary. The principle was sound but it made less sense in 1957 as two of the Wallasey steamers, *Leasowe* and *Egremont* had been built with only one gangway door each side. Birkenhead backs immediately went up when it was suggested that Birkenhead's gangways should be altered rather than Wallasey's on the quite logical grounds that there were fewer of them to alter, thus reducing the cost of the exercise. Two new vessels, then in the planning stage, could have been designed to the required dimensions. Wallasey had eight gangways, two each at Seacombe and New Brighton and four at Liverpool whilst Birkenhead had two on each bank of the river. Wallasey suggested that, instead of converting two old boats, Birkenhead should rely on Wallasey boats for spares. Alderman Ashton's proposals were made available to the press, resulting in a counter-statement being issued by Birkenhead, ending with the following:-

'It was obvious that if Birkenhead were left with two boats only it would not be possible for Wallasey to hire a boat from Birkenhead. All the hiring would have to be done by Birkenhead, and as they have now got all the cover they require by retaining the third boat at the cost of an annual survey, there did not appear to be any real value in the Wallasey proposals. It was for this reason that Birkenhead stated that there appeared to be no useful purpose in discussing the matter further. We are always ready to discuss any proposals with the Wallasey Corporation that will lead to real economies in the operation of the Ferry undertaking, but are reluctant to undertake heavy expenditure when the prospects of future economies are extremely nebulous and indefinite.'

Perhaps with a little more tact, some progress might have been made as, by 1957, a combined Mersey ferry fleet made economic sense and within 13 years it was to become fact. But while Tunnel financial support existed, Birkenhead had no incentive to make fundamental, far-reaching economies.

Woodside ferry approach in the 1960s. The century-old terminal building is unchanged but the vessel crossing to Liverpool is diesel-powered. The islands and bus queue-barriers were installed during the 1939-45 war. Buses were parked on the north side to save mileage to and from the depot at Laird Street between peaks; they are parked on the site of the original stone quay which still lies below the surface. By that date Birkenhead's bus fleet, under the same management as the ferries, largely consisted of Leyland PD2 buses though a Guy Arab is nearest the camera.

The condition of the landing stage was another serious problem and a programme of patching up was carried out over a period of several years. D. V. Buck and Partners were appointed as consultants and, in a report submitted in August 1965, they recommended a three-phase programme of reconstruction. This covered renewal of the decking and replacement of a number of the pontoons. A new screen was provided between the passenger stage and the now disused goods stage, the old warehouse demolished and a new ticket office built in 1967. However the defects continued to develop. In January 1969 the Transport Committee was told that since the completion of the second phase in July 1967, two further fractures had developed in the kelsons. The estimated cost of phase 3 was £11,000.

Although rail traffic had declined and most long distance trains to and from Woodside had been withdrawn over the previous decade, the closure of Woodside railway station and the truncating of the Chester line at Rock Ferry from 4th November 1967, was a further blow to the ferries, as all rail traffic was automatically routed on to the Mersey Railway.

Full employment brought further problems, as there was a shortage of suitably qualified seamen for promotion to officer rank. In 1969 there was difficulty in manning the vessels during the summer season because of the lack of relief men for senior members of the crews.

At the time of handover to the PTE, the Birkenhead Corporation Ferries were undoubtedly the most senior municipal transport undertaking with an enviable record of 127½ years continuous public service. Until 1934, the ferries had been very profitable and, whilst several changes in the presentation of the accounts make it difficult to say exactly without ambiguity by how much the rates were relieved, the sum was considerable. The first contribution of £1,600 was in 1847-48; this represented a return on sales of 8.17%. There was a gap of three years and then, except in 1855-56, regular payments were made to the township. In 1864-65, the 'dividend' was equivalent to a 30.36% return on sales. From 1882-83, by which time £137,641 had been paid over, payments were made into the 'Interest Rate Fund' from which interest payments were also made so that, without a great deal of research, the exact 'profit' is hard to calculate. However, until 1935-36 there was a trading loss only in 1920-21 and 1921-22. Thereafter, during the remainder of the municipal period, the MTJC paid over £2,752,163 to make good ferry losses, an average of £78,635 per year.

The PTE Years

The Transport Act 1968 was designed to ease the burdens on public transport caused by the changes in social habits and one of the measures proposed was the creation of Passenger Transport Authorities in conurbations. Merseyside was one of the first four areas selected, and the Merseyside Passenger Transport Area (Designation) Order 1969 was discussed by the Birkenhead Municipal Transport Committee at their meeting on 26th February 1969. The Authority consisted of representatives of the local councils in the designated area while the Executive comprised professionals charged with implementing the Authority's policy. The Executive was appointed on 1st November 1969 and on 1st December acquired the passenger transport undertakings of Liverpool, Birkenhead and Wallasey, including the ferries of the last two. For the record, under local government reorganisation in 1974, the Merseyside County Council became the Authority and the bus undertakings of St. Helens and Southport were absorbed on 1st April 1974.

Understandably, the municipalities kept expenditure to a minimum during their last months of stewardship and the PTE inherited much dereliction and serious financial problems.

Seven vessels passed into the combined fleet, *Overchurch*, *Mountwood* and *Woodchurch* from Birkenhead and *Egremont*, *Leasowe*, *Royal Iris* and *Royal Daffodil* from Wallasey. All were diesel propelled except the cruise ship *Royal Iris* which was diesel-electric.

Eventually, in 1973, the Seacombe gangways were modified to permit the use of the ex-Birkenhead boats on the Seacombe service and all the Wallasey boats except *Royal Iris* were sold.

The PTE had serious and expensive problems with landing stages. Patching up work continued at Woodside and also at Seacombe, a much newer structure commissioned in 1926. Further fractures developed in the main kelsons at Woodside and potential danger to users was a source of some concern. In November 1970, the Dock Board gave notice of their intention to abrogate their responsibility for George's landing stage, setting off the train of events described in detail in Chapter 12. The disruption caused by diversion of the vessels during reconstruction at Liverpool and suspension of the service following the sinking of the new George's landing stage in 1976 resulted in a further permanent loss of traffic to the ferries.

Further decking was replaced at Woodside stage in 1973 and the passenger shelter renewed. There were now major fractures in the kelsons requiring immediate attention. Patching continued and in 1976 further work was authorised to cost £13,000 including £6,000 for temporary repairs to the bearings of the passenger bridge.

The PTE was less parochial in its attitude to the ferries. Despite pressure from the MTJC, Birkenhead Corporation had maintained a rather nostalgic civic pride in the ferries undertaking. The PTE adopted a policy of railway

Overchurch, *built in 1962, with green and black funnel.*

extension and went ahead with an expensive scheme to reroute the Mersey Railway on to a new loop line under Liverpool city centre, serving the commercial and shopping areas much more comprehensively; a new junction was built at Hamilton Square, Birkenhead, effectively doubling line capacity by eliminating conflicting train movements.

The Mersey Tunnel (Liverpool/Wallasey etc) Act 1965 had authorised the construction of a second road tunnel and had amended earlier legislation governing ferry revenue support. This was to terminate 40 years after the opening of the first tunnel viz: 18th July 1974. In the 4½ years between the formation of the PTE and that date, the MTJC had paid over £1,152,340, bringing the grand total of tunnel support to £3,904,340 or an average of £97,613 per year. Faced with the full financial burden of the ferries, in 1974, the PTE commissioned an assessment by the Centre of Transport Studies at Cranfield Institute of Technology

on the future need for surface transport facilities across the Mersey. The Wallasey road tunnel had opened on 28th June 1971 and the first local tunnel bus service was running between Liverpool city centre, Liscard and New Brighton.

The study concluded that the withdrawal of all ferry services would alleviate some of the PTE's financial problems as the other cross-river services had the capacity to cope with all existing ferry traffic which, by that time, had fallen to 4.000 — 5,000 passengers a day at Woodside and Seacombe combined, a number which would have been carried in 40 minutes on one ferry in earlier times. The study team recognised the sentimental viewpoint and made a number of suggestions for reducing operating losses without lowering the level of service, by cutting the fleet size, using smaller vessels and introducing automatic ticketing. The use of catamarans, hydrofoils or hovercraft was rejected as not viable, though later on, in 1982, a catamaran, *Highland Seabird*, was tried out unsuccessfully. The study team examined the possibility of introducing new ferry crossings and concluded that the only possibility lay in a direct link to Speke but only if Liverpool airport was allowed to realise its full potential.

The Future in Doubt

In 1974 the question of the future of the ferries came before the new Merseyside County Council. The Passenger Transport Committee nad already voted to discontinue the service which was losing £800,000 per year and on purely economic grounds there was no case for retention. However in the face of a storm of popular protest, the County Council voted to retain the ferries on a reduced frequency, the fares to be related to bus and rail fares when the new Liverpool landing stage came into service.

The Woodside fare had been increased from 4d to 6d in 1970 and was decimalised as 2½p in February 1971; on 31st January 1972 the fare was increased to 4p. Thereafter fares followed the pattern of increases on the buses and trains, having reached 40p by 1989. Contracts were superseded by inter-modal zone tickets from 29th October 1978.

In the 1976-77 Parliamentary session, the Merseyside Passenger Transport Bill was presented by Eric Ogden, MP for West Derby, to give the PTE power to discontinue ferry services and introduce penalties for overriders on buses. Meanwhile in April 1977, the Leader of the County Council told transport interest groups that the ferries' future lay in pleasure trips only. However on 11th July 1977 the Bill was talked out in a 2½ hour speech by David Hunt, MP for Wirral West. A great victory was claimed by the Friends of the Ferries, a group founded in 1974 to promote the retention of the ferries which continued to promote the ferries' cause.

Integration of the Birkenhead and Wallasey ferries was finally completed following the destruction by fire of the Woodside ferry workshops in May 1980, resulting in the loss of almost all the vessels' spare parts. New workshops and stores were already being built at Seacombe and ferries

administration was transferred there in March 1981. Passengers on Woodside ferry declined from 750,000 in 1979-80 to 608,000 in 1980-81.

On 6th April 1981, the Woodside and Seacombe services were reduced to a basic 40-minute service worked by one boat, additional peak hour trips being provided by the cruise ship, *Royal Iris*. *Woodchurch* was laid up. In 1983 it was agreed that responsibility for the formulation, promotion and marketing of ferry leisure services should, from 1984, be assumed by the County Council's Tourism Committee, operational control remaining with the PTE. It was also decided that the 40-minute service was self-defeating and, from 28th November 1983, *Woodchurch* was brought back into service and the off-peak and Saturday frequencies on both Woodside and Seacombe services were doubled to every 20 minutes—30 minutes on Sundays—requiring one boat on each service and one in reserve.

The ferries had a momentous year in 1984. A landing stage was built at Otterspool for the Garden Festival and between 3rd May and mid-October a special service was run from Liverpool to Otterspool via Woodside at a flat fare of 25p. Unfortunately the depth of water in the Garston Channel at Otterspool was such that the service could run only at high tide and the number of trips at hourly intervals varied between two and five per day. *Overchurch*, painted in a somewhat garish red, white and blue livery was mainly used on this service, an unexpected revival of the South End ferry of the 1860s.

The appearance in the Mersey of the ships engaged in the Tall Ships Race from 1st to 4th August brought patronage to the ferries on a scale unknown for nearly 40 years. 250,000 passengers were carried on the four days and the Woodside service was suspended between 12.30 and 8.30pm on 4th August 1984, the day of the Grand Parade of sail, all the vessels being used as grandstands.

Woodside Refurbished

Following a report by marine consultants, D. V. Buck and Partners, the County Council decided that there was no

Overchurch, berthed at the Garden Festival landing stage, Otterspool on 30th June 1984

Woodside landing stage in course of dismantlement during the summer of 1985. The southern end is still in use by the Woodside passenger ferry. Note the derelict lairages in the right foreground and the north bridge originally used for cattle.

alternative but to renew the Woodside landing stage and reconstruct the terminal buildings. The 1864 booking hall, of wooden construction on brick foundations, was a listed building and was refurbished in the existing style, many of the timbers being replaced. The timber terminal building behind was demolished and replaced by a tubular steel-framed structure with a glazed barrel roof with a concourse in clay paviors on a reinforced concrete slab, supported on ground beams and 25ft. piles which were necessary because of uneven settlement of the ground over the original stone pier with its two slipways. The work was estimated to cost the County Council £2.6 million of which £1,482,000 was paid by the European Regional Development Fund. However the total cost was approximately £3.2 million of which £244,000 was for the booking hall restoration.

During the summer of 1985, the northern section of the landing stage, disused since the cattle trade ceased, and the northern bridge, were removed in a two-part operation and towed to Garston for breaking up. The ferry service ceased with the last sailing on Saturday 31st August 1985 but the last vessel to use the old stage was *Royal Iris* on a cruise to and from the Ellesmere Port Boat Museum the following day. During the next week, the passenger bridge was lifted and the remaining part of the passenger stage

detached from its moorings and towed to Liverpool North Docks for breaking up.

The new stage, built by Die-Biesbosch at Dordrecht in the Netherlands, arrived in the Mersey on the afternoon of 6th September, towed on the 700 mile passage by the tug *Ardneil*. It was joined in the estuary by the Mersey tug *Rowanmore* and welcomed officially off New Brighton by *Overchurch* with the mayor of Wirral, Cllr. G. C. Lindsay and other dignitaries and invited guests on board. The new bridge and boom, 151ft. long, were stowed on the stage and installation proceeded during the following two weeks, the 200-ton crane *Mammoth* being hired to lift the bridge and boom on to their bearings. Just after 11.00am on Monday 23rd September, the chairman of the Merseyside County Council, Counc. Edith Lawrenson, headed a party which boarded *Overchurch* at Liverpool and crossed to Woodside, where she became the first passenger to disembark at the new stage. Having cut a tape on the new bridge, she declared the new ferry terminal open and public service between Woodside and Liverpool resumed with the 11.55am sailing, following the longest suspension of the Woodside ferry service on record.

There are no kelsons in the new landing stage which is a welded steel box with plated structural tees forming the bulkheads; it measures 171ft. by 79ft. by 10ft. 6in. deep.

The old Woodside passenger bridge being floated away for breaking during suspension of the ferry in September 1985. The boom in the foreground was added in 1955 to provide stability after the removal of the floating roadway.

The new Woodside landing stage soon after installation in 1985. The tall tower on the left provided hydraulic power for the lifts at Hamilton Square underground railway station while those seen above the barrel-roofed booking hall at the shore end of the bridge are ventilating shafts for the original road tunnel of 1934. The strengthening buttresses in the river wall were found to be necessary in the 1930s due to uneven settlement of the infilling of the 1860s.

Overchurch in red, white and blue paint, displaying a retention campaign banner for Merseyside County Council in August 1984.

the terminal bridge and waiting room are all of glazed barrel-roof construction. Several features of the old stage were incorporated in the new one including the fog bell and bollards. The cast-iron ornamental pillars and archways of the gangways had been sent to Holland and were in position on arrival as were the gangway recesses. The crown finials, symbolic of Edward III's Charter, were later restored. Three decorative lamp standards were re-installed without their globes at the northern end whilst the decorative three-light bracket was replaced at the south end. Work on the bridge canopy and the terminal building continued throughout the winter and on 13th March 1986 Counc. Mrs Lawrenson returned to Woodside to open formally the new terminal building and unveil a commemorative plaque. Three of the five columns supporting the shortened canopy are truncated tramway standards, disused since 1937. The demolition of buildings on the north side had enabled the Council to lay out a promenade area, comprising the end of the old stone pier, on which still stands the lighthouse, albeit now surmounted by a light which previously adorned the bell tower. For the first time in 125 years, a full vista of the river could be obtained from Woodside.

A New Role

With further local government changes and abolition of the Merseyside County Council, the PTE once more fell under the control of an Authority consisting of the elected representatives of the five District Councils. Fears that deregulation of public road transport would lead to the demise of the ferries proved to be unfounded though many more buses now run through both road tunnels. The ferries remained the responsibility of the Merseyside PTE, ultimately through a subsidiary company, Mersey Ferries Ltd and, as the costly prospect of fleet replacement loomed, it was decided to commission L & R Leisure plc to carry out a project to adapt the Mersey ferries to a purely tourist role, augmented by some cross-river peak hour journeys. The 'core product' would be cruising. A Business Plan, completed in 1989, was opposed by the ferries staff and referred back to the consultants. A decision was made

129

*The size of the modern ferry vessels is dramatically emphasised by this view of MV **Woodchurch** alongside **Queen Elizabeth 2** off Woodside on 24th July 1990. The occasion was the centenary of the Cunard Line.*

to refurbish *Mountwood* and *Woodchurch* and, from 1st April 1990 a half-hourly triangular ferry service was inaugurated with *Overchurch* between Liverpool, Woodside and Seacombe, operating clockwise in the morning peak and thereafter anti-clockwise. There was a 45-minute Sunday service. This was subsequently amended to give a less frequent but longer off-peak cruise, the vessels sailing further up and down stream on each circuit.

Memories of the great days of the ferries linger on — days when a ferry trip was an essential element in the journey to work and home again. The fug in the smoking saloon on a cold winter's morning; the spontaneous anti-clockwise march, five or six abreast, round and round the promenade deck; the dexterity of the deck hands as they flung the pilot rope ashore and then skilfully manipulated the mooring ropes, figure-eight style round the twin capstans; the ting of the ship's bell and the last-minute clatter of running footsteps on the slatted gangways; all these will be remembered for many years to come. Remembered too by the older people are the choking fogs, now happily only

a memory, and the slow progress of the boats across the dangerous waters, their masters guided only by the monotonous bells and foghorns on each side of the river.

Gone are the days when the river was full of shipping but the reprieve of the ferries when all seemed lost, and the preservation of many historic masterpieces of the port, may yet herald an era of new prosperity for a part of Britain which has suffered more than its share of misfortunes.

11 THE MERSEY FERRY BOATS

The design of ferry boats for any estuary or bay tends to take on a family resemblance, as all the vessels plying their trade are influenced by a number of common factors. On the Mersey, these factors were the swift flowing tide, the 32ft. tidal range, the limitations of the landing arrangements and, as traffic increased following industrialisation and population growth, the need for relatively high speeds, rapid acceleration and expeditious loading and unloading.

When steam power was first applied to the Mersey ferries during the euphoria of the post-Napoleonic War era, the vessels were little more than adaptations of the sailing vessels of old. There were exceptions, of course, such as the twin-hulled *Etna* but experience proved that existing boatbuilding skills could be adapted to the new mode of propulsion and there was really no need for radical changes in design. Wooden ships continued to be the norm in the earliest days and because of the very low power of the early simple steam engines (*Etna's* nhp was only 22), sail assistance was common. Competition and public demand for regularity and good timekeeping led to the building of longer, more powerful boats with twin cylinder oscillating engines. Length increased from around 80ft. to 125ft. in the space of 20 years. The additional stresses generated by engines of 70-80nhp demanded iron construction which was almost universal by the 1840s.

In the 19th century, there were many small shipyards on both banks of the Mersey but shipbuilding on the Lancashire shore was finally killed off by the Dock Board's refusal to grant freehold rights. As ships became larger and more complex, the smaller yards could not compete nor could they risk the capital investment needed for iron shipbuilding, as the danger of the Dock Board taking their yards for more dock extensions was ever present. They either closed down or merged with the survivors until building was concentrated in an area on the Cheshire shore south of Woodside. Shipbuilding was always highly competitive and, despite the wide choice of local yards, many Mersey ferry steamers were built elsewhere from quite early times. Engines and hulls often came from different sources.

Until the 1850s, little provision was made for passenger amenities and in boisterous weather, travellers would huddle against the tiny deckhouse and paddle-boxes or try to get some warmth from the spindly funnel; some boats had cramped cabins below deck and Woodside of 1853 had a 'glass saloon' on deck but, by all accounts it was a pokey ill-ventilated affair to be used only as a last resort. Although the Laird family had enormous influence in Birkenhead, they seem to have contributed very little to ferry boat design and evolution and relatively few orders went to their yard. The great breakthrough came with the availability of safe floating landing stages on both sides of the river. Larger, more powerful boats were now practicable and these further stimulated the growth of traffic.

It is not known when the red and black funnels of the Birkenhead steamers became standard. The funnel was, in fact, red with a broad black band at top and bottom and a

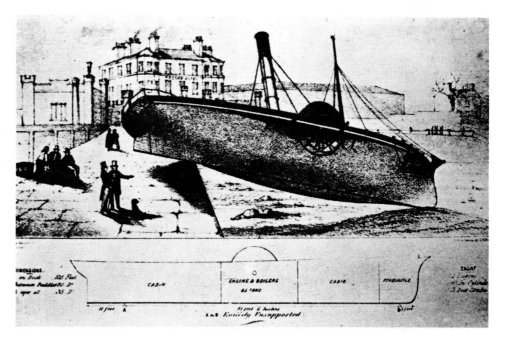

*In April 1856, **Queen** was grounded on the Woodside quay at low tide but was so well-built by John Laird in 1844 that she suffered no permanent damage and she continued in service until 1881. The luckless master, John Jones, was held to blame and reduced to a hand. The diagram shows how the vessel was supported at points 81ft. 6in. apart out of her total length of 105ft, the weight of engines and boilers amidships being given as 65 tons.*

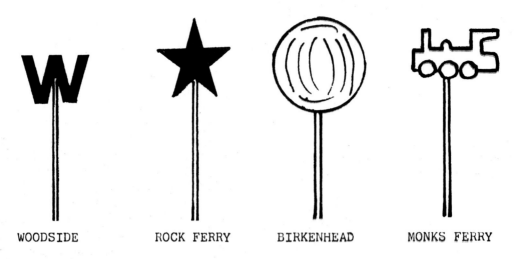

WOODSIDE   ROCK FERRY   BIRKENHEAD   MONKS FERRY

In the early days of steam, when vessels of many different ferries scrambled for berths and many passengers were illiterate, there was a need for an easy means of identifying the various ferries. Masthead signs were certainly in use in the early 1840s and probably much earlier. They died out when regular berths were provided. The W and locomotive signs for Woodside and Monks Ferry are self-explanatory. The others are more enigmatic. The star for Rock Ferry may have been connected with the vessel of that name which worked the passage for a time and one can speculate that the sphere was the sign of James Ball, a proprietor of Birkenhead ferry in the 1820s.

*The twin-funnelled **Cheshire** of 1864 marked a turning point in ferry boat design but caused economic problems because of its high coal consumption.*

*This rare view of **Liverpool** of 1855, tied up behind the south end of Woodside stage, clearly shows the austere accommodation aboard the early steamers. At the stage is one of the first cabin vessels, **Cheshire, Lancashire** or **Woodside** of the 1860s with funnels athwartships. The wording on the paddle boxes is **Fare One Penny, Birkenhead Park and Docks and Street Railway, Woodside**.*

Heavily loaded ferry steamers leaving Liverpool, probably on a fine Sunday or Bank Holiday. The Eastham **Fairy Queen** *is tied up at the southern end of George's stage and the twin-funnelled Woodside steamer appears to be either* **Lancashire** *or* **Woodside** *both of which were withdrawn in 1891. The others cannot be identified but probably include Tranmere and Wallasey boats.*

narrow black ring in between.

Cheshire and *Lancashire* had four-cylinder compound engines but there was a reversion to two-cylinder simple oscillating engines for *Woodside*.

A 10-minute service between Woodside and Liverpool could be worked by two large new boats and one small old boat instead of four of the smaller boats. Unfortunately the new boats consumed enormous quantities of coal and new boiler technology was tried when a further boat was ordered from R. & J. Evans in 1872. At the time a number of Liverpool shipowners were experimenting with water-tube boilers for deep sea vessels which were complex in design but promised much improved fuel consumption. *Birkenhead* of 1872 came with Roots boilers made by the Patent Steam Boiler Co of Birmingham and although her four-cylinder diagonal engines, supplied by J. Jones of Liverpool, were similar to those in the 1860s vessels, she consumed between 17 and 25% less coal, despite running

at 40 psi rather than her design pressure of 60 psi. In fact the reduced boiler pressure was fortunate as *Birkenhead's* boilers gave endless trouble. The idea was correct but the circumstances were wrong. Because of the vessel's shallow draught and flush deck, the headroom in which to install the boiler was insufficient. Impure water was used for the first few months leading to overheated tubes until an adequate fresh water tank was fitted. Even then the bottom row of tubes burnt out and the vessel was frequently out of service for retubing. The large, slow-stroke paddle engine tended to empty the tubes of water each time it gulped steam and priming was encouraged by the lack of height. The boilers did not like the frequent stopping and starting either and after three years of breakdowns, the water-tube boilers were replaced by ordinary plant made by James Taylor & Co.

These clumsy steamers of the 1860s and 1870s set the standard for passenger amenities for many years. The

WATER-TUBE MARINE BOILERS.

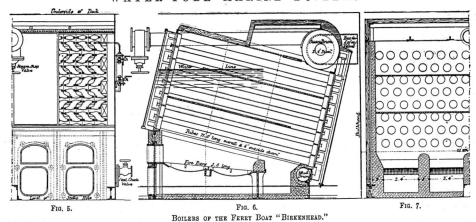

The water tube boilers of the steamer **Birkenhead**, *were of advanced design but not well adapted to the vessel.*

FIG. 5. FIG. 6. FIG. 7.

BOILERS OF THE FERRY BOAT "BIRKENHEAD."

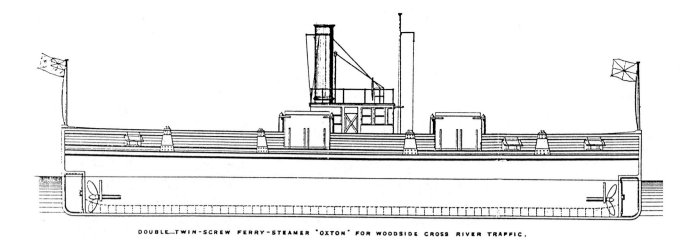

DOUBLE-TWIN-SCREW FERRY-STEAMER "OXTON" FOR WOODSIDE CROSS RIVER TRAFFIC.

General drawing of the first purpose-built vehicle ferry on the Mersey, **Oxton** *of 1879.*

saloon on the main deck provided separate accommodation for smokers forward and non-smokers amidships with a ladies' saloon aft. The promenade deck was the same width as the saloons. The position of the gangway doors was determined by the protrusion of the paddle-boxes. Their lack of response to the helm resulted in minor collisions. *Lancashire* was involved in three in 1869-70 whilst on 30th July 1873 *Birkenhead* was in collision with the Tranmere Ferry steamer of the same name.

Claughton of 1876, built by D. & W. Henderson & Co had two bell-mouthed funnels athwartships, one behind the starboard paddle and the other before the port paddle. Her dimensions were little different from those of *Birkenhead* and she was equipped with simple diagonal four-cylinder engines.

The steamers of the 'sixties and 'seventies tended to have shorter working lives at Birkenhead than those which came later as the last quarter of the 19th century was a time of great technological advances in marine engineering and they were overtaken by obsolescence before they wore out.

Oxton was launched at the yard of W. Simon & Co Renfrew, on 9th June 1879. At first the Commissioners refused to accept her, (they were often pernickerty about new boats) as the vessel could not attain the specified speed of 10 knots. However after a second trial with 30 tons of cargo on deck and 20 tons of coal on board, she was accepted on 1st August. She was the first example on the Mersey of a ferry steamer propelled by four screws, two forward and two aft, but with one rudder aft. She was specially designed to speed up the handling of vehicular traffic, which was revolutionised when she took up service in 1879. Stem and stern were squared off and the absence of paddle-boxes ensured an uncluttered deck, though a central deckhouse and bridge surrounded the spindly funnel. With four screws, the vessel could cross the river with her head set obliquely to the current; she could also spring out from the landing stage, an advantage when leaving the embayment at Liverpool.

Berthage limitations kept her length down to 130ft. but the beam was increased to 45ft. and the draught averaged 7ft. 6in. With the hull divided into eight watertight compartments, she was virtually unsinkable. The four gangways, two each side, were 17ft. wide and were raised and lowered by two donkey engines controlled by levers on deck through worm gears and friction cones. Propulsion was by two pairs of compound surface-condensing inverted vertical engines; the high and low pressure cylinders were respectively 19in. and 36in. in diameter with a stroke of 24in. They worked at 100rpm with a steam pressure of 65 psi. Superheaters were attached to the two 10ft. by 10ft. 6in. multi-tubular boilers. Steam-powered starting and steering gear was fitted.

The economic results of placing *Oxton* in service are described in Chapter 7. Suffice it to say that a second vessel, *Bebington*, to a somewhat similar specification, was built in 1880 by W. Allsup & Co, Preston, who also constructed a vessel of the same type for Wallasey Local Board the following year. *Tranmere* built by W. A. Stevens of Canada Works, Birkenhead, followed in 1884. The same yard secured the contract for a new passenger steamer *Cheshire* in 1889, the earlier vessel of the same name having been withdrawn in 1887, converted to a tug by Liverpool Steam Tug Co. and renamed *America*. The new *Cheshire* was to be the first steel paddler in the fleet and, at 137ft., was slightly shorter than her immediate predecessors. W. A. Stevens became insolvent and a liquidator, George Nicholson, supervised completion of the job but, following trials, the Corporation declined to take delivery on the grounds that the speed was 8-9 knots compared with a specification of 12 knots, the draught was over 6ft instead of 5ft. 9in. and the steering was inefficient. After much acrimonious correspondence, the Corporation decided to take over the boat and sell it through brokers C. H. Kellock, a reserve price of £7,000 being fixed. Eventually agreement was reached with the creditors; St. Clare Byrne was engaged as consultant and various modifications made, whereupon the vessel was placed in service.

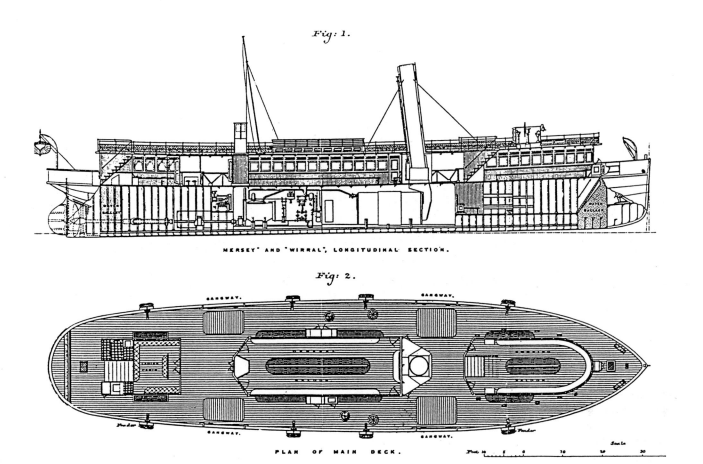

Fig: 1.

MERSEY AND WIRRAL, LONGITUDINAL SECTION.

Fig: 2.

PLAN OF MAIN DECK.

Mersey and **Wirral**, *the first twin-screw steamers for the Woodside passenger service, helped the ferries to overcome competition from the Mersey Railway. The graph of displacement related draught to tonnage, 8ft. being required for 600 tons.*

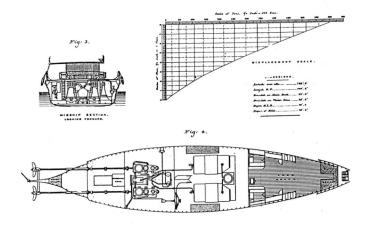

Because of the financial crisis which followed the opening of the Mersey Railway, the Corporation's specifications were well nigh impossible of achievement at an affordable price and, when further tenders were invited late in 1889, there was no response. The Corporation was seeking to replace three of the old slow, coal-eating boats with two fast, economical vessels and a private approach was made to the Liverpool firm of John Jones & Sons. Charles Jones, the designer, in a paper given to the Institution of Civil Engineers in the 1893-94 session, stated that a contract was made for two boats, the only conditions being those of length, draught of water, height of deck from water-line, a mean speed of 12 knots and a Board of Trade passenger certificate for 600. There was to be no interference with the builders by the Corporation and the boats were to be retained by Jones if the conditions were not fulfilled. This was an over-simplification, as there were other items specified including the appointment of James Taylor to supervise the work at £52-10-0d per boat.

Best quality Siemens-Martin steel was used for the hulls which were divided into 11 watertight compartments. The vessels were propelled by two sets of triple-expansion engines, each driving a screw of 7ft. 9in. diameter. They

had a normal trim of 5ft. forward and 7ft. aft and water ballast trimming tanks were placed fore and aft. The mast was aft of the single funnel and the steering position was well forward on the promenade deck. The vessels were named *Mersey* and *Wirral* and, on the trial trip of *Mersey* on 10th November 1890, a mean speed of 13.06 knots was achieved over four runs. There was excessive vibration, which was cured by replacing the original two-blade propellers by four blades, and some difficulty in springing away from the stage. On *Mersey*, the engine room controls were not grouped to permit of operation by one man. The Corporation had numerous alterations done by Clover & Co and a dispute with Jones almost went to arbitration. Another noteworthy innovation was the adaptation of

Mersey and *Wirral* of 1890 helped to recover some of the traffic lost to the Mersey Railway from 1886. Note the forward steering position, unprotected from the elements on the upper deck.

some of the upper deck seats as life rafts, a system invented by Capt. Pinhey, which became standard practice. A boat, lifebuoys and buoyant apparatus for about half the certificated capacity were provided on all boats.

Despite these teething troubles, the new boats were a great success. Their speed enabled two boats to run the Woodside service instead of three and Charles Jones claimed that coal consumption was 5½cwt per hour compared with 9¾cwt used by the old paddlers. Their motion in bad weather was steadier and they probably contributed to the increase in passengers during the 1890s. The decision to build another paddler in 1894 was all the more inexplicable. This vessel, *Birkenhead*, was of similar dimensions to the 1872 boat of the same name but built of steel by J. Scott & Co Kinghorn, Fife who took *Claughton*

in part exchange and sold her to the Liverpool Steam Tug Co. as the tug *Australia*. The machinery was similar to that of *Cheshire*. *Birkenhead*, which achieved 11.7 knots on her trials, was destined to be the last paddler and was retained for only 13 years, being sold in 1907 to White Star Line, renamed *Gallic* and used as a tender at Cherbourg until broken up at Garston in 1913. *Cheshire* went to the Great Western Railway in 1904 for similar work at Plymouth.

Mechanical Steering

One way of improving manoevrability of the larger steamers was the fitting of power steering. The first *Cheshire* was equipped with Brown Bros. patent hydraulic steering and reversing machinery in 1871 and an offer to

Mersey and *Wirral* were relegated to the South Ferries after a few years. The former is shown in company with the training ship HMS *Conway*, moored off Rock Ferry. Note the stern mounted lifeboat as fitted to all ferry vessels.

install it in *Birkenhead*, then building, at the same price was accepted. Nothing more was done until 1880 when the Committee decided to invite tenders to fit steam or hydraulic steering gear to one or two of the Woodside steamers. Nothing further seems to have happened until March 1882 when the Harrison Patent Steering Engine Co. of Ocean Works, Cross Lane, Salford was awarded the contract to equip *Bebington* and *Lancashire*; *Oxton* was fitted from new and *Woodside* was done early in 1884. Thereafter it became standard when a new boat was ordered.

There was some public alarm when *Cheshire* was sunk in a collision in 1874 and it was proposed to build additional bulkheads and fit a 'rubber' round the hull, a substantial protective belt of timber to take the initial impact. This was also done to *Woodside* and became normal practice. Repairs to *Cheshire* were estimated at £4,000 and were not finished until 1876. New decks, overhaul of the hull and machinery and a new boiler and fittings were needed and it was probably at this time that she was converted to a luggage boat. Following the success of *Oxton*, the Committee proposed to convert *Lancashire* from paddle-wheels to double twin-screws but the more cautious town council insisted on an independent report to ensure her stability. Two marine surveyors, St. Clare J. Byrne and Daniel Mylchreest, said it might be possible but the main deck would be below the level of the landing stage and potentially dangerous to passengers. The resolution was rescinded; *Lancashire* was given new boilers by James Taylor & Co and other repairs were carried out by the Corporation who had a well-equipped workshop. The practice at the time was to have five passenger boats available for Woodside; three were run continuously for nine weeks, one was on survey and one in reserve. *Lancashire* now became the fifth steamer.

Another necessary improvement was bridge accommodation for captains and steersmen as the old practice of steering from the promenade deck was no longer acceptable. A two-level screened platform was proposed, immediately forward of the funnel with the steersman on the lower level and the captain above him. However, many years were to elapse before navigating officers and steersmen were given any protection from the elements.

Electric Light

Gas lighting had been installed in the Wallasey Local Board's steamer *Mayflower* in 1862. Town gas was piped aboard and stored in what was, in effect, a miniature gas holder and various other Mersey steamers were also fitted. At least one Woodside steamer was equipped with gas as the 1863-64 accounts show expenditure of £7-2-5d on gutta-percha for gas bags and it seems likely that these were for *Cheshire*. Oil lamps were also fitted for emergency use. By the 1880s, lighting by electricity was sufficiently far advanced to be considered as an alternative to gas for saloon lighting; there was adequate power to drive a dynamo and no risk of fire or explosion. *Claughton* was fitted as an experiment and interest in the subject was such

that the Dock Board laid down a code of practice in bye-laws in 1884. In July of that year, the Ferry Committee decided to install electric light in *Lancashire*, *Cheshire*, *Birkenhead* and *Woodside*, the work being entrusted to the Manchester and District Edison Electric Light Co Ltd. The system was obviously undeveloped and there was endless trouble; it was apparently abandoned in 1886. However new developments brought greater reliability and the steamers built in the 1890s and subsequently were all electrically lit from small high-speed steam dynamos, though until modern times, all vessels also had oil lighting for use when not in steam. The three luggage boats were converted to electric light in the mid-nineties.

The New Century's Steamers

In 1899 Birkenhead Corporation ordered two new twin screw steamers, subsequently named *Lancashire* and *Claughton*, from J. Scott and Co. Kinghorn; these vessels were a big improvement on *Mersey* and *Wirral*, setting the standard for the remainder of the steam era. They had two four-cylinder engines each with cylinders of 17in., 23in. and 28in. (2), and a stroke of 18in. ihp was 1200. With a length of 150.5ft. and a breadth of 41ft., all of which was usable as there were no paddle boxes, they had passenger certificates for 1,300 passengers and a speed of 12½ knots. Access to the promenade deck was by two wide stairways, one at the bow and one at the stern. These powerful boats gave good service on the Woodside passage for 30 years. Both were fitted with improved steam whistles and had their navigation cabs enclosed in 1926. *Lancashire* was bought by the Galway Harbour Commissioners in 1929, refitted by Cammell Lairds and renamed *Cathair-na-Gallime*, being finally broken up, aged 50, at Cork in 1949. *Claughton*, after being strategically renamed *Old Claughton* in 1930, was sold for scrap and broken up at Preston the same year. A further pair of vessels was ordered

*Woodside passenger steamer **Lancashire** of 1899 set the standard for the next 40 years. Seen with her in the river are the Seacombe luggage boat **Wallasey** and Wallasey passenger steamer **John Herron**.*

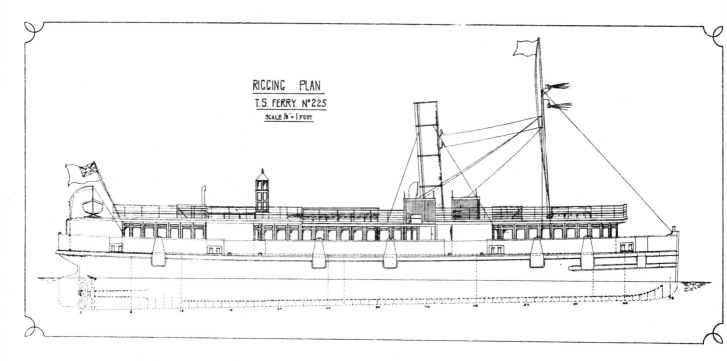

RIGGING PLAN
T.S. FERRY. N° 225
SCALE ⅛" = 1 FOOT

Storeton was built for Rock Ferry in 1910 and resembled contemporary Woodside steamers except for her narrow beam.

in 1903 from Londonderry Shipbuilding Co. These were *Bidston* and *Woodside*, closely resembling their predecessors in all respects but the passenger certificates were for 1,603 passengers. Their two surface condensing triple expansion engines, built by Central Marine Engineering Works at West Hartlepool had 15½in., 23 and 28in. cylinders and a stroke of 18in. *Woodside* had an uneventful career on the Mersey but, following withdrawal in 1930, she went to Bermuda where she saw further service for many more years.

The fleet modernisation was completed in 1910 when *Storeton* was built specifically for the South Ferries. Whilst almost as long as the Woodside boats, she was considerably narrower at 32.1ft., passenger accommodation being reduced to 1,075. She was built by Ailsa Shipbuilding Co of Ayr and was the last vessel to have the central stairway to the promenade deck. She survived the closure of Rock Ferry and was sold to the Leith Salvage and Towing Co in May 1940.

In 1906 the Corporation ordered a further purpose-built luggage boat from Caledonia Shipbuilding Co Preston. Her dimensions and machinery were very similar to those of *Tranmere* built in 1884. She was named *Liverpool* but on her trials was found to be too low for the landing stages and was returned to her builders. Very extensive modifications were necessary to make her acceptable and when she finally entered service in 1908, she had been renamed *Prenton*.

Problems of Inflation

In the post 1914-18 war years there was an urgent need for new luggage boats, both as replacements and to enable the four-boat service to be introduced. The Committee

decided to invite tenders in February 1920 but, because of inflation, the amount of £57,000 in the Depreciation and Boat Fund was insufficient, another £150,000 being required. A Provisional Order was needed to authorise the raising of a loan and, at first, the Ministry of Health (the department responsible for local authority loans) declined to accept the Order for consideration in the current Parliamentary session. However they bowed before pressure. A special meeting on 26th May 1920 accepted the tender of H. and C. Grayson for two boats, subject to Parliamentary sanction. Because of inflationary pressures, no firm price could be quoted, the basis of the tender being the cost of labour and materials, 20% for establishment charges and 10% profit; the estimate was £100,000 each but the builders were virtually given a blank cheque.

The new vessels were to be longer, wider and much more powerful than their predecessors, the principal dimensions being length 142.5ft., beam 50.1ft., depth 13.7ft., gross tonnage 724, nhp 253. Triple expansion 6-cylinder engines were to be supplied by D. Rollo and Sons. The Provisional Order having been granted, a model was inspected and contract terms agreed on 18th August 1920. The shipbuilders were busy so work could not start immediately. The Committee chose the names *Barnston* and *Churton* and the new vessels were launched at Garston on 7th July and 3rd October 1921 respectively. *Barnston* was in service by 19th October. The general layout closely followed that of *Oxton* of 1879 with twin screws fore and aft but with a completely uncluttered deck except for the funnel and bridge amidships. However their greater engine power gave them a working speed of 11 knots compared with the 8-8½ knots of the original luggage boats and the 10 knots of *Prenton*. On the debit side, they consumed 6½ tons of coal daily against the old

Bebington in mid-river in the 'thirties. Built by Cammell Lairds in 1925, this was the ultimate in vehicular ferry design on the Mersey with no wasted space on deck.

boats' three tons. The extra width and absence of a deckhouse, enabled motor lorries with trailers to manoevre which had been very difficult with the old boats. These factors and the increase in speed helped to alleviate the congestion. Problems now arose with an overrun of costs. *Barnston* cost £123,198 and *Churton* £121,299, a total of £244,497, which was reduced to £243,690 after discussion. The authorised sum of £200,000 was paid but the balance could not be handed over until the Government had authorised the additional borrowing, so the builders had to wait for their money for almost a year. The Corporation retained all six goods vessels in the fleet.

In October 1924, by which time prices had fallen very considerably, Cammell Laird's tender of £200,000 was accepted for four boats. This was £43,000 less than the cost of the two 1921 luggage boats. Two of the four boats were to be goods vessels almost identical to their 1921 predecessors. They were to be *Bebington*, the third of that name, and *Oxton*, the second; in order to retain the names,

the registrations of the existing vessels of those names were changed to *Old Bebington* and *Old Oxton*, a ploy used by the Corporation from time to time. *Bebington* was launched on 21st August 1925 and *Oxton* the following day. At her trials on 30th September, *Bebington* achieved 10.75 knots. Both vessels were in service by October and tenders were invited for four old steamers—the luggage boats *Old Oxton*, (1879), *Old Bebington* (1880) and *Tranmere* (1884) and the passenger steamer *Mersey* (1890). Robert Smith and Son, Birkenhead, offered £1,850 for the first three and they were duly broken up for scrap.

The new passenger boats were *Hinderton* for Woodside and *Upton* for Rock Ferry where *Mersey* of 1890 was still in service. The dimensions and machinery of these boats were similar to those of *Bidston* and *Storeton* respectively, except that the promenade decks extended for the full width of the vessels and they were reached by four stairways, two either side, conveniently located near the gangway doors.

Thurstaston, dating from 1930, on the Woodside service on 30th August 1958. The former Great Western goods depot at Morpeth Dock is visible behind the foremast and, to its right, the Wallasey Landing Stage (cattle stage).

Claughton of 1930, which epitomised the Woodside fleet for many years, is seen towards the end of her life on 15th June 1957.

In 1929 the Corporation decided that the last of the nineteenth century steamers should be replaced and orders were placed with Cammell Laird for two steamers, similar to *Hinderton*, to replace *Lancashire* and *Claughton* of 1899. *Lancashire* was to be sold for £3,000 with passenger certificate renewed, whilst *Claughton* went for scrap at £1,125. Prior to disposal, the Corporation protected the name by renaming the vessel *Old Claughton* and the new steamers were named *Claughton* and *Thurstaston*. Both entered service in August 1930 and it was then decided to sell *Woodside* of 1903. She went through C. W. Kellock & Co Ltd to Bermuda Transportation Co Ltd for £3,500. The new vessels differed from *Hinderton* by having higher wheelhouses and improved auxiliary machinery. All had framework on the promenade deck to accommodate a canvas awning aft of the funnel.

With a new fleet, the Corporation was able to offer a speedy service as, with their twin screw 4-cylinder triple expansion engines, their vessels were the fastest on the river and, being narrower in the beam, were noticeably more manoeuvrable than the contemporary Wallasey steamers. The last vessel to enter service before the 1939-45 war was *Bidston* of 1933 to replace the 1903 vessel of the same name. The original specification called for an increase of 3ft. in beam, a new system of ventilation and a navigation bridge but when she entered service on 27th

February 1933, she was virtually identical to her predecessors. The old boat, renamed *Old Bidston* was sold through Kellocks for £1,750 to Blackpool Pleasure Steamers Ltd who renamed her *Minden*. She went for scrap at Preston at the end of the 1937 season.

These vessels served Woodside ferry through the war years and the 1950s. By the end of that decade, despite the financial plight of the ferries, Birkenhead Corporation felt that it had no alternative but to replace the ageing coal-fired fleet with modern diesel-propelled vessels.

The Change to Diesel

The changeover from coal-fired steam to direct drive diesel propulsion was controversial and was not favoured by the ferries management. In a report to the Committee in 1951, the manager pointed out that with steam there had been one breakdown in service in 25 years, whilst diesel engines were considered to be unreliable, thereby making it essential to install more than one engine. Reference was made to two new pilot boats, each with two engines and the Wallasey cruise vessel *Royal Iris* with four.

A motor vessel would require a crew of six compared with the current level of nine but there were other problems. To quote the report:- 'Since the opening of Queensway and the closing of the Rock Ferry and Goods

The helm of a ferry steamer. It is suspected that this is, in fact, a Wallasey ferry boat but the arrangement was typical.

Services all the younger members of our staff have obtained work elsewhere, leaving the senior officers and casual labour. At the moment the average age of the Engineers is 56 and that of the Assistant Engineers 49. All have been in our service since boys and do not hold Ministry of Transport Certificates hence three engineers would have to be engaged for each motor vessel operated and paid higher salaries for the extra qualifications'.

The workshop and its staff were unsuitable for diesel engine maintenance which would need to be contracted out. The manager concluded with an observation that a dozen new tugs were all steam propelled 'a fact that gives rise to considerable speculation regarding the advisability of installing diesel engines in Mersey River craft'. As described elsewhere, the closure and subsequent removal of the Woodside floating roadway on 14th February 1955 severed the route by which coal was taken to the landing stage and ashes removed, and means had to be found to

use the passenger bridge. This procedure was costly, cumbersome and potentially dangerous and, to say the least, a great nuisance. Wallasey Corporation already had one diesel-electric and three direct diesel vessels with speeds of up to 13 knots.

In 1958 the Tunnel Committee, under pressure from Birkenhead Corporation, agreed to a reversal of the 'make do and mend' policy. This followed the laying-up of *Hinderton* after two mid-river collisions which resulted in her plates above the waterline being condemned. She finally left the Mersey on tow on 9th September 1958, destined for a scrapyard near Antwerp. Tenders were invited for two new vessels and the bid of Philip & Son, Dartmouth for £482,278 was accepted. The Corporation would have preferred to place the order with Cammell Laird but they pleaded other commitments. Philips had built the Wallasey diesel vessels, *Leasowe* (1951) and *Egremont* (1952) which were similar in general design to the

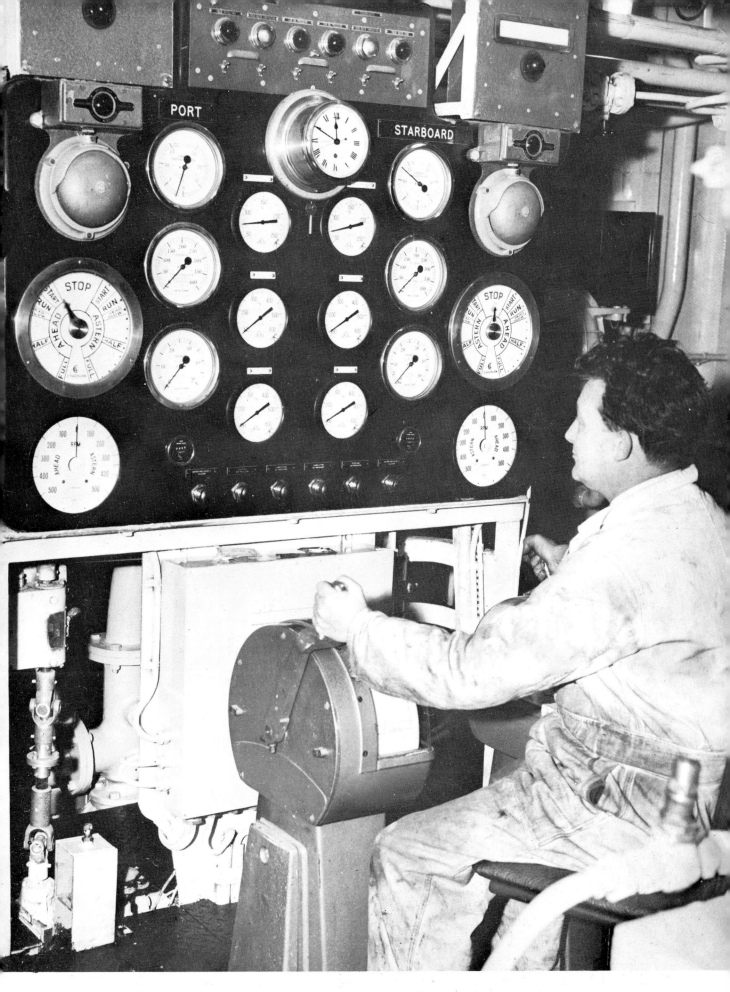

*'Driving position' in the engine room of **Mountwood**.*

The annual survey was an important element in ferry economics. **Overchurch** *in dry dock at West Float, Birkenhead in January 1970.*

Birkenhead specification.

The traditional re-use of old names was abandoned and the new vessels were given the names *Mountwood* and *Woodchurch* after post-war housing estates. They were in all respects identical, with a length of 152ft. 3in., breadth of 40ft. 6in. and depth of 12ft. 5in. with 5ft. 5½in. freeboard. There was direct diesel propulsion by two Crossley engines developing 680 bhp per shaft with bridge control of the main engines. Automatic air brakes were fitted. Auxiliary machinery was powered by Ruston and Hornsby engines. Passenger capacity of 1,200 was far in excess of likely requirements; for the first time, accommodation was on three levels with provision for a refreshment saloon below the main deck and partially enclosed promenade deck. A third ship of very similar design and almost identical dimensions, *Overchurch* (another post-war housing estate), was built by Cammell Laird in 1962.

The last steam ferry boat in the Birkenhead fleet was *Claughton*, the third of her name, which left the river on tow on 21st September 1962 to be broken up at Ghent. The last steam ferry of all on the Mersey was Wallasey Corporation's *Wallasey* which went to Ghent for breaking in 1964.

The ferry boats could now be fuelled through a pipeline laid down on the passenger bridge and one fill-up lasted for several days. Crews were reduced from nine to seven and some land-based staff became redundant.

All three diesel vessels passed to the Merseyside Passenger Transport Executive on 1st December 1969 and, following the reduction in ferry service frequencies and the sale of the Wallasey boats, they have worked both the Woodside and Seacombe services. In 1989 it was decided to extend the life of *Mountwood* and *Woodchurch*. *Overchurch* maintained the service while they were completely refurbished.

12 GEORGE'S LANDING STAGE

Just as the introduction of steam power was the first major turning point in the development of the Mersey ferries, so the adoption of floating landing stages was the second. Before they were brought into use, embarkation and landing could be extremely hazardous to the extent that a river crossing was only to be undertaken as a matter of dire necessity. The ferry boats departed from various stone steps and slips in the inlets which were built in the vicinity of what was to become Liverpool Pier Head, though at an unknown date during the eighteenth century, a wooden pier, jutting straight out into the river, was built which could be used by ferry boats at low tide. It was demolished in connection with the construction of George's Dock, opened in 1771 and George's Dock Basin, which gave access to George's and later Prince's Docks, then provided sheltered accommodation for ferry boats. The seventh Liverpool Dock Act 1811 authorised the construction of an L-shaped basin to the west of George's Dock and this became known as George's Ferry Basin. The berths were alongside 'Parade Slip'. This basin was specifically designed for ferry purposes but not all the boats moved there. According to *Gore's Directory*, in 1821 there were five recognised landing places for ferry boats viz:

1. North side of George's Dock Basin
2. George's Ferry Basin or Parade Slip
3. Stairs at West Side of Nos. 2 and 3 Graving Docks
4. Stairs at West Side of King's Dock
5. Basin and slips at West end of No. 1 Graving Dock

The advent of larger steam vessels gave rise to further problems as they were often unable to reach the slip or steps at low tide and an 'extension stage' was built, probably in the 1820s. This was an early example of the 'running out stage' comprising a stage and walkway which was hauled up and down a sloping slip by chains. When not in use this telescopic structure was housed in a tunnel in the river wall. Records do not explain whether it was hand-operated by windlass or powered by a stationary steam engine. Writing in The Porcupine in 1867, J. A. Picton described the difficulties experienced by passengers whilst using this device at low tide.

'It was no unusual thing to have five or six steamers lying outside of it, over which, or some of them at all events, (one) had to scramble with great inconvenience, and often at considerable risk, to reach the outlying boats.'

As an alternative to the stone slips or steps used when there was adequate depth of water, there were wooden landing slips pivoted at the landward end but these were particularly vulnerable in bad weather. A report in the *Daily Courier* of 22nd January 1840 describes conditions during a 'particularly bad hurricane' on the previous day:

'The floating wooden landing slips were knocked to and fro in a manner that excited considerable apprehension for their safety. Sometimes they were completely buried in the frothy waters but they rose again to be buffeted and they stood all the force of the wind and water gallantly though their unwieldy proportions did not promise such worthy behaviour. The ferry steamers, during the period of which we are speaking, suspended their operations and we believe we are correct in stating that but few trips were made in the course of the afternoon.'

Cubitt's Landing Stage

Although floating landing stages had been suggested as early as 1811, it was not until December 1842 that the first permanent structure connected to the land by a proper bridge was installed. This was placed at the north of the Seacombe Ferry Basin, an inlet on the south side of Prince's Parade, and its obvious superiority convinced Liverpool Corporation of the need to improve landing facilities generally. Premiums were offered for the design of a stage capable of handling all the ferry traffic. Strangely, no suitable design was submitted and William Cubitt, C.E. was engaged by the Corporation to design a structure which he did with great success. This attracted the attention of the eminent engineer, Sir John Rennie. In the course of his Presidential address to the Institute of Mechanical Engineers in 1846, Rennie said:-

'Cubitt has also proposed to adopt wrought iron on a great scale, for constructing landing platforms at Liverpool where the difficulty of building docks or quays which large steam vessels can approach at all times of the tide, render works of this kind necessary to accommodate the immense traffic frequenting Liverpool. The landing platform designed by Cubitt, and now in course of construction, consists of a wooden frame, 500ft. long by 80ft. wide, floated upon a number of wrought iron pontoons, each 80ft. long, 10ft. wide and 6ft. deep; it is connected with the shore by two bridges, each formed of two hollow wrought iron beams, 150ft. long, carrying the platform of the bridge; the attachment with the shore and the stage is made so as to admit of motion both vertically and horizontally to accommodate

St. Georges Baths Liverpool
and Cheshire Ferry Boats

An engraving of St. George's Baths on the river wall at Liverpool Pier Head prior to the installation of the first landing stage in 1847. The artist has depicted a primitive pier with lifting section in the background.

George's Landing Stage being floated into position with the aid of seven tugs in 1847.

Prince's Landing Stage with its four bridges depicted soon after it was brought into use in 1857.

itself to the rising, falling, ebbing and flowing of the tide, which there rises about 30ft.'

Cubitt's George's Landing Stage was brought into use on 1st June 1847. It was 508ft. long and 82ft. wide and rested on 39 pontoons strapped to 40,000cu.ft. of timber 3ft. 6in. thick. A contemporary report estimated that 40,000 people could find standing room. The stage cost about $50,000, an enormous sum in 1847.

To reduce resistance to the tide, the deck was tapered at each end like the prow of a ship. At each end there was a small lighthouse with powerful reflectors and a waiting shed for passengers. The use of the basins declined. Whilst this stage was a great improvement, its mixed use by passengers, goods, horses and cattle soon resulted in intolerable conditions both on the approaches and upon the landing stage itself. Vessels of ten ferries jostled other craft for berths and the steep roads down from the town were narrow and congested, direct access to the waterfront being obstructed by George's Dock. Liverpool Corporation had gone to Parliament in 1855 for powers to improve the approach but nothing had been done. In 1855, Cubitt was commissioned to design a second platform of somewhat

Cross-section of George's Landing Stage about 1866.

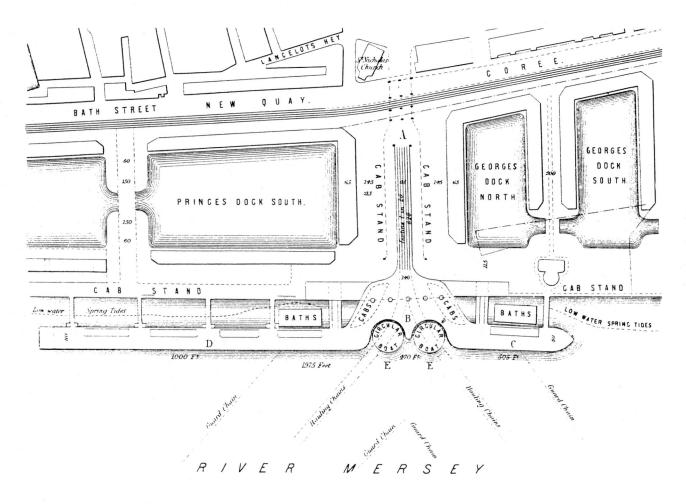

G. F. Lyster's plan for circular chain ferries and the original embayment. Note that the scheme also provided for the division of both Prince's and George's Docks into two sections

similar construction (Prince's Landing Stage), to be placed to the north of George's Basin. Built at Birkenhead by Thomas Vernon and Sons at a cost of £130,000, the stage measured 1,002ft. by 81ft. 4in. and was opened on 1st September 1857. The goods steamers left George's for the new stage and congestion at the ferry berths was temporarily eased.

The formation of the Mersey Docks and Harbour Board in 1858 created one authority responsible for port installations on both sides of the river and the Mersey Docks (Ferry Accommodation) Act 1860 conferred powers 'to erect floating bridges and other works at Liverpool and Birkenhead and for other purposes'.

John Laird MP continually brought pressure to bear on the Dock Board and G. Fosbery Lyster, the Board's Engineer, is said to have prepared five different schemes for the Pier Head area. One of the most interesting, published in 1866, envisaged the joining of the Prince's and George's Landing Stages (which, of course, was later done) and the construction of the floating roadway in the position which it later occupied. At its foot, where the two

landing stages joined, there were to be two semi-circular embayments for use by specially designed circular ferry boats capable of carrying both goods and passengers to Woodside and Seacombe. These were to have been chain ferries as described in Chapter 7.

Strangely, the idea of an embayment caught on, though, in practice, with vessels free to manoeuvre, it was a hindrance rather than a help to navigation. Laird countered this with a scheme to fill in George's Dock, creating 41,000 sq. yds. for buildings and 56,700 sq.yds. for dock purposes. His floating roadway would have been built at Mann Island

The 1874 Stage

The Mersey Docks (Various Powers) Act 1867 gave powers to close and fill up the whole or part of George's Basin, Seacombe Basin and the passage between George's Basin and Prince's Dock and to construct a floating roadway and ferry goods stage. However, controversy still raged as to the exact position of the floating roadway. In 1869 a plan

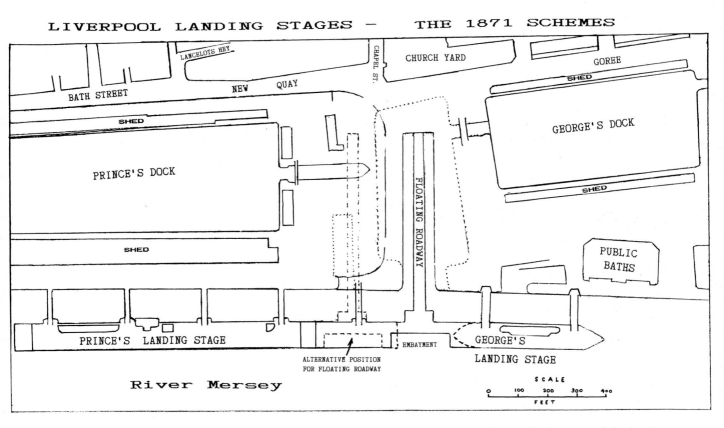

The deliberations of the Dock Board in the late 1860s produced alternative schemes for the development of the landing stages. This map shows the floating roadway in the position in which it was built and the alternative position which Parliament refused to approve.

was drawn up to site it opposite St. Nicholas' churchyard, almost exactly on the centre line of George's Basin. George's and Prince's Landing Stages were to be joined, either by a new stage costing £143,400, or by using part of the stage to be removed from the Low Water Basin (cost £116,350). An embayment approximately 200ft. long was to be provided for goods steamers opposite the floating roadway. It was believed by all concerned, including the Birkenhead Commissioners and Wallasey Local Board, that cart traffic could not be safely handled without the shelter afforded by the embayment. However there was controversy about the whole plan and the Dock Board deposited two Bills, one with plans based on the 1869 proposals and the other with plans locating the floating roadway and embayment approximately 250ft. further north, provision being made for Prince's Landing Stage to be extended by about 300ft. to accommodate these works. George's Basin would have remained and there would have been no connection with George's Stage; Seacombe Basin and Prince's Channel would have been arched over. After listening to the evidence in Committee, the House of Lords approved the original plan of 1869, George's Basin being filled except to the extent necessary to provide room for the floating roadway. Birkenhead Commissioners had opposed the revised plan, but the House of Lords Committee said that they would

have rejected it in any case as falling short of the Parliamentary obligations of 1860, 'the works not being worth the money it was proposed to expend upon them'. These plans were authorised by the Mersey Docks (Liverpool River Approaches) Act 1871 and the joining of the two stages and the provision of the floating roadway was approved by the Dock Board on 9th May 1872. A new, lengthened George's Landing Stage was also sanctioned. The old stage was removed on 23rd July 1874 and the new one, 600ft. long and built at Canada Works, on the West Float was floated into position the next day.

The stage consisted of iron pontoons on which were placed five large wrought iron kelsons or box girders about 20ft. apart, running longitudinally for the whole length. Across these kelsons were placed pine beams the width of the stage, varying in thickness from 16in. to 14in. by 12in. Upon these beams were fastened the longitudinal pine deck or planking, 6in. by 4in. and crossing this again were greenheart sheathing planks 6in. by 2in. The whole of this was caulked and pitched to make it impervious to the action of the water and weather.

It was opened to the public on 27th July 1874 but, on the following afternoon, it caught fire whilst repairs were being made by a gas fitter under the deck. The structure was highly inflammable and the flames quickly spread from end to end, all efforts to extinguish the fire being in vain.

The burnt out structure with its booms and bridges was towed to the head of the Great Float where repairs were entrusted to Canada Works. The large wrought iron girders were found to be twisted and broken in numerous places by the heat and these had to be cut, straightened and repaired. Long disused pier steps were brought back into use for the ferries, some old steamers being moored to serve as temporary stages.

During reconstruction, iron beams were substituted for the original wooden ones and pine deck planking was replaced with greenheart. The bridges were strengthened with plates running the whole length on both the top and bottom with a view to facilitating covering them at some future date.

On 27th July 1875, the renewed stage was towed down to the Alfred Dock and the bridges and booms were brought across the river and temporarily moored in readiness for connecting them with the stage. Early the following day, exactly a year after the fire, the stage was towed across the river and secured in position, but repair work was not fully completed until April 1876.

The cut-away section known as the embayment at the foot of the floating roadway was controversial even before it opened. Its original concept, as the sheltered terminus of Lyster's chain ferries, was sound but for steamers free of chains, it was a navigational nightmare. After the fire, strong representations were made to the Dock Board to rebuild the stage without the embayment but to no effect. A contributor to the periodical *Engineering* in April 1876 wrote:-

'I regret to say the embayment has been retained in its original form notwithstanding the efforts which were made after the fire to have it done away with in the reconstruction. This might have been effected at a very slight extra cost. I have enquired personally from several of the Captains of both these steamers and boats who are constantly going to and from the stage and each one of them condemns it. One Captain told me that no steamer could get out of it in a westerly gale. This I can vouch for, as I have seen the boats, unable to start direct from the stage, having to slide along it to the end and thus get ahead of the wind.'

The matter was raised again in 1882-83, Wallasey joining with Birkenhead in urging the Dock Board to fill it in. By this time the Board wanted to move the goods berth further north but the Cheshire authorities were adamant that the solution lay in the abolition of the embayment.

The Pier Head in July 1904 on the occasion of the visit of King Edward VII and Queen Alexandra to lay the foundation stone of the Anglican Cathedral. The fleet is at anchor in the river and New Brighton Tower, taller than Blackpool's, is clearly visible. There is a crowded vessel at the Woodside berth on the left, with two Wallasey boats astern and a Woodside luggage boat further north.

Finally, in 1888 the Dock Board agreed and asked Birkenhead and Wallasey to support the Bill for the extension of Prince's Landing Stage, which would include filling in the embayment, though Birkenhead Commissioners maintained that the Board already had powers to do this under the 1860 Act. Full agreement was reached in May 1889 but it was 1894 before the embayment finally went.

The Combined Landing Stage

A new Prince's Landing Stage was built in Wallasey Dock in 1895-96 by Pearson and Knowles of Warrington and towed across to Liverpool in one piece. When joined to the George's Stage, the full structure measured 2,478ft., almost half a mile. The goods berths were moved slightly north, a curved road being laid out on the stage to guide traffic to and from the floating roadway.

The Mersey Docks Consolidation Act 1858 required the Dock Board to maintain a depth of 6ft of water at George's Landing Stage but during the 1880s and 1890s, there were many occasions when ferry steamers were unable to use the southern berths at low tide because of the northward advance of the Pluckington Bank which endangered the stage itself. There was a continuous running battle of words between the Corporation and the Dock Board who steadfastly refused to take action for several years despite severe disruption of ferry services on many occasions. A series of sluices was built in the quay wall behind George's Stage through which water was discharged at low tide, the theory being that sufficient depth would be maintained by a scouring action, unassisted by dredging. In practice, the sand was driven from under the stage only to deposit itself 30ft. to 50ft. westward right in the track of the Woodside passenger boats. In 1890 during a period of 123 days, the boats were moved from their normal berths on 79 days, usually twice daily. Later the Dock Board, having improved access to the port by dredging the bar, turned their attention to dredging in the river and 30ft. of water was provided alongside the stage at low water springs.

In all, nine bridges connected the stage to the shore. The Prince's bridges, 110ft. long, served also as booms, being fixed to the main girders of the stage. The George's bridges were 150ft. long and free to slide at the stage end.

The passenger bridges were eventually covered by curved glazed roofs and embellished with advertisements.

PASSENGER BRIDGE AT THE GEORGE'S LANDING-STAGE, LIVERPOOL.

MR. A. G. LYSTER, M. INST. C. E., LONDON, ENGINEER; MESSRS. FRANCIS MORTON AND CO., LIMITED, GARSTON, LIVERPOOL, CONTRACTORS.

(For Description, see Page 264.)

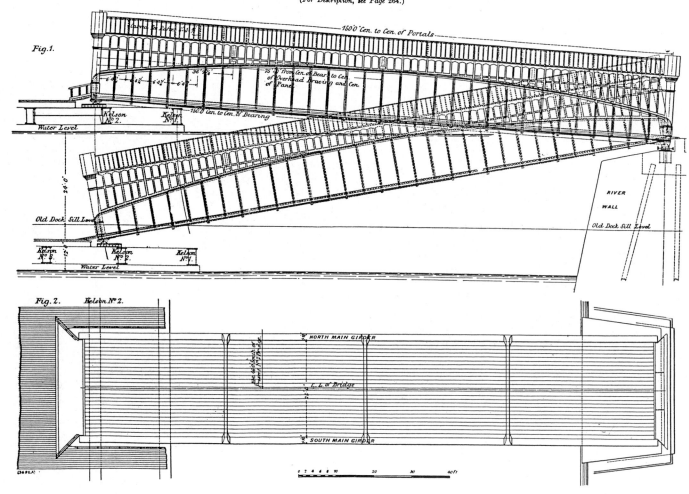

Detail of No. 1A passenger bridge at George's Landing Stage, installed in 1913 to alleviate pedestrian congestion on the approaches to the landing stage.

But they were soon too narrow to handle the enormous volume of ferry traffic. Relatively few people used the outside footwalks which were added, mounted on outriggers. By 1910, the congestion was so serious that people trying to make their way against the main passenger flow at peak times had difficulty in doing so and Wallasey took the initiative in suggesting the provision of an additional passenger bridge, strategically placed to handle the Seacombe, Egremont and New Brighton traffic, which reached enormous proportions at holiday times.

Birkenhead Corporation agreed to participate financially and the result was a tripartite agreement between the Dock Board, Birkenhead and Wallasey Corporations dated 27th February 1911, whereby No. 2 bridge was to be moved to a new position 90ft. south and a new 25ft.-wide bridge was to be placed approximately in the existing position of No. 2. In consideration of this, Wallasey was to pay £300 and Birkenhead £200 per annum for 20 years. However in March 1912, consequent on a Pier Head improvement scheme proposed by Liverpool Corporation whereby the position of the tramway termini would be altered, new positions were agreed viz: No. 2 bridge to be moved 69ft. northward and

the new bridge (No. 1A) to be 46ft. south of the old No. 2 bridge.

The new bridge was designed by A. G. Lyster and built at Garston by Francis Morton and Co Ltd. Weighing 110 tons without the glazing etc, it was assembled at the Pier Head and launched on a temporary track with 14.75 tons of ballast on the landward end. As the tide rose, the bridge was moved forward so that the outer end rested on temporary pontoons which lifted with the water so that the bridge could slide on to the stage. This operation was carried out on 8th July 1913 and the bridge was roofed in situ and brought into service during the autumn.

Lengthening

In an attempt to overcome congestion on the Woodside goods ferry, it was agreed in 1921 that the stage be extended by 55ft. and the passenger berths moved southwards to accommodate a second goods berth. This was done during 1922 by removing the tapered southern end and inserting a new length of stage. Shelters were built on the extension later. The end berth was to be shared by the Rock Ferry and Eastham boats. The curved roadway

No. 1A bridge being manoeuvred into position. No. 2 bridge, seen to the right, was moved further north.

(Below) The south end of George's Landing Stage in December 1922 after the insertion of an additional 55ft. section immediately south of the twin booms. A boat for Woodside has just left, while another can be seen turning to head across the river towards Liverpool. A Corporation tram and two taxis are to be seen, while a pilot cutter is moored on the landward side of the stage, almost opposite the two Rock Ferry loading gates.

Crowds on George's Landing Stage at a busy summer weekend in the 'thirties. The Woodside boat is moored on the left. Note the fogbell tower which was renewed in the 'twenties and has been preserved.

was removed as the goods berth was now opposite the foot of the floating roadway.

The ferry landing stage had now reached the form which became familiar to thousands of passengers for five decades. The ferry berths were well established, with the luggage boats occupying the section between Prince's and George's Stages and then, from north to south, the berths for New Brighton/Egremont, Seacombe, Woodside, Rock Ferry/New Ferry and Eastham. The municipal berths were identically equipped with two counterweighted gangways, serving the fore and aft saloons on the main deck and similar but smaller gangways, at the head of a single or double staircase, gave direct access to the promenade deck, being used only to speed up loading at peak hours.

Permanent gangways were first fitted to the new stage at Woodside early in 1862 and, in July of that year, the Dock Board granted permission for a similar one to be fitted at George's Landing Stage. High level gangways were first fitted in 1883 and cost £148 at Woodside (single staircase) and £202 at Liverpool (double staircase) when new. The space below the steps provided shelter for the stage hands who man-handled the mooring ropes and lowered the gangways. New and enlarged main gangways, fitted in 1896, cost £164-17-0d each. At the vehicular ferry berths, the gangways needed to be much larger and heavier and were mounted on the decks of the steamers where power was available to raise and lower them.

At Liverpool a wooden tower, between the Seacombe and Woodside berths, housed the fog bell which was renewed in 1926 at a cost of £75 to each ferry authority. The complete tower and bell is preserved at the Maritime Museum.

There were refreshment rooms, a bookstall, a railway booking office and rather comfortless shelters but the services were so frequent that few people waited for long, except in the night hours, and in fine weather the endless panorama of shipping on the river was a constant source of interest to the onlooker.

The Concrete Stage

With the liners gone and the port in decline, the Dock Board was in serious financial trouble and it was obvious that anachronistic statutory duties, imposed when the port was expanding in the mid-nineteenth century, could no longer be justified. It was proposed to reorganise the Board as the Mersey Docks and Harbour Company and a Bill was deposited in Parliament for the 1971 session. In November 1970, the Board had notified the Merseyside Passenger Transport Executive, which had inherited the Birkenhead and Wallasey ferries 11 months earlier, that the Bill would repeal MDHB obligations to provide and maintain George's Landing Stage for the use of the ferries and it was proposed to make a charge of about £77,000 per year for the right to use the stage.

The stage was in a dilapidated state as lack of funds had resulted in minimum maintenance for several years. Three berths were still in use, two (Woodside and Seacombe) regularly and one (New Brighton) only casually; the New Brighton service ceased on 26th September 1971. During that year discussions between the parties concluded with agreement by the PTE to pay 25% of the capital cost of a new landing stage and a monthly sum for maintenance. Meetings were held to decide details of the design of the stage on which it was hoped to start work in 1972. However disagreement between the PTE and MDHC on both technical and financial matters delayed the scheme for a year. The new stage was to have two ferry berths at the south end and a berth for Isle of Man steamers at the north end, with provision for beam loading of motor vehicles which would have access by way of the floating roadway. It was to be of pontoon construction in concrete to the Harbour company's design and built by their contractors, Peter Lind.

Work started on 16th July 1973 with the demolition of the old stage. The ferries were temporarily transferred to Prince's Landing Stage where shelters were erected and a pedestrian bridge placed across the floating roadway to give easier access to and from the Pier Head bus station.

The new stage comprised six thin-walled reinforced concrete pontoons, 197ft. long by 59ft. wide, divided by concrete walls into watertight compartments and linked together by pre-stressed tendons, passing through holes cast in the adjoining vertical faces. The pontoons were assembled in Dublin and towed across the Irish Sea to Liverpool; the cost of the stage was £1.7 million. The ferries section comprised the southern two pontoons and services resumed from George's Landing Stage on 13th July 1975. The three Pier Head bridges were replaced by one, a second bridge, secured to Prince's Parade, being designed to carry vehicular traffic for the Manx steamers in a gyratory traffic scheme to speed loading and unloading of passenger accompanied cars, the floating roadway, refurbished in 1953 being used in the other direction.

The year 1976 opened with storms of unusual violence, tides at Liverpool reaching 35ft., six feet above the predicted level and, making an inspection at noon on Saturday 3rd January, Peter Lind's project manager noticed a tilt in the northern ferry pontoon where ducts had been left open to enable it to be chained to the Isle of Man stage later in the month. After it was discovered that the pontoon was partially flooded, the ferry service was suspended and attempts by the fire brigade to pump the northern box dry were unsuccessful. At low tide the north box lay on the river bed and the south box, now three quarters full of water, was tilting about 30 degrees. The bridge walkway had been twisted and one of the booms securing the stage to the river wall had been dislodged. The south box was then deliberately fully flooded to avoid it breaking its back as it rose with the tide.

Ferry service was resumed on 12th January 1976 from the Isle of Man berth but on 20th, the booms carrying this section of the landing stage were carried away during further severe storms and the services were again suspended, being resumed from temporary berths at Prince's Landing Stage on 11th February.

The concrete pontoons salvaged and connections with the river wall restored, normal ferry services from the new stage were resumed on 13th April 1976; the stage grounded in January 1978 due to insufficient dredging which did nothing to restore public confidence. It seems an amazing coincidence that two George's Landing Stages should both have been struck by disasters, separated by almost a century, within a short time of being commissioned.

The peak hour and holiday crowds which thronged the landing stage in days gone by are no more and the Prince's Landing Stage has also gone. But with new landing stages at Liverpool and Woodside, the future of the ferry service as a reminder of the past, seems assured for some years to come.

APPENDIX 1

The text of an advertisement placed in a local newspaper by Hugh Williams, proprietor of Woodside ferry in 1834. Note the special attention given to facilities to and from North Wales. Immigration to the Merseyside towns had already established a strong community of interest.

WOODSIDE ROYAL MAIL FERRY

Golden Lion Inn General Coach Office
Dale Street
Morgan's St. George's Inn & Eagle Hotel Coach Office
Fenwick Street, Liverpool
Feathers Coach Office, 1 James Street,
(opposite St.George's Church)
Bear's Head Inn Coach Office
Water Street
and
Woodside Royal Mail Ferry

HUGH WILLIAMS

begs to inform the Nobility, Gentry and Public in general that the following coaches leave Woodside Hotel daily:-

LONDON — The 'Albion', every morning at a quarter before 7 (Sundays excepted). Route: Chester, Malpas, Whitchurch, Newport, Ivetsy Bank, Walsall, Birmingham, Coventry, Dunchurch, Daventry, Stony Stratford, St.Albans, to the Bull and Mouth, Bull and Mouth Street near the G.P.O.

NB: Passengers for London by this conveyance have the option of sleeping in Birmingham and proceeding the following morning, without additional charge.

BIRMINGHAM — The 'Albion Celerity' at a quarter before 7 (Sundays excepted). Route: Chester, Malpas, Whitchurch, Newport, Ivetsy Bank, Walsall to the Albion Hotel.

SHREWSBURY — The 'Cheshire Hero', through Chester, Whitchurch, Wem, at a quarter before 10 in the morning (Sundays excepted).

HOLYHEAD — The 'Holyhead Mail', through Chester, Hawarden, St. Asaph, Abergele, Conway, Bangor and Mona, at a quarter past 5 every evening.

WELSHPOOL — The 'Nettle' at a quarter past 8 (Sundays excepted), to the Royal Oak at 6 in the evening. Route: Chester, Wrexham, Ruabon, Chirk, Oswestry and Llanymynech.

HOLYWELL — The 'Lord Mostyn' at a quarter before 4 pm (Sundays excepted). Route: Neston, Lower King's Ferry, Flint and Bagillt.

BANGOR — The 'Lady Mostyn' at a quarter before 8 a.m. (Sundays excepted). Route: Neston, Lower King's Ferry, Flint, Bagillt, Holywell, St. Asaph, Abergele, Conway, Aber, to the Penrhyn Arms by 7 the same evening.

N.B. Passengers for Holywell, Bagillt and neighbourhood, will observe that great accommodation is afforded by the 'Lord and Lady Mostyn' coaches. Passengers by the 'Lord Mostyn' will arrive in Liverpool at a quarter before 12, and leave again at a quarter before 4 in the afternoon, allowing four hours to remain in Liverpool. The 'Lady Mostyn' returns to Liverpool at a quarter before 7 in the evening, allowing three hours in Holywell and neighbourhood.

Posthorses, carriages, chaises, cars etc, supplied on the shortest notice.

Steam packets, 'Francis', 'Kingfisher', 'Ribble', 'Ann', half-hourly.

APPENDIX 2

BIRKENHEAD FERRIES—CREW WAGES

as at 1st January 1847

| | | PER WEEK | | INCREMENTS AFTER | | |
	1st Class	2nd Class	3rd Class	5yr	7yr	10yr
CAPTAINS	£1-12-0	£1-10-0	-	1/6	1/-	2/6
HELMSMEN	£1- 4-0	£1- 3-0	-	1/-	1/-	1/6
SEAMEN, FIREMEN	)					
AND SLIPMEN	) £1- 2-6	£1- 0-0	-	1/-	1/-	1/6
ENGINE DRIVERS	£1-17-0	£1-12-0	£1- 0-0d	2/-	1/-	2/6
TOLL COLLECTORS	£1-15-0					

	FLATS:-	CAPTAINS	£1-10-6
		SEAMEN	£1- 4-0

WEEKLY WAGES OF OFFICERS AT VARIOUS DATES

1862	Senior Captain	£1-19-0,	Junior Captain	£1-17-0

Mate	1863	£1-8-0,	1873	£1-10-0,	1876	£1-12-0		
Passenger Captain	1873	£2-2-0,	1881	£2-5-0,	1883	£2-5-0,	1899	£2-10-0
Goods Captain	1873	£2-0-0,	1881	£2-0-0,	1883	£2-5-0,	1899	£2-7-6

In 1899 the following increases in wage rates were granted:-

Helmsman	from £1-12-0 to £1-15-0
Engine Driver	from £2-2-0 to £2-7-6
Asst.Engine Driver	from £1-12-0 to £1-14-0
South Ferry Captain	from £2-3-0 to £2-5-0.

APPENDIX 3

FERRY EMPLOYEES—1892 & 1927

Occupation	No.	1892 Average Length of Service(Yrs)	1892 Average Wage	No.	1927 Average Wage
Manager	1	21	£300 pa	1	£1,000 pa
Accountant/Chief Clerk	1	44	£240 pa	1	£425 pa
Clerks	3	8	£66 pa	10	£209 pa
Chief Engineer	1	22	£220 pa	1	£338 pa
Chief Inspectors/Inspectors	2	23	£132-10-0 pa	10	£4-0-0
Captains	7	28	£2-5-0	19	£5-7-5
Engineers	10	20	£2-2-0	43	£4-12-0
Asst. Engineers	4	17.5	£1-12-0		
Yard Engine Attendt.	1	41	£1-10-0		
Mate	7	13	£1-12-6	23	£4-0-0
Seaman	22	11.6	£1-4-4	70	£3-4-0
Fireman	14	12.4	£1-5-7	48	£2-19-6
Stageman	5	25	£1-7-0	25	£3-6-6
Constable	4	15	£1-10-9		
Collectors & Goods Clerks	13	17	£1-6-0	23	£3-4-0
Tradesmen	15	16	£1-16-3	81	£2-15-6
Apprentices	3	4	10-0		
Other	9	19	£1-2-0	45	£2-0-0
Boys	3	2.7	10-0		
	125	16		400	
Per Boat Owned	17.86			33.33	

Wages are weekly unless otherwise stated.

The 1927 figures are not entirely compatible with those for 1892 as Assistant Engineers, Assistant Firemen, Junior Firemen and Junior Seamen are grouped with the full grade. Apprentices are almost certainly grouped with tradesmen thus bringing down the average wage considerably. Some of the additional staff in 1927 were accounted for by the South Ferries but most of the increase was caused by the reduction in working hours in March 1919.

APPENDIX 4

STATEMENT
WITH REFERENCE TO
THE DEBT ON THE FERRIES

In accordance with the resolution of the Ferries Committee of the 17th ult., instructing the Borough Treasurer to prepare a statement with reference to the Debt on the Ferries, and the manner in which such Debt has been accumulated, the Treasurer begs to submit to the Ferries Committee the following statement showing the debt in an epitomized form.

The figures so far as the 'Old Debt' is concerned, agree with the record in the account books kept at Woodside Ferry.

WOODSIDE FERRY OLD DEBT

Covering the period from the year 1842 to the year 1855, the amounts paid by the Birkenhead Improvement Commissioners on behalf of the Ferry Committee are as follows, viz:-

1842	For Fee Simple	£44,000	0	0
"	" Goodwill	15,000	0	0
"	" Buildings	1,500	0	0
"	" Boats, &c	15,470	3	8
1843	" Cash (for alterations)	588	16	11
1844	" Cash (new boats)	9,840	0	0
	making a total of	£86,399	0	7

In April 1855, the above amount of £86,399 0s. 7d., standing to the debit of Woodside Ferry Capital Account in the Ledger, was cancelled, and on the same date the Woodside Ferry Capital Account was debited as follows:-

To General Property Account for Fee Simple	£44,000	0	0
" Bond given to F. R. Price, transferred from other securities*, at 4 per cent	53,976	0	0
" 2½ years interest at 4 per cent	5,397	12	0
	£103,373	12	0

The result of this change being an additional charge to the Ferry Account of £16,974 11s. 5d.

Total as above	£103,373	12	0
Add various sums advanced by the Commissioners from 1864 to 1868 for New Boats and Works amounting to...	38,244	7	4
	£141,617	19	4

* Parks

In the notes on particulars relating to the Old Ferry Debt, prepared by the Ferries Accountant in December last, is the following:-

'It remained at this figure £141,617 19s. 4d. until 1880, or until the Incorporation of the Town, at which date another re-arranging of the Finances took place (owing to the necessary shewing of the Debt, etc., for the passing of the 1881 Act), and it would appear that this sum of £141,617 19s. 4d. is the true total of cash advanced by the Township to the Ferry, including the amount spent on Parks and Cemetery, but the newly created Council, after much deliberation in valuing the Ferry, agreed (1st March 1879) that the sum of £103,373 should be taken as the capital of Ferry on Bond, and amount advanced for Sea Wall, New Works, etc., £56,225 12s. 3d., making a total Debt of £159,598 12s. 3d.

'The following is a copy of the Journal Entry of this alteration (Journal, page 259, 26th March , 1890):-

WOODSIDE FERRY, DR.

TO CORPORATION OF BIRKENHEAD

For amount as paid by Act of Parliament, 1850, as Capital of Ferry on Bond Debt.........................	£103,373	0	0
For advanced on New Works (Sea Wall, etc.).........	56,225	12	3
(*Total of Ferry's Indebtedness to the Township*)........	£159,598	12	3

The Treasurer has no reason to doubt the accuracy of these figures, which increases the debt by the sum of £17,980 12s. 11d. (apparently accounted for thus):-

Cost of New Works and Land, etc., at Ferry...........	£4,321	6	3
Cost of Sea Wall south of Woodside Pier.............	13,659	6	8
	£17,980	12	11

After deducting the sum of £20,000 received as compensation from the Mersey Railway Company in the year 1886, the debt stood at £139,598 12s. 3d., and this agrees with the sum mentioned in the schedule of the Birkenhead Corporation Act, 1897.

NET RESULT:-

Amount added to the Ferry Debt and credited to the Birkenhead and Claughton Debt as previously shown but paid for out of cash provided by the Ferry Revenue..	£16,974	11	5
Ditto Ditto	17,980	12	11
	£34,955	4	4

The Treasurer wishes to record his obligations to the Ferry Accountant for the assistance rendered by him in this matter.

A Statement showing the position of the Debt at 31st March 1902 is annexed hereto.

BOROUGH TREASURER'S OFFICE
BIRKENHEAD, 13th January, 1903

THOMAS SUMNER
Borough Treasurer

APPENDIX 5

WOODSIDE GOODS SERVICE
SELECTION OF TOLLS 1876—1880

	Sep. 1876	Feb. 1879	Oct. 1879	1880
Carriage with two horses, family, servants and luggage	10/-	10/-		
do (without family etc.)	8/-	7/-		
Cart with 2 horses	8/-	8/-	3/6	1/9
Cart with 1 horse	6/-	6/-	3/-	1/6
Corpse	2/6	2/6	2/6	2/6
Hearse, one way	10/-	8/-	4/-	1 horse 2/- 2 horses 3/- 4 horses 5/-
do return trip	5/-	4/-	2/-	
Light 4-wheel phaeton with 2 horses	6/-	8/- Ret.	3/-	1/6
do with 1 horse	5/-	6/- Ret.	2/-	1/-
Wheelbarrow with one man	4d	4d	4d	4d
do loaded	8d	6d		
Parcels	1d	1d	1d	1d
Horse	1/-	1/-		9d (with man)
Cow or Bull	1/-	6		6d
Pigs or sheep, dead or alive	1½d	1d	1d	1d
Oakum per bundle	2d	2d		
Handcart, any size		1/- Ret.		
Mourning Coach		3/- One way 4/6 Ret.		
Horse gig and man		1/6 One way 2/- Ret.		

This is a selection of items from a very lengthy tariff. Where no figure is given the item was not specifically mentioned in contemporary documents.

APPENDIX 6

DEFINITION OF LIVERPOOL FERRY BERTHS

Summary of parts of a Supplemental Agreement between Birkenhead Corporation and Mersey Docks & Harbour Board dated 7th July 1921.

1. The Ferry Goods Stage shall be considered as extending for 470ft. southwards from the south end of Prince's Stage.

2. The George's Stage shall be considered as extending (including the proposed 55ft. southward extension) for 690ft. southwards from the southern end of the Ferry Goods Stage.

Ferry Goods Stage

A. No. 1 or North Berth 155ft. long—for use by Wallasey Corporation

B. No. 2 or South Berth 315ft. long—for use by Birkenhead Corporation.

George's Stage

A. An unappropriated space of 20ft. southwards from Ferry Goods Stage

B. No. 1 or North Berth 335ft. long—for use by Wallasey Corporation (New Brighton, Egremont and Seacombe)

C. An unappropriated space of 10ft. southwards from No. 1 berth

D. No. 2 or Middle Berth 170ft. long—for use by Birkenhead Corporation for Woodside steamers

E. No. 3 or South Berth 171ft. long—for joint use by:-

    1. Birkenhead Corporation for New Ferry and Rock Ferry steamers

    2. Eastham ferry vessels

    3. LNW/GW vessels and any other ferry vessels

APPENDIX 7

BIRKENHEAD CORPORATION FERRIES

SUMMARY OF VEHICLES CONVEYED BY GOODS STEAMERS
BETWEEN LIVERPOOL & WOODSIDE (BOTH WAYS)

Between 12 midnight 17th March and 12 midnight 18th March 1932
(Grand National Day)

	Horse	Steam	Commercial Motor	Motor Cars	Misc.*	Total (Both Ways)
0001-0400	1	--	7	32	--	40
0401-0800	10	12	176	26	7	231
0801-1200	27	26	525	427	54	1059
1201-1600	25	27	448	277	38	815
1601-2000	13	19	340	547	46	965
2001-0000	--	1	42	223	8	274
	76	85	1538	1532	153	3384
Percentage	2.25	2.51	45.45	45.27	4.52	100

* Includes Motor cycles, Charabancs etc.

*The old order and the new — **Thurstaston** of 1930, seen in 1957, and **Mountwood**, seen on her first day in service, 30th January 1960.*

APPENDIX 8

TOLLS AND CHARGES—BIRKENHEAD CORPORATION FERRIES
1st FEBRUARY 1922

Woodside Goods Boats Service.

	†Ordinary Rate		Empty Vehicle Rate	
Horse Vehicles—	s	d	s	d
Brougham or Cab	2	0	—	
Cart (2 wheels)	2	0	1	6
Float	2	0	1	6
,, exceeding 9ft.	3	0	2	6
Hearse	6	6	—	
Lorry or Wagon	2	6	2	0
,, ,, exceeding 18ft....	3	6	3	0
Oil Tank Wagon.........................	3	6	—	
Trap	2	0	—	
Van—Furniture	4	0	3	0
,, Parcels Delivery (2 wheels)...........	2	6	2	0
,, ,, ,, (4 wheels)......	3	0	2	6
,, Undertakers	2	6	—	
Wagonette or Omnibus	3	0	—	
Handcart	1	0	—	
Truck (hand), Small	0	5	—	
,, Large	0	9	—	
Wheelbarrow	0	7	—	

If extra horses are used, an additional rate of 8d. per horse to be payable.

Motor Vehicles—				
Ambulance	2	6	—	
Bicycle and Trader's Side-Car	0	9	—	
Car or Chassis not exceeding 11ft....	1	6	—	
,, ,, ,, 14ft........	2	0	—	
,, ,, exceeding 14ft.	2	6	—	
,, 3 wheels, 2 seats	1	0	—	
Car by Passenger Steamer when Goods Boats are not running	*10	0	—	
*(15/- on Sundays)				
Char-a-banc or Omnibus (Small)	4	6	—	
,, ,, (exceeding 14 seats)	7	6	—	
Delivery Van, up to 20 cwt....	2	0	1	6
,, ,, over 20 cwt...........	2	6	2	0
Furniture Van	4	0	3	0
Hearse	6	6	—	
Lorry or Wagon	3	6	2	6
,, ,, with Trailer	6	6	4	0
Oil Tank Wagon	3	6	—	
Taxi Cab	2	0	—	
Tractor Engine	7	6	—	
Steam Vehicles—				
Lorry or Wagon	3	6	2	6
,, ,, with Trailer...............	6	6	4	0
Roller...	7	6	—	
Tractor Engine	7	6	—	
,, ,, and Crane Trailer	10	0	—	

† Special Tolls on Sundays and Holidays.

Floating Roadways, Liverpool and Birkenhead.

Under Mersey Docks and Harbour Board Regulations the following motor-cars, vehicles and trailers are forbidden to use the Liverpool Landing Stage or the Floating Roadways (Liverpool and Birkenhead)—

(a) Motor-cars or vehicles which with or without load exceed 12 tons weight, or 9 tons on any one axle ; and

(b) Trailers which with or without load, attached to any motor-car or vehicle exceed 6 tons in weight.

Woodside Goods Boats Service.

	Ordinary Rate	
Conveyance of Live Stock—	s	d
Calves, per head...........................	0	3
Cattle, ,, ...	0	7
Horse or Donkey	0	8
Sheep or Pig (dead or alive)	0	1½
,, ,, per 100...	10	0

Woodside and South Ferries.
Conveyance of Light Goods and Parcel Traffic
(At Owner's Risk).

		s	d	
Weight not exceeding 14lbs.		0	4	and 3d. for each additional 28lbs.
,, ,, 28lbs.		0	6	
,, ,, 56lbs.		0	8	
,, ,, 84lbs.		0	10	
,, ,, 112lbs.		1	0	

LIGHT GOODS AND PARCELS may be left at the Woodside Goods Office, or at the Liverpool Goods Office (Landing Stage) for delivery in Birkenhead. Light Goods and Parcels so left at Liverpool are carried to Woodside and handed over to reliable carriers, at owner's risk, for delivery. The above rates do not include delivery.

Passenger Fares.

Between Liverpool and	Single Fare		Workmen's Return Fare Note "A"		Night Boats Single Fare Note "B"
	Adults	*Children		and Bicycle	
Woodside	2½d.	1d.	2½d.	5d.	9d.
Rock Ferry......	2½d.	1½d.	3d.	6d.	—
New Ferry	3d.	2d.	4d.	7d.	—

* Children over 3 and under 12 years of age.

Note " A "—Issued before 8 a.m. to return at any time on day of issue. Workmen's Tickets are not issued on Sundays, Christmas Day, Good Friday, or Bank Holidays.

Note " B "—In operation between the hours of 12-30 a.m. and 4-0 a.m. inclusive.

Pleasure Party Fares (Return).

		Children	Adults
WOODSIDE................................A		1½d.	4d.
ROCK FERRY ....A		2½d.	4d.
NEW FERRY ....A		3d.	5d.
BIDSTON HILL ....B		5d.	9d.

A. Minimum 25 Passengers.
B. Minimum 50 Passengers. (Not issued on Saturdays, Sundays, or Bank Holidays).

TOLLS AND CHARGES—BIRKENHEAD CORPORATION FERRIES
1st FEBRUARY 1922

Passenger Rates.

	Woodside		Rock Ferry		New Ferry	
	s	d	s	d	s	d
ssenger and Bassinette, Mailcart or Go-cart	0	4	0	4	0	5
,, Bath Chair	0	5	0	5	0	6
,, Bicycle	0	5	0	5	0	6
,, Dog	0	4	0	4	0	5
,, *Handcart (Small)	1	0	1	0	1	3
,, Motor Bicycle	0	6	0	6	0	7
,, Motor Bicycle (Sundays)	0	9	0	9	0	10
,, Motor Bicycle & Trailer or Side-car	0	9	0	9	0	10
,, Motor Bicycle & Trailer or Side-car (Sundays)...	1	0	1	0	1	2
,, *Motor Car, three wheels, two seats	1	0	1	0	1	3
,, Motor Car, three wheels, two Seats (Sundays) ...	2	0	2	0	2	3
,, Truck (Small)	0	5	0	5	0	6
,, Truck (Large)...............	0	9	0	9	1	0
,, Wheelbarrow	0	7	0	7	0	8
ntractor and Bicycle............	0	2½	0	2½	0	2½
,, Motor Cycle	0	3½	0	3½	0	3½
ssenger's Excess Luggage (not personal) per package (small)	0	2	0	2	0	3
ssenger's Excess Luggage (not personal) per package (large)	0	4	0	4	0	6

*Handcarts and three-wheeled Motor Cars (2 seats) will not be carried on the Woodside Passenger Steamers when the Goods Boats are running.

Availability of Tickets.

Workmen's and single journey tickets are available on day of issue only, and ordinary return tickets on day of issue or following day, ordinary return tickets issued on a Saturday, are available to return the following Monday.

For the convenience of Cyclists, and to save time, tickets are sold on the Liverpool Stage to New Ferry and Rock Ferry on Saturdays and Sundays during the Summer season.

Landing and Embarking Charges.

A Toll or charge of One Penny will be made in respect of each person landing from any Boat on to any pier, Landing Stage, or other property of the Corporation, and a similar toll or charge will be made in respect of each person embarking therefrom.

Cloak Rooms.

Cloak Rooms are provided at Woodside, Rock Ferry, and New Ferry, for the convenience of passengers wishing to leave parcels, &c.

Season Ticket Rates.

Contract Tickets will only be issued during the first fifteen days of each month.
Contract Tickets date from the first day of any month, and must be given up on expiry.

Liverpool and Woodside Ferry.

	12 Months	6 Months	3 Months	1 Month
Adult	52/-	29/-	16/-	6/-
For bona fide Apprentices and Scholars (not exceeding the age of 18 years)...	26/-	—	—	—
Night Boat Contracts (additional)	25/-	15/-	8/6	3/6

Liverpool and Rock Ferry.
(Available at Woodside Ferry).

	12 Months	6 Months	3 Months	1 Month
Adult	57/-	31/-	17/-	6/6
For bona-fide Apprentices and Scholars (not exceeding the age of 18 years)...	26/-	—	—	—

Liverpool and New Ferry.
(Available at Rock Ferry and Woodside Ferry).

	12 Months	6 Months	3 Months	1 Month
Adult	60/-	33/-	18/-	7/-
For bona-fide Apprentices, and Scholars (not exceeding the age of 18 years)...	26/-	—	—	—

For Children under twelve years of age, half the above charges respectively (Apprentices, Scholars, Monthly, and Night Boat Contracts excepted).
For conditions of issue see Form of Application.

Storage Rates (at Owner's Risk).

[Locker accommodation is not provided at Rock Ferry or New Ferry.]

	12 Months	6 Months	3 Months	Per Day
Bicycle	15/-	9/-	5/-	4d.
,, (including Locker)	17/6	10/6	6/-	—
Motor Cycle	20/-	12/6	7/6	6d.
,, (including medium Locker)	22/6	14/6	8/6	—
,, (including Large Locker)............	23/6	15/6	9/6	—
,, and Side-Car	—	—	—	9d.

NOTICE.—These Tolls and Charges are payable to the Collectors of the Corporation on the Ferry Premises or on the Ferry Steamers.

APPENDIX 9

TOLLS AND CHARGES—BIRKENHEAD CORPORATION FERRIES
1st DECEMBER 1938
(CARD OVERSTAMPED TO MARK ROCK FERRY CLOSURE 30th JUNE 1939)

County=Borough of Birkenhead.

CORPORATION FERRIES.

TOLLS & CHARGES

FOR THE CONVEYANCE OF
VEHICLES, GOODS, &c.,
PASSENGER FARES,
AND
SEASON TICKET RATES.

WOODSIDE FERRY
.. AND ..
ROCK FERRY.

1st December, 1938, and until further notice.
(CANCELLING ALL PREVIOUS LISTS.)

NOTICE.—These Tolls and Charges are payable to the Collectors of the Corporation on the Ferry Premises or on the Ferry Steamers.

All tickets are issued subject to the Ferries Bye-laws, Rules and Regulations *vide* notices, and are not transferable.

For further particulars
Telephone Birkenhead 3080
Extension Numbers—Manager's Office 246
General ,,   247
Goods Office - 249

R. S. COWAN,
WOODSIDE.
4094. 4/35. 1m.bal. 4/39.   GENERAL MANAGER.

1

The rates charged by the Corporation are for providing means of crossing the River. The Corporation will not be liable for any loss or damage from any cause whatsoever (including amongst other things loss or damage by negligence of the Corporation, their Employees, or Agents, robbery or theft by their Employees, Agents, Passengers, or by any other persons whomsoever, or damage by fire or water howsoever caused) whether any such loss or damage arises during loading, landing or transit.

DANGEROUS GOODS.

Extract from Byelaws with respect to the Ferries dated 5th July, 1929.
Confirmed by the Ministry of Transport 11th July, 1929.

Byelaw No. 27. Goods Declared to be Dangerous. The Corporation hereby, under the powers and for the purposes of Section 229 of the Birkenhead Corporation Act, 1881, declare the following goods to be of a dangerous nature, namely: aquafortis, vitriol or vitriolic substance, naphtha, carbide of calcium, benzine, petroleum, gun cotton, gun powder, lucifer matches, muriatic acid, dynamite, nitro-glycerine, chlorate mixture fulminate, ammunition, acetylene, picric acid, picrates; or any explosive within the meaning of the Explosives Act, 1875, as amended by the Explosives Act, 1923, or any Orders in Council made thereunder; or any explosive substance as defined by the Explosive Substances Act, 1883, or any Orders in Council made thereunder; or any other explosive or explosive substance declared to be such by any other statute or any Orders in Council made thereunder; or any oils or bituminous substance; or any products of petroleum mentioned specifically or otherwise referred to in the Petroleum Acts or Orders in Council made thereunder; and any person who sends or conveys by any of the boats any such goods as aforesaid without distinctly marking their nature on the exterior of the outermost covering of the package containing the same or otherwise giving notice in writing to the book-keeper or other servant of the Corporation with whom the same are left at the time of sending, will, in accordance with the provisions of the said Section, be liable to a penalty not exceeding Ten Pounds for every such offence.

NOTICE.—If any person knowingly or wilfully refuses or neglects to pay his Fare or Toll for using the Ferry when the same is payable, every such person will be liable to a penalty not exceeding forty shillings, and in the case of an offence after a previous conviction, to a penalty not exceeding £5.

ERNEST W. TAME,
1st December, 1938.   Town Clerk.

2

WOODSIDE VEHICLES AND GOODS BOAT SERVICE.

Schedule of Tolls and Charges for the Conveyance of Motor and Steam Vehicles, Goods, etc.

No additional charge will be made for the Driver and other person or persons required by law to be carried on the vehicle or trailer. Other persons conveyed in or on vehicles will be charged as follows :—

Children under 14 years of age - 1d.   Other persons   2d.

The Corporation reserve the right for their Vehicle and Goods Steamer to call at Wallasey Cattle Stage for traffic as and when required.

HORSE DRAWN VEHICLES

	TOLL per Vehicle
	s d
1. Goods Vehicles	
Not otherwise specified. (Unladen weight)	
(a) Not exceeding .. .. 20 cwts. ..	1 0
(b) Exceeding 20 cwts. but not exceeding 30 cwts. ..	1 6
(c) Exceeding .. .. 30 cwts. .	2 0
2. Hackney Vehicles	
(Seating Capacity, excluding Driver)	
(a) Not exceeding .. .. .. 4 persons ..	1 6
(b) Exceeding 4 persons, but not exceeding 8 persons ..	2 0
(c) Exceeding .. .. .. 8 persons ..	2 6
3. Miscellaneous	
Ambulance..	2 0
Caravan	2 6
Furniture Van	3 0
Hearse	3 6
Tank Wagon	3 0
Handcart and Passenger	1 0
Truck, Small (4 feet and under) and Passenger ..	0 5
„ Large (over 4 feet) and Passenger „..	0 9
Tricycle, Pedal, with Box (Commercial) and Passenger ..	0 9
Wheelbarrow and Passenger	0 7

If extra horses are used, an additional rate of 6d. per horse to be payable.

Woodside Stage—Pull-up Horses.

Charges		s d	
One Horse		1 0	to Shore Road
Team (2 Horses)		1 6	do.
One Horse		1 6	to Town Hall
Team (2 Horses)		2 0	do.

Motor and Steam Vehicles, etc.

	TOLL per Vehicle	Trailer Additional Charge per Trailer
	s d	s d
1. Goods Vehicles		
Not otherwise specified (Unladen Weight)		
(a) Not exceeding .. .. 20 cwts.	1 0	1 0
(b) Exceeding 20 cwts. but not exceeding .. 30 cwts.	1 6	1 6
(c) Exceeding 30 cwts. but not exceeding .. 2 tons	2 0	2 0
(d) Exceeding 2 tons do. do. .. 4 tons	2 6	2 6
2. Motor Tractors (Unladen Weight)		
(a) Not exceeding .. .. .. 2 tons	1 0	2 0
(b) Exceeding 2 tons but not exceeding .. 4 tons	2 0	2 0
(c) Exceeding .. .. 4 tons	3 0	2 0
3. Steam Propelled Vehicles		
(a) Goods Vehicle { (1) not exceeding .. 4 tons	2 6	2 0
{ (2) exceeding .. .. 4 tons	3 0	2 0
(b) Roller	5 0	—
(c) Tractor	3 0	2 0
4. Motor Cars (Taxed according to Horse-power)		
(a) Not exceeding .. .. .. 8 H.P.	1 0	1 0
(b) Exceeding 8 H.P. but not exceeding .. 12 H.P.	1 6	1 6
(c) Exceeding .. .. 12 H.P.	2 0	1 6

3

Motor and Steam Vehicles, etc.—*continued.*

	TOLL per Vehicle	Trailer Additional Charge per Trailer
	s d	s d
5. Hackney Vehicles. (Seating capacity, excluding Driver)		
(a) Not exceeding .. .. .. 4 persons	1 6	—
(b) Exceeding 4 persons but not exceeding .. 8 „	2 0	—
(c) Exceeding 8 persons but not exceeding .. 14 „	2 6	—
(d) Exceeding 14 persons but not exceeding .. 26 „	3 6	—
(e) Exceeding .. .. 26 „	5 0	—
6. Miscellaneous		
Ambulance	2 0	—
Furniture Van	3 0	2 0
Hearse	3 6	—
Motor Bicycle	0 6	—
Motor Bicycle and Side-car	0 9	—
Motor Car—3 wheels, 2 seats	1 0	—
Pedal Cycle (with passenger)	0 3	—
Showman's Special Vehicle	2 6	2 6
Tank Wagon	3 0	—

The Goods Steamer is not allowed to sail with the gangway or gangways down without special permission from the Ferries General Manager.	**Special Charges.**
	An Additional charge will be made or overhanging loads on the following scale—
	5 feet and under 10 feet .. .. 6d.
	10 feet and under 15 feet . .. 9d.
	15 feet and under 20 feet 1/-
	Over 20 feet 2/-

Traffic not specified in Schedule.

Tolls as nearly as may be equivalent to the Tolls for the most similar description of traffic specified in the Schedule.

Conveyance of Live Stock—

	Ordinary Rate
	s d
Calves, per head..	0 3
Cattle, ...	0 6
Dogs, each	0 1
Horse or Donkey	0 6
Sheep or Pig (dead or alive)	0 1½
„ or Pigs, per 100	10 0

The tolls for the conveyance of Animals include the Fare for the Drover and his dog.

Woodside Ferry and Rock Ferry.

Conveyance of Light Goods and Parcel Traffic
(At Owner's Risk).

	s d	
Weight not exceeding 14lbs.	0 2	and 3d.
„ „ 28lbs.	0 3	for each
„ „ 56lbs.	0 4	additional
„ „ 84lbs.	0 5	56lbs. or
„ „ 112lbs. ... .…	0 6	part thereof.

LIGHT GOODS AND PARCELS carried to or from Liverpool are stored free of warehouse rent for 24 hours at owner's risk, after which storage rent will be charged at the rate of 1d. per package per day.

4

Continued on page 168

ROCK FERRY CLOSURE 30th JUNE 1939

ROCK FERRY CLOSURE – 30th JUNE 1939.

Rates by Passenger Steamers.

FARES Between Liverpool and	Single Ordinary Fares			Workman's Return Fare Note "A"		Night Boat Single Fare* Note "B"
	Adult		* Child		and Bicycle	
	Single	"C" Day Ret'n				
Woodside	2d.	—	1d.	2d.	3d.	9d.
Rock Ferry	2½d	4d	1½d.	3d.	5d.	—

* Child over 3 and under 14 years of age, by Night Boat 3d.
Note "A"—Issued before 8 a.m. to return at any time on day of issue. Workmen's Tickets are not issued on Sundays, Christmas Day, Good Friday, or Bank Holidays.
Note "B"—In operation between the hours of 12·35 a.m. and 4·0 a.m. inclusive.
„ "C"—Available on Day of Issue only.

	Woodside Ferry			Rock Ferry	
	Day Boats		Night Boat	Single	Return
	Single s d	Return s d	Single s d	s d	s d
Passenger	0 2	—	0 9	0 2½	—
„ Day Return Ticket (available day of issue only)	—	—	—	—	0 4
Child (over 3 and under 14 years of age)	0 1	0 2	0 3	0 1½	0 3
„ „ „ and Pedal Bicycle	0 2	—	0 4	0 3	0 5
Passenger and Bassinette, Mailcart, Go-Cart, Pavi-Car or Bath Chair	0 3	0 6	1 0	0 4	0 8
„ and Pedal Bicycle	0 3	0 5	0 10	0 4	0 5
„ and Pedal Tandem Bicycle or Tricycle (1 passenger only)	0 4	0 6	0 11	0 5	0 6
„ and Pedal Tandem Bicycle and "Baby" Sidecar (1 passenger only)	0 5	0 7	1 0	0 6	0 7
„ and Pedal Tandem Bicycle with extra passenger	0 6	0 8	1 8	0 7½	0 8
„ and Pedal Tandem Bicycle and "Baby" Sidecar with extra passenger	0 7	0 9	1 9	0 8½	0 9
„ and Motor Bicycle	0 6	—	1 1	0 6	—
„ and Motor Bicycle and Sidecar or Trailer	0 9	—	1 4	0 9	—
„ and Motor Car, 3 wheels, 2 seats	1 0	—	1 6	1 0	—
„ and Truck (small) 4 ft. and under	0 5	—	1 0	0 5	—
„ „ (large) over 4 ft.	0 9	—	1 0	0 9	—
„ and Wheelbarrow	0 7	—	1 0	0 7	—
„ and Dog	0 3	—	1 0	0 4	—
„ and Handcart	1 0	—	1 6	1 0	—
Passenger's Excess Luggage (not personal) per package (small)	0 2	—	0 3	0 2	—
„ Excess Luggage (not personal) per package (large)	0 4	—	0 6	0 4	—
Contractor and Pedal Bicycle	0 1	—	0 1	0 2	—
„ and Motor Bicycle	0 4	—	0 4	0 4	—

Special Tolls will be charged on Parcels, etc., carried by the Passenger Night Boat between the hours of 12·35 a.m. and 4·0 a.m. (inclusive).

Pleasure Party Fares (Return).

	Children Each	Adults Each
WOODSIDE ...... } Minimum {	1½d.	3d.
ROCK FERRY ... } 20 Passengers {	2½d	4d.

Apply for Party Authority Form.

Availability of Tickets, &c.

Workmen's and single journey tickets are available on day of issue only, and ordinary return tickets on day of issue or following day; ordinary return tickets issued on a Saturday are available for return the following Sunday or Monday.

The return halves of Rock Ferry tickets are also available *via* Woodside.

The return halves of cyclists' tickets are available on day of issue or following day at either Woodside or Rock Ferry (except Workmen's Return Cycle Tickets).

For the convenience of Cyclists, and to save time, tickets are sold on the Rock Ferry Steamers on Sunday mornings and Bank Holidays and on Liverpool Landing Stage on Saturday afternoons during the Summer season.

For the convenience of Workmen with cycles, return tickets are issued on the Woodside Ferry Steamers (from Liverpool only) between 7 a.m. and 8 a.m. inclusive.

NOTICE.—Cyclists from Liverpool by Woodside Ferry are requested to leave the Woodside Stage by the Goods Section and Floating Roadway.

On Saturdays, Sundays and Bank Holidays after 6 p.m. during the Summer season, cyclists travelling to Liverpool are requested to proceed down the Floating Roadway to Woodside Stage.

ROCK FERRY SERVICE. On Sundays and Bank Holidays gentlemen cyclists are requested to place their cycles on the upper decks of the steamers as directed, in order to facilitate the loading of other cycles in the available space.

Season Ticket Rates.
Liverpool and Woodside Ferry.

	12 Months	6 Months	3 Months	1 Month	Weekly
Adult	45/-	25/-	13/-	4/6	1/3‡
Contractor's Wife	27/-	18/-	—	—	—
For bona fide Apprentices and Scholars (not exceeding the age of 21 years)	22/6	12/6	6/6	—	—
Night Boat Contracts (additional)	25/-	15/-	8/6	3/6	—
Passenger & Pedal Bicycle	70/-	38/-	20/-	7/-	—
Passenger and Motor Cycle	95/-	51/-	26/6	9/6	—
Passenger and Motor Cycle and Side-car	145/-	77/-	40/-	14/6	—
Private Motor Cars by Goods and Vehicle Steamer	£16	£9	£5	£2	12/6†

Liverpool and Rock Ferry.
(Available at Woodside Ferry.)

	12 Months	6 Months	3 Months	1 Month	Weekly
Adult	57/-	31/-	17/-	6/6	1/9‡
Contractor's Wife	35/-	22/-	—	—	—
For bona-fide Apprentices and Scholars (not exceeding the age of 21 years)	26/-	14/6	7/6	—	—
Passenger & Pedal Bicycle	82/-	44/-	24/-	9/-	—
Passenger and Motor Cycle	107/-	57/-	30/6	11/6	—
Passenger and Motor Cycle and Side-car	157/-	83/-	44/-	16/6	—

† Issued at the Turnstiles. No form required. Available Sunday to Saturday.

† Available Monday to Sunday.

Contract Tickets (Weekly Tickets excepted) will only be issued during the first fifteen days of each month, dating from the first day of any month, and all contract tickets must be given up on expiry.

For Children under fourteen years of age, half the "Adult" Rates. (Monthly and Weekly Contracts excepted.)

A Contractor's Wife's ticket must expire on the same date as the first ticket.

For conditions of issue see Form of Application.

Cloak Rooms.

Cloak Rooms are provided at Woodside and Rock Ferry, for the convenience of passengers wishing to leave parcels, &c.

Storage Rates (at Owner's Risk).

Tenants to be Ferries contractors or toll-paying passengers.

	12 Months	6 Months	3 Months	Per Day
Pedal Bicycle	15/-	9/-	5/-	4d.
„ (including Locker)	17/6	10/6	6/-	—
Motor Cycle	20/-	12/6	7/6	6d.
„ and Side-Car	40/-	25/-	15/-	9d.
„ (including medium Locker)†	22/6	14/6	8/6	—
„ (including Large Locker)	23/6	15/6	9/6	—
Motor Car (Runabout) 2 seats, 3-4 wheels†	60/-	37/6	22/6	9d.
„ „ Ford "8"†	60/-	37/6	—	—

† Not at Rock Ferry.

Landing and Embarking Charges.

A Toll or charge of One Penny will be made in respect of each person landing from any Boat on to any pier, Landing Stage, or other property of the Corporation, and a similar toll or charge will be made in respect of each person embarking therefrom.

5

6

Continued on page 169

CHEAP DAY EXCURSIONS

From LIVERPOOL Landing Stage (via Woodside Ferry Day Boats and Motor-Bus) and

Arrowe Park Gates, Arrowe House Farm, Barnston, Bidston Village, Bromborough Cross, Bromborough Pool, Eastham Village, Heswall, Landican Lane, Leasowe (Reed's Lane), Lower Bebington Village, Moreton, Oaklea Road (near Irby), Pensby, Spital Cross Roads, Thingwall Corner, Thurstaston, Town Lane, and Upton Village.

See EXCURSION PROGRAMME

	Adults	Children under 14
Arrowe Park Gates	10d	5d
*Arrowe House Farm	10d	5d
Barnston (via "Crosville" only) ...	1/2	6d
Bidston Village	8d	4d
Bromborough Cross	10d	5d
Bromborough Pool Lane End ...	8d	5d
*Eastham Village	1/-	6d
*Heswall	1/4	7d
Landican Lane	8d	5d
Leasowe, Reeds Lane ...	8d	4d
Lower Bebington Village	8d	5d
Moreton, via Arrowe	1/-	6d
Moreton, via Bidston	10d	5d
Oaklea Road, near Irby	1/-	6d
Pensby (via "Crosville" only) ..	1/2	6d
Spital Cross Roads	8d	5d
*Thingwall Corner	1/-	6d
Thurstaston (via Irby)	1/2	6d
Upton Manor (via Arrowe) ..	10d	5d
Upton Cricket Ground	10d	5d
Upton Station	8d	5d

* Also available via "CROSVILLE" Buses.

Available for return by Passenger Day Boats, on day of issue or following day. Tickets issued on Saturdays are available for return on the following Sunday or Monday.

Book at the Turnstiles, Woodside Ferry.

NO LUGGAGE ALLOWED.

7

Through Return Fares between Liverpool Landing Stage and various Corporation Motor Bus Stages.

Cheap Return Tickets are issued daily by Motor Bus and Ferry Steamer via Woodside, or by Motor Bus and Ferry Steamer via Rock Ferry.

The Tickets are issued at any time of the day, either way, available for return by passenger day boats on day of issue or following day. No luggage allowed.

Tickets issued on Saturday are available for return on the following Sunday or Monday. Book at the Turnstiles.

Via WOODSIDE — BUSES. 5d.

RETURN FARE to and from LIVERPOOL.

ROUTE	STAGE
Eastham Village	Bedford Road (New Chester Road)
Heswall	Fire Station (Borough Road)
Lower Bebington ..	Union Street (Old Chester Road)
Moreton (via Bidston) ..	Park Entrance (Conway Street)
Moreton Shore (via Arrowe)	Fire Station (Borough Road)
New Ferry (via Kings Road) ..	Fire Station (Borough Road)
North Circle.. ..	Duke Street (Cleveland Street)
North Circle	Park Road East (Claughton Road)
Oxton Circle	Fire Station (Borough Road)
Oxton Circle	Park Road East (Conway Street)
Prenton	Fire Station (Borough Road)
Thurstaston (via Frankby) ..	Park Entrance (Conway Street)
Tranmere	The Convent (Church Road)

Via WOODSIDE — BUSES. 6d.

RETURN FARE to and from LIVERPOOL.

ROUTE	STAGE
Eastham Village	New Ferry Toll Bar
Heswall	Prenton Dell Road
Lower Bebington ..	Bebington Station
Moreton (via Bidston) ..	Hurrell Road
Moreton Shore (via Arrowe)	Prenton Dell Road
New Ferry (via Kings Road) ..	Village Road
North Circle	Any point between
(Alight at Upton Road for Bidston Hill)	Shrewsbury Road and Ilchester Road
Oxton Circle ..	Any point between Park Road East and Fire Station (either way)
Prenton	Prenton Terminus
Thurstaston (via Frankby) ..	Noctorum Road
Tranmere	Village Road (Higher Bebington)

Via Rock Ferry (Week-days only).

Bus Route to and from Rock Ferry Pier	STAGE		Through Return Fare
MORETON	Mount Road		5d
	Duke Street		6d
Bus Service from Rock Ferry Pier arrive	8-0 a.m. to 11-20 a.m only	see	
.. ,,	8-35 a.m. to 10-53 a.m. only	timetable	
PORT SUNLIGHT	King's Lane		5d
	Terminus		6d

FLOATING ROADWAYS, LIVERPOOL & BIRKENHEAD

Under the Mersey Docks and Harbour Board Regulations, 1930, the following are the maximum weights of vehicles allowed to use the Liverpool Landing Stage or the Floating Roadways (Liverpool and Birkenhead).

7. Without the previous permission in writing of the General Manager of the Board, or of an Assistant General Manager.

(1) Vehicles (excluding Trailers) on not more than two axles shall not use the Floating Roadway if (a) the total weight of the vehicle with or without load exceeds .. .. .. 12 tons
or if (b) the weight on any one axle exceeds .. .. 9 ,,

(2) Vehicles (excluding Trailers) on more than two axles shall not use the Floating Roadway if (a) the total weight of the vehicle with or without load exceeds .. .. 15 ,,
or if (b) the weight on any one axle exceeds .. .. 9 ,,
or if (c) the combined weight on any two adjacent axles exceeds .. .. 12 ,,

(3) TRAILERS shall not use the Floating Roadway if the total weight of the trailer with or without load exceeds .. 6 ,,
Provided that if the trailer is being drawn by a vehicle the weight of which whether loaded or unloaded does not exceed 6 tons, then the weight of the trailer with or without load shall not exceed .. .. 12 ,,
and the weight on any one axle of the trailer shall not exceed .. .. 9 ,,

For the purposes of this Regulation two or more axles in line with each other across the vehicle shall be deemed to be one axle and a tractor and a trailer, where the front end of the trailer is carried upon the tractor, shall be deemed to be a vehicle.

8. Notwithstanding the provisions of Regulation 7, no locomotive-roller or vehicle with caterpillar tracks shall use the Floating Roadway without the previous permission in writing of the General Manager of the Board, or of an Assistant General Manager.

8

APPENDIX 10

TOLLS AND CHARGES—BIRKENHEAD CORPORATION FERRIES
1st APRIL 1948

COUNTY BOROUGH OF BIRKENHEAD

SCHEDULE OF
Tolls and Charges, Woodside Ferry
From 1st APRIL, 1949, and until further notice (cancelling all previous lists)

PARTICULARS	Day Boats	Night Boats
	s. d.	s. d.
Adult	2½	9
Child (over 3 and under 14 years)	1	3
Child (under 14 years) and Pedal Cycle	2½	6
Passenger and Bassinette, Mailcart, Go-cart, Pavi Car or Bath Chair	4	1 0
Passenger and Pedal Cycle	4	1 0
,, ,, Pedal Cycle (Return)	7	—
,, ,, Pedal Tandem Bicycle or Tricycle (1 passenger only)	5½	1 3
,, ,, Pedal Tandem Bicycle or Tricycle (1 passenger only) (Return)	10	—
,, ,, Pedal Tandem Bicycle and 'Baby' Sidecar (1 passenger only)	6½	1 5
,, ,, Pedal Tandem Bicycle and 'Baby' Sidecar ,, (Return)	1 0	—
,, ,, Pedal Tandem Bicycle with extra passenger	8	2 0
,, ,, Pedal Tandem Bicycle with extra passenger (Return)	1 3	—
,, ,, Pedal Tandem and 'Baby' Sidecar with extra passenger ...	9	2 2
,, ,, Pedal Tandem and 'Baby' Sidecar with extra ,, (Return)	1 5	—
,, ,, Motor Bicycle	6	1 4
,, ,, Motor Bicycle (Return)	11	—
,, ,, Motor Bicycle and Sidecar or Trailer	9	1 10
,, ,, Motor Bicycle and Sidecar or Trailer (Return)	1 5	—
,, ,, Motor Car, 3 wheels, 2 seats	1 4	3 0
,, ,, Truck (small) 4 ft. and under	5	1 2
,, ,, Truck (large) over 4 ft.	9	1 10
,, ,, Wheelbarrow	7	1 6
,, ,, Dog	4	1 0
,, ,, Handcart (small) 4 ft. 6 ins. and under	1 0	2 4
,, ,, Handcart (large) over 4 ft. 6 ins.	1 9	3 10
Passengers' Excess Luggage (not personal) per package (small)	2	3
,, Excess Luggage (not personal) per package (large)	4	6
Contractor and Pedal Bicycle	1½	3
,, and Motor Bicycle	4	8
Pleasure Party Fares (Return) Adults } Minimum 20 passengers ..	4	—
,, ,, (Return) Children }	1½	—
Workmen's Return	2½	—
,, ,, (and Bicycle)	5	—

Return halves of Cyclists' Tickets (except Workmen's Return Cycle Tickets) are available on day of issue or following day, and such tickets, issued on a Saturday, are available for return on the following Sunday or Monday.

FOR SEASON TICKET AND PARCEL RATES SEE OVER

TOLLS AND CHARGES—BIRKENHEAD CORPORATION FERRIES
1st APRIL 1948

CONVEYANCE OF LIGHT GOODS AND PARCEL TRAFFIC (at Owner's Risk)

LIGHT GOODS and PARCELS carried to or from Liverpool are stored free of warehouse rent for 24 hours at owner's risk, after which storage rent will be charged at the rate of 1d. per package per day.

							s.	d.	
Weight not exceeding	14 lbs	...	...	...	...	...	0	2	and 3d. for each additional 56 lbs. or part thereof
,, ,,	28 lbs	...	...	...	...	...	0	3	
,, ,,	56 lbs	...	...	...	...	...	0	4	
,, ,,	84 lbs	...	...	...	...	...	0	5	
,, ,,	112 lbs	...	...	...	...	...	0	6	

SEASON TICKET RATES

		12 Months	6 Months	3 Months	1 Month	Weekly
		£ s. d.	£ s. d.	£ s. d.	£ s. d.	s. d.
Adult	Day ...	2 12 0	1 9 0	0 16 0	0 5 10	1 8
	Day and Night...	3 17 0	2 4 0	1 4 6	0 9 6	—
Contractor's Wife	Day ...	1 10 0	1 0 0	—	—	—
	Day and Night	2 17 0	1 16 6	—	—	—
Apprentice, Scholar (under 21 years) or Child (under 14 years)	Day ...	1 6 0	0 14 6	0 8 0	—	—
	Day and Night...	2 12 0	1 10 0	0 17 0	—	—
Passenger and Pedal Cycle	Day ...	4 1 0	2 4 0	1 4 6	0 9 0	—
	Day and Night..	5 4 6	2 18 6	1 12 0	0 12 6	—
Passenger and Motor Cycle ...	Day ...	5 10 0	2 19 0	1 12 6	0 12 4	—
	Day and Night...	6 12 0	3 12 6	1 19 0	0 15 6	—
Passenger, Motor Cycle and Side-car ...	Day ...	8 7 6	4 9 6	2 9 0	0 18 10	—
	Day and Night	9 7 0	5 1 0	2 14 6	1 1 6	—

NOTICE—These Tolls and Charges are payable to the Collectors of the Corporation on the Ferry Premises or on the Ferry Steamers.

All tickets are issued subject to the Ferries Byelaws, Rules and Regulations, *vide notices*, and are not transferable.

For further particulars:—Telephone **Birkenhead 7000**

Extension Numbers:—Manager's Office **246**   General Office **247**

R. S. COWAN,   Chief Clerk **248**   Goods Office **249**
General Manager.

The rates charged by the Corporation are for providing means of crossing the River.

The Corporation will not be liable for any loss or damage from any cause whatsoever (including amongst other things loss or damage by negligence of the Corporation, their Employees, or Agents, robbery or theft by their Employees, Agents, Passengers, or by any other persons whomsoever, or damage by fire or water howsoever caused) whether any such loss or damage arises during loading, landing or transit.

NOTICE—If any person knowingly or wilfully refuses or neglects to pay his Fare or Toll for using the Ferry when the same is payable, every such person will be liable to a penalty not exceeding Forty Shillings, and in the case of an offence after a previous conviction, to a penalty not exceeding £5.

ERNEST W. TAME,
Town Clerk.

5068-368 1m 3-49

APPENDIX 11

FERRY FLEET LIST

1.WOODSIDE (including Birkenhead Corporation steamers used at NEW FERRY (1897-1922) & ROCK FERRY(1899-1939)

Date (built) Acquired	Type	Name & Number	Gross Tonnage	Dimensions (L x B x D) feet	Shipbuilders
(1816) 1822	Wood PS	COUNTESS OF BRIDGEWATER	67	85.3 x 16.9 x 7.10	A. McLachlan Dumbarton
1822	Wood PS	ROYAL MAIL	?	L 72.0	Bland & Chaloner
1825	Wood PS	FRANCES	54	74.6 x 17.0 x 7.7	Lomax & Wilson, Tranmere
(1828)	Wood PS	HERCULES	46		
(1822) 1828	Wood PS	ST. DAVID	45	72.4 x 14.10 x 6.10	Mottershead & Hayes
1830	Wood PS	KINGFISHER	120	77.0 x 16.7 x 7.8	J & R Fisher
(1829) 1832	Wood PS	RIBBLE	50 $\frac{20}{94}$	77.9 x 16.0 x 6.7½	Mottershead & Hayes
1834	Wood PS	ANN			
(1834) 1834?	Wood PS	ENTERPRISE	22.31	60.5 x 13.7 x 6.3	? Preston
(1825) 10/1835	Wood PS	HELENSBURGH	82	100.3 x 16.2 x 8.6	Wm.Denny Dumbarton
1836	Iron PS	ELIZA PRICE			J.Laird
1836	Iron PS	CLEVELAND	95 (later 98)	86.3 x 18.1 x 7.9	Page & Grantham
?	?	HIRONDELLE			
1835	Iron PS	ALEXANDRA	83	84.6 x 13.6 x ?	Hurry & Milcrest
(1836) 1841?	Wood PS	TOBERMORY		80.1 x 11.7 x 8.2(?)	Scott, Sinclair & Co
1844	Iron PS	QUEEN	173	113.0 x 22.2 x 10.9	J. Laird
1845	Iron PS	PRINCE 48764	182	112.0 x 22.0 x 10.9	J. Laird
1846	Iron PS	WIRRAL (1)	192	126.0 x 22.5 x 9.9	J. Laird
1847	Iron PS	LORD MORPETH 48765	193	116.6 x 22.1 x ?	Hodgson, Liverpool
1853	Iron PS	WOODSIDE (1)	115	108.2 x 19.7 x 7.0	Jordan & Getty
1855	Iron PS	LIVERPOOL (1)	157	124.3 x 22.2 x 9.1	J. Laird
1855	Iron PS	EMPRESS EUGENIE	157	124.3 x 22.2 x 9.1	J. Laird
(1853) c.1860	Iron PS	NEWPORT	163	128.1 x 23.2 x 9.1	Fenton & Smeaton Perth
1863	Iron PS	CHESHIRE (1)	421	150.0 x 30.0 x 11.0	H. M. Laurence & Co, Liverpool
1865	Iron PS	LANCASHIRE (1) 51494	389	150.0 x 32.2 x 10.9	C. J. Mare & Co Northfleet
1865	Iron PS	WOODSIDE (2) 51488	373	150.6 x 32.2 x 10.9	C. J. Mare & Co Northfleet
1872	Iron PS	BIRKENHEAD (2) 65952* (See Note)	448	148.8 x 30.0 x 11.7	R. & J. Evans
1876	Iron PS	CLAUGHTON (1) 74491	437	150.0 x 31.2 x 12.9	D. & W. Henderson & Co Glasgow

Engine Builders	Machinery	nhp	Disposal and Notes
D. McArthur		32	Formerly GREENOCK. Probably chartered from Ellesmere & Chester Canal. Withdrawn 1822
Fawcett			?
			1844. Broken up.
			1844. to James Hutchinson
J.Rigby			1832
Rigby Hawthorn		65	1856-62. 620 passrs.
		25	2/1841.
Fawcett		34	?
			4/1841.
Robt. Napier	Simple Lever 1 cyl.	52	Ex Stevenson & others 1835 Withdrawn 1844. May have become landing stage 1855.
Mather, Dixon		50 (later 75)	To coal hulk 1865. 620 passrs. Hired. Laid up by 3/1846
J. Rigby	1 cyl.	40	Ex Morecroft, Rock Ferry. ?1840 Hired until March 1846.
G. Forrester	Simple Oscillating 2-cyl. 31"36"	60	New boiler 1866. 589 passrs. To T. Redhead 2.5.1881 for £300.
G. Forrester	Simple Oscillating 2-cyl. 31"36"	60	To E. H. Clayton 12.3.1881 for £267.10.0d 589 passrs.
G. Forrester	Simple Oscillating	60	To T. Redhead 1868. 589 passrs.
Fawcett Preston	Simple 2-cyl.34"36"	70	1870 to Shropshire Union Rly & Canal Co. 1873 to Willoughby, Tranmere. 665 passrs.
		70	Withdrawn 1865.To Willoughby 1873. 573 pass.
	Simple Oscillating 2-cyl. 36"48"	80	1882 to Tranmere Ferry.774 passrs.
	Simple Oscillating 2-cyl. 36"48"	80	Did not enter service. Sold 1855 to Admiralty as THAIS.
		70	Luggage Boat.Ex Scottish Central Rly.Co. On fire 1864. Sold to T. C. Gibson. 727 pass.
	Simple Oscillating 4-cyl. 33"42"	100	New boilers 1878. 1612 passrs. To Liverpool Steam Towing Co. 1887 as tug AMERICA.
	Simple diagonal 4-cyl. 34"48"	120	Sold by auction 9.4.1891. Boilers to CLAUGHTON before sale. 1500 passrs Broken up at Tranmere.
	Simple Oscillating 2-cyl. 34"48"	154	12/1891 to Wallasey Local Board as SHAMROCK. Scrapped 1901.
J. Jones & Sons	Simple diagonal 4-cyl. 32"48"	130	New boiler 1875. Sold by auction 18.12.1890. Broken up.
	Simple diagonal 4-cyl. 30"48"	120	1894 Taken in part exchange for BIRKENHEAD(3). To Liverpool Steam Towing Co as tug AUSTRALIA.

Date (built) Acquired	Type	Name & Number	Gross Tonnage	Dimensions (L x B x D) feet	Shipbuilders
1879	Iron DTSS	OXTON (1) 81287	431	130.0 x 45.2 x 12.0	W. Simons & Co, Renfrew
1880	Iron DTSS	BEBINGTON (2) 84050	435	130.0 x 45.2 x 12.4	W. Allsup & Co, Preston
1884	Iron DTSS	TRANMERE 87986	435	130.0 x 45.2 x 12.3	W. A. Stevens Canada Works
1889	Steel PS	CHESHIRE (2)	380	137.3 x 28.0 x 11.4	Canada Works
1890	Steel TSS	MERSEY (4) 97825	308	145.1 x 32.0 x 10.4	J. Jones & Sons
1890	Steel TSS	WIRRAL (2)	308	145.1 x 32.0 x 10.4	J. Jones & Sons
1894	Steel PS	BIRKENHEAD (4)	434	150.0 x 28.2 x 10.3	J. Scott & Co, Kinghorn
(1887) 1897	Steel SS	FIREFLY	165	133.5 x 18.2 x 8.5	J. F. Waddington & Co, Seacombe
1899	Steel TSS	LANCASHIRE (2) 110549	469	150.5 x 41.0 x 11.4	J. Scott & Co, Kinghorn
1899	Steel TSS	CLAUGHTON (2) 110580	469	150.5 x 41.0 x 11.3	J. Scott & Co, Kinghorn
1903	Steel TSS	BIDSTON (1) 118008	444	150.0 x 41.0 x 10.9	Londonderry Shipbbuilding Co
1903	Steel TSS	WOODSIDE (3) 118009	445	150.0 x 41.0 x 10.9	Londonderry Shipbuilding Co
(1906) 1908	Steel DTSS	LIVERPOOL(2)/ PRENTON 127918	487	129.2 x 45.4 x 13.0	Caledonian Shpbldg Co, Preston
1910	Steel TSS	STORETON 131272	342	145.5 x 32.1 x 10.5	Ailsa Shpbldg Co Ltd, Ayr
1921	Steel DTSS	BARNSTON 145883	724	142.5 x 50.1 x 13.7	H. & G. Grayson Garston
1921	Steel DTSS	CHURTON 145904	724	142.5 x 50.1 x 13.7	H. & G. Grayson Garston
1925	Steel DTSS	BEBINGTON (3)	732	142.9 x 50.0 x 13.8	Cammell Laird & Co Ltd
1925	Steel DTSS	OXTON (2)	732	142.9 x 50.0 x 13.8	Cammell Laird & Co Ltd.
1925	Steel TSS	HINDERTON	484	158.5 x 42.6 x 11.5	Cammell Laird & Co Ltd.
1925	Steel TSS	UPTON 85819	374	151.2 x 33.5 x 11.4	Cammell Laird & Co Ltd
1930	Steel TSS	THURSTASTON	487	158.5 x 42.6 x 11.5	Cammell Laird & Co Ltd.

Engine Builders	Machinery	nhp	Disposal and Notes
	Compound 4-cyl. 19″; 34″24″	98	New boilers 1893 and 1923. New engines 1897. Renamed OLD OXTON 1925 and scrapped.
	Compound 4-cyl. 19″; 34″24″	98	New boilers 1895 and 1919. Renamed OLD BEBINGTON 1925 and scrapped.
	Compound 4-cyl. 18″; 36″24″	108	New boiler 1898. Scrapped 1925.
E. & S. Co Ltd	Comp.diagonal 4-cyl. 24½″; 47″42″	107	To Great Western Rly. 1904 as a tender at Plymouth.
	Triple expansion 2x3 cyl.15½″, 22″, 36″18″	960ihp	1925
	Triple expansion 2x3 cyl.15½″,22″, 36″18″	960ihp	1914?
	Comp.diagonal 4-cyl. 22″; 40″48″		1907 to White Star Line as tender GALLIC. Broken up at Garston 1913
		57	Ex-R.A.Macfie, New Ferry 1897. Sold to E. T. Brown & Co. London 1904
	Triple expansion 2x4 cyl.(2)17″, (2) 23″, (4)28″18″	300	1929 to Galway Harbour Commissioners as CATHAIR-NA-GALLIME. 1315 passrs.
	Triple expansion 2x4 cyl.(2)17″, (2) 23″,(4)28″18″	300	1930 renamed OLD CLAUGHTON. Broken up at Preston 1930. 1305 passrs.
Central Marine Eng.Works W. Hartlepool	Triple expansion (2)15½″ (2)23″, (4)28″18″	183	1603 passrs. 1933 to Blackpool Pleasure Steamers Ltd. as MINDEN. Scrapped at Preston 1937.
Central Marine Eng.Works W. Hartlepool	Triple expansion (2)15½″ (2)23″ (4)28″18″	183	1930 to Bermuda Transportation Co.
	Compound 4-cyl. 18″; 36″24″	135	1908 Renamed PRENTON before entering service. 1934 broken up at New Ferry.
	Triple expansion (2)13″ (2)21″ (4)23½″20″	127	28.8.1940 to Leith Salvage & Towing Co. Ltd. 1075 passrs.
D. Rollo & Sons Liverpool	Triple expansion 6-cyl. 17¾″, 27½″ 45¼″24″	253	1939 to Dutch owners.
D. Rollo & Sons Liverpool	Triple expansion 6-cyl. 17¾″, 27½″ 45¼″24″	253	1939 to Dutch owners.
	Triple expansion 6-cyl. 17¾″, 27½″ 45¼″24″	253	1949 Broken up.
	Triple expansion 6-cyl. 17¾″, 27½″ 45¼″24″	253	1949 Broken up.
Cammell Laird & Co Ltd	Triple expansion 8-cyl. (2)15½″(2)24″ (4)28½″18″.	1300ihp	1433 passrs. Withdrawn 13.5.1956 1958 to Antwerp for breaking up.
Cammell Laird & Co Ltd	Triple expansion 8- cyl.(2)13¼″(2)21¼″ (4)24½″18″.		1113 passrs. 1946 to Red Funnel Steamers, Southampton. Broken up 1953.
Cammell Laird & Co Ltd	Triple expansion 8-cyl.(2)15½″(2)24″ (4)28½″18″.		1433 passrs. 1961 to Dutch owners.

Date (built) Acquired	Type	Name & Number	Gross Tonnage	Dimensions (L x B x D) feet	Shipbuilders
1930	Steel TSS	CLAUGHTON (3)	487	158.5 x 42.6 x 11.5	Cammell Laird & Co Ltd.
1933	Steel TSS	BIDSTON (2)	487	158.5 x 42.6 x 11.5	Cammell Laird & Co Ltd.
1960	Steel TSMV	MOUNTWOOD	464	152.3 x 40.5 x 12.5	Philip & Son, Dartmouth
1960	Steel TSMV	WOODCHURCH	464	152.3 x 40.5 x 12.5	Philip & Son, Dartmouth
1962	Steel TSMV	OVERCHURCH	468	152.5 x 40.6 x 12.5	Cammell Laird & Co Ltd.

2. MONKS FERRY (1837-46 & 1868-78).

Date (built) Acquired	Type	Name & Number	Gross Tonnage	Dimensions (L x B x D) feet	Shipbuilders
1837	Wood PS	MONK	71	88.4 x15.9 x 7.0	W. Seddon, Birkenhead
1838	Wood PS	ABBEY (2)	53	87.8 x 15.3 x ?	Humble & Millcrest, Birkenhead
1840	Iron PS	NUN 48762	187	108.0 x 20.3 x 9.9	John Laird
(1834) 1840	Iron PS	DOLPHIN	63	93.2 x 15.2 x 8.0	J. Lang, Dumbarton
(1836) ?	Wood PS	JAMES DENNISTOUN	76(?)	104.8 x 14.6 x 9.0	Hunter & Dow Glasgow

Railway Steamers

1868	Iron PS	THAMES	125	106.0 x 20.1 x 8.6	Bowdler, Chaffer & Co, Seacombe
1868	Iron PS	MERSEY (3)	125	106.0 x 20.1 x 8.6	Bowdler, Chaffer & Co, Seacombe
1868	Iron PS	SEVERN	125	106.0 x 20.1 x 8.6	Bowdler, Chaffer & Co, Seacombe

Engine Builders	Machinery	nhp	Disposal and Notes
Cammell Laird & Co Ltd	Triple expansion 8-cyl.(2)15½"(2)24" (4)28½"18".		1433 passrs. 1962 to Ghent for breaking up.
Cammell Laird & Co Ltd	Triple expansion 8-cyl.(2)15½"(2)24" (4)28½"18".		1433 passrs.
Crossley Bros. Ruston & Hornsby (auxiliaries)	Direct diesel propulsion Bridge control of main engines. Fitted with automatic air brakes.	1360bhp (680 per shaft)	1200 passrs.
Crossley Bros. Ruston & Hornsby (auxiliaries)	Direct diesel propulsion Bridge control of main engines. Fitted with automatic air brakes.	1360bhp (680 per shaft)	1200 passrs.
Crossley Bros. Ruston & Hornsby (auxiliaries)	Direct diesel propulsion Bridge control of main engines. Fitted with automatic air brakes.	1360bhp (680 per shaft)	1200 passrs.

Engine Builders	Machinery	nhp	Disposal and Notes
Johnson & Co.		45	21.7.1843
		50	1845
		60	
Forrester & Co	Single Beam 78hp 48"×36"	60	To Birkenhead Commissioners 1847 1860 To Thos.Redhead. 604 passrs.
Caird & Co. (reeng.by Johnson)		42	1845
R. Napier		?	?
Fawcett, Preston	Simple Oscillating 2cyl. 34"×42"	70	Withdrawn 31.3.1878 To GWR then to LT&S Rly Co
Fawcett, Preston	Simple Oscillating 2cyl. 34"×42"	70	Withdrawn 31.3.1878 To LNWR for service in N. Ireland. Broken up 1894.
Fawcett, Preston	Simple Oscillating 2cyl. 34"×42"	70	Withdrawn 31.3.1878 To LNWR for service in N. Ireland. Broken up 1894.

Date (built) Acquired	Type	Name & Number	Gross Tonnage	Dimensions (L x B x D) feet	Shipbuilders

Note: The involvement of some owners with both ferries at certain times makes attribution of vessels difficult.

JAMES BALL (later JAMES BALL & SONS), 1817-38

Date (built) Acquired	Type	Name & Number	Gross Tonnage	Dimensions (L x B x D) feet	Shipbuilders
(1817) 1817	Wood PS	REGULATOR			
1826	Wood PS	JAMES	48	68.4 (or 76.4) x 16.5 x 7.5	Mottershead & Hayes
1826	Wood PS	HERO	63	80.3 x 16.5 x ?	? Tranmere
1827	Wood PS	BRITANNIA (1)	80	67.6 x 14.7 x 6.7	Mottershead & Hayes
1829	Wood PS	WILLIAM FAWCETT	47.8 (net)	74.3 x 15.1 x 8.4	Mottershead & Hayes

BATMAN, LA FRENCH & OTHERS

Date (built) Acquired	Type	Name & Number	Gross Tonnage	Dimensions (L x B x D) feet	Shipbuilders
1817	Wood Twin Hull PS	ETNA (or AETNA)	75	63.0 x 28.0 x ?	Dawson & Pearson Liverpool
1819	Wood PS Twin Hull?	MERSEY (1)	80		Dawson & Pearson Liverpool
1822	Wood PS	ABBEY (1)	54	76.3 x 16.8 x 7.6	Chas. Grayson
1823	Wood PS	VESUVIUS	43		Gladstone & Foster, Liverpool

LIVERPOOL CORPORATION (To E. G. & S. Willoughby August 1851)

Date (built) Acquired	Type	Name & Number	Gross Tonnage	Dimensions (L x B x D) feet	Shipbuilders
(1846) 1848	Iron PS	FANNY	78	110.6 x 16.8 x 7.2	Barr & McNab
1849	Iron PS	CATO	89	109.7 x 17.9 x 8.4	Cato Miller & Co.
1849	Iron PS	VERNON	85	135.0 x 16.9 x 8.0	T. Vernon

WILLOUGHBY'S & FROM 1873 TRANMERE FERRY CO.

Date (built) Acquired	Type	Name & Number	Gross Tonnage	Dimensions (L x B x D) feet	Shipbuilders
1841	Iron PS	MERSEY (2)	107	87.5 x 16.4 x 7.9	Grantham & Page
(1833) 1845	Wood PS	ABBEY (2)	53 net	87.7 x 15.3 x 7.0	Humble & Milcrest
1846	Iron PS	BIRKENHEAD (1)	132	100.7 x 17.1 x 10.0	Hawarden Iron Works Co
1847	Iron PS	BRITANNIA (2)	124	114.0 x 17.6 x 9.2 or 111.6 x 17.0 x 8.5	Jas. Hodgson & Co
(1838) c1846	Iron PS	ROYAL VICTORIA	58	106.8 x 14.1 x 7.3	Barr & McNab
(1837) 1855	Iron PS	CURLEW	82	95.0 x 15.2 x 8.3	Napier, Glasgow
(1845) 1865	Iron PS	STAR	92	90.3 x 15.4 x 8.6	John Rigby
(1853) 1866	Iron PS	WOODSIDE (1)	115	108.2 x 19.7 x 7.0	Jordan & Getty
1869	Iron PS	SEYMOUR	110	121.6 x 18.0 x 7.8	Bowdler
1872	Iron PS	BIRKENHEAD (3) * See Note	448	148.8 x 30.0 x 11.7	R. & J. Evans
(1847) 1873	Iron PS	LORD MORPETH	275 143?	116.6 x 22.1 x ?	Jas. Hodgson
(1853) 1873	Iron PS	SUPERB	108	102.6 x 18.2 x 9.4	T. D. Marshall South Shields
(1862) 1876	Iron PS	KINGSTOWN	158	151.0 x 20.1 x 7.3	T. Wingate & Co. Whiteinch

Engine Builders	Machinery	nhp	Disposal and Notes
			1818
			1853
Foster & Gladstone			1832
	2-cyl.	20	1853
		60	
Fawcett, Littledale & Co.		22	c1832
Fawcett, Littledale & Co.			1826
		22	
		45 or 48	1857
Fawcett, Preston & Co	Simple Oscillating 2-cyl. 30″36″	60	1873
Fawcett, Preston	Simple Oscillating	60	? After 1866

Engine Builders	Machinery	nhp	Disposal and Notes
		45	1881
		60	1851
		130 or 60	
		55 or 100	
		65	c1855
		39	ex Glencoe 1855, ex Loch Lomond
		45	ex Hetherington 1870-78
Fawcett, Preston & Co.		70	ex Birkenhead Commissioners
Fawcett	Simple Oscillating 2-cyl. 33″36″	60	To Wallasey Local Board 1872
J. Jones		130 or 140	c1881
Fawcett, Preston & Co.	Simple lever 2-cyl.34″36″	70	ex Birkenhead Commissioners 1873
			1879
	Simple Diagonal 2-cyl 36″36″	86	1883-84

Date (built) Acquired	Type	Name & Number	Gross Tonnage	Dimensions (L x B x D) feet	Shipbuilders
(1858) 1877	Iron PS	VICTORIA	92	135.8 x 15.6 x 6.6	R. Napier, Govan
(1861) 1879	Iron PS	HARRY CLASPER	103	115.6 x 16.7 x 7.5	J.Rogerson & Co. St. Peter's
(1879) 1882	Iron PS	MOLLINGTON	98	128.2 x 15.1 x 6.1	Jn. Reid & Co. Port Glasgow
(1855) 1882	Iron PS	LIVERPOOL (1)	157	124.3 x 22.2 x 9.1	John Laird

4. ROCK FERRY (1831-91)

Date (built) Acquired	Type	Name & Number	Gross Tonnage	Dimensions (L x B x D) feet	Shipbuilders
?	Wood Sail	WILLIAM			
(1825) 1832	Wood PS	AIMWELL	63	81.5 x 17.8 x 8.3	?, Dumbarton
1835	Iron PS	ALEXANDRA	83	84.6 x 13.6 x ?	Hurry & Milcrest, Chester
1837	Iron PS	CHESHIRE WITCH	88	84.5 x 15.0 x 8.4	Kelsick, Wood & Sons, Maryport
1841	PS	BEBINGTON (1) or BEVINGTON			
1840	Iron PS	ALBERT	130	124.6 x 20.6 x 7.9	R. Napier
(?) 1843	PS	PRINCE OF WALES	40		John Rigby, Sandycroft
1845	Iron PS	STAR	92	90.2 x 15.4 x 8.6	John Rigby, Sandycroft
(1840) 1847	Iron PS	FLAMBEAU	80 NRT	139.2 x 19.2 x 10.2	J. Ward, Hoby & Co. Greenock
1849	Iron PS	SYLPH (1)	128	112.8 x 16.8 x 8.8	
1851	Iron PS	NYMPH	90	113.3 x 17.9 x 7.8	Thos. Vernon, Liverpool
1855	Iron PS	ANT	102	122.6 x 18.1 x 7.5	Blackwood & Gordon, Paisley
1855	Iron PS	BEE	102	122.6 x 18.1 x 7.5	Blackwood & Gordon, Paisley
1858	Iron PS	WASP	130	128.0 x 16.6 x 7.6	Blackwood & Gordon, Paisley
1865	Iron PS	FAIRY QUEEN	149	135.0 x 20.0 x 7.7	Harland & Wolff
1865	Iron PS	GIPSEY QUEEN	149	135.0 x 20.0 x 7.7	Harland & Wolff
1866	Iron PS	ALEXANDRA No.2	114	142.0 x 17.2 x 6.7	? Govan
1877	Iron PS	QUEEN OF THE MERSEY	222	140.6 x 21.1 x 8.1	
(1862) 1886	Iron PS	MAYFLY	241	155.6 x 20.1 x 8.8	Lawrence, Liverpool

5. NEW FERRY

Date (built) Acquired	Type	Name & Number	Gross Tonnage	Dimensions (L x B x D) feet	Shipbuilders
1826	Wood PS	HARRIET	48	91.0 x 26.0 x 7.6 (?)	Humble & Hurry
1864	Iron PS	SPRITE	166	126.7 x 16.6 x 8.3	C. & R. Miller
1864	Iron PS	SYLPH (2)	110	126.7 x 16.5 x 7.7	C. & R. Miller
1864	Iron Flat	SOUTH END	255	121.5 x 31.3 x 6.9	Bowdler, Chaffer
1866	Iron PS	SYREN	126	128.0 x 16.6 x 7.8	Preston
1887	Steel PS	FIREFLY	165	133.5 x 18.2 x 18.5	J. F. Waddington & Co, Seacombe

Engine Builders	Machinery	nhp	Disposal and Notes
Hawks, Crawshay	Simple Oscillating 2-cyl.	40	1881
	Simple Diagonal 2-cyl. 24″36″	40	c1895
		50	1904 To Portuguese owners
			ex Birkenhead Corporation 1882
			1887

Engine Builders	Machinery	nhp	Disposal and Notes
John Rigby	Simple 1 cyl	40	To Birkenhead Commissioners 1835
		50	185?
		80	1858
		80	1858 To Eastham
		38	Rebuilt 1843
			c1850
		45	1865 To Willoughby, Tranmere
		?	1851
		60	1854
		50	1865
		60	1883
		60	1883
		70	1866 To Eastham
Blackwood & Gordon		70	1876-80 To Eastham
Blackwood & Gordon		70	1889 To Eastham
		50	1889
		80	1880
			1893 Ex Wallasey Local Board MAYFLOWER.

Engine Builders	Machinery	nhp	Disposal and Notes
		45?	1846
Fawcett		35	1876?
		35	1876
----	----	--	Landing Stage. To Wallasey Local Board 1876
Fawcett		35	1876
		57	To Birkenhead Corporation 1897

6. EASTHAM

Date (built) Acquired	Type	Name & Number	Gross Tonnage	Dimensions (L x B x D) feet	Shipbuilders
1816	Wood PS	PRINCESS CHARLOTTE	19		Mottershead & Hutchison
1821	Wood PS	LADY STANLEY	61	77.0 x 17.7 x 7.0	Mottershead & Hayes
1824	Wood PS	MARIA (1)		Mottershead & Hayes	
1826	Wood PS	MARIA (2)	60?		John Wilson, Chester
1833	Wood PS	LADY BULKELEY			
1834	Wood PS	SIR THOMAS STANLEY	100	85.3 x 15.9 x 7.0	Thos. Wilson
1837	Wood PS	WILLIAM STANLEY	81	93.6 x 15.8 x ?	
(1836) 1846	Iron PS	ROYAL TAR	79 net	125.7 x 16.6 x 8.8	Tod & McGregor
(1827) 1847	Wood PS	CLARENCE	70	92.0 x 16.0 x ?	Wm. Denny
(1845) 1854	Iron PS	LOCHLOMOND	68	126.0 x 16.3 x 6.7	Wm. Denny
18??	PS	EASTHAM FAIRY (1)			
(1837) 1857	Wood PS	THOMAS ROYDEN	108	90.7 x 15.1 x 7.4	T. Royden
(1840) 1858	Iron PS	ALBERT	120	124.6 x 20.6 x 7.9	R. Napier, Glasgow
(1854) 1860	Iron PS	TOWARD CASTLE	49.57 net	106.2 x 15.5 x 7.5	
1861	Iron PS	EASTHAM FAIRY (2) 42594	115	125.0 x 19.2 x 7.7	Nathaniel Cox, Chester
1881	Iron PS	SWIFTSURE	115	125.0 x 19.2 x 7.7	Nathaniel Cox (?), Chester
(1850) 1863	Iron PS	RICHMOND (ex PRINCE ALBERT)	109	142.2 x 17.1 x 7.0	Wm. Denny & Bros, Dumbarton
(1858) 1866?	Iron PS	WASP	130	131.9 x 19.0 x 8.5	Blackwood & Gordon
(1865) 1876?	Iron PS	FAIRY QUEEN	149	135.0 x 20.1 x 7.7	Harland & Wolff Belfast
(1865) 1889	Iron PS	GIPSEY QUEEN	149	135.0 x 20.1 x 7.7	Harland & Wolff Belfast
1890	Iron TSS	ATHLETE	260	147.4 x 22.8 x 12.1	T. W. Thompson, Birkenhead
(1882) 1897	Steel PS	ONYX (ex NORFOLK)	114	140.0 x 17.5 x 6.9	Thames Ironworks Co
1897	Steel PS	PEARL	171	130.0 x 22.0 x 8.0	J. Jones, Liverpool
1897	Steel PS	RUBY	171	124.0 x 22.0 x 8.0	J. Jones, Liverpool
1898	Steel PS	SAPPHIRE	223	140.0 x 24.1 x 8.1	J. Jones, Liverpool
(1864) 1898	Iron PS	EAGLE	208	219.5 x 20.5 x 7.3	C. Connell & Co

* NOTE 1. The numbers shown below the names of the vessels are the official ships' numbers as shown in Lloyd's List from 1871. The numbers of many old vessels have not been traced and, in some cases, it seems that names have been changed but not registered.

NOTE 2. There were two vessels named BIRKENHEAD which are identically described, that owned by Tranmere Ferry Co. appearing in Lloyds Register and the other, owned by the Birkenhead Commissioners, appearing in official records. It seems unlikely that the two vessels were identical in all respects but the existence of two vessels is confirmed by an entry in the Commissioners' accounts recording payment of £25, the cost of repairing the Tranmere ferry steamer BIRKENHEAD after being in collision with the Commissioners' steamer BIRKENHEAD on 30th July 1873.

Engine Builders	Machinery	nhp	Disposal and Notes
		28	18??
Brunton, Birmingham		20	18??
			1826?
		30	18??
			1834
Fawcett	Lever 1-cyl.	40	1855-57
			1845
			1852
		45	1849?
			1862
		45	1865
		80	1861
		50	
		60	
		60	1861
Caird & Co.		60	18??
	Simple 2-cyl. 33″45″		1895-97 New boiler 1891 Ex Rock Ferry
Blackwood & Gordon	Simple 2-cyl. 35″42″	70	1895-97 New boiler 1890 Ex Rock Ferry
Blackwood & Gordon	Simple 2-cyl. 35″42″	70	1895-97 New boiler 1884 Ex Rock Ferry
Canada Works Birkenhead		99	1894
Young & Son	Oscillating 1-cyl. 30″33″	50	1905-12
J. Jones Liverpool	Compound Diagonal 2-cyl 20″, 38″42″	80	1929
J. Jones Liverpool	Compound Diagonal 2-cyl 20″, 38″42″	80	1929
J. Jones Liverpool	Compound Diagonal 2-cyl 21″, 39″42″	65	1929
W. King & Co	Diagonal 1-cyl. 50¼″56″	85	1899?

TABLES

BIRKENHEAD FERRIES
NO. OF PASSENGERS CARRIED

TABLE 1
WOODSIDE

The figures for 1840-49 are best estimates based on revenue and are unreliable. Various official sources give different figures.

These figures include contract ticket holders, the official basis of estimation by 1941 being as follows:-

Weekly	3 journeys per day for 6 days
Monthly	3 journeys per day for 28 days
3-monthly	3 journeys per day for 78 days
6-monthly	3 journeys per day for 156 days
Yearly	3 journeys per day for 312 days

The accuracy of these estimates can be questioned but they are based on the assumption that some ticket holders made four daily journeys and others two. A number of social or recreational journeys are also assumed to have been made.

From 1980 Zone and Saveaway ticket passengers are estimated at 70%.

Figures exclude passengers carried on the Goods Ferry.

* denotes change of financial year — 11 months only. Years end on 24th April until 1878 then on 31st March.

Overchurch, in the PTE green funnel livery, approaching Liverpool landing stage in July 1976.

Year Ending	No.of Pass.	Year Ending	No.of Pass.	Year Ending	No.of Pass.
1840	1 052 900	1890	5 259 280	1940	11 386 936
1841	1 170 300	1891	5 759 048	1941	10 008 008
1842	1 584 100	1892	5 702 398	1942	7 930 416
1843	1 568 100	1893	5 856 697	1943	8 843 052
1844	2 238 700	1894	7 116 584	1944	9 079 913
1845	2 849 000	1895	7 143 088	1945	9 156 322
1846	3 184 000	1896	7 547 980	1946	9 309 497
1847	2 832 400	1897	7 613 098	1947	9 436 005
1848	3 536 400	1898	7 980 540	1948	11 268 923
1849	3 832 600	1899	8 206 078	1949	11 400 795
1850	4 262 200	1900	8 026 962	1950	11 098 928
1851	4 644 000	1901	7 944 566	1951	9 926 235
1852	4 708 000	1902	9 418 619	1952	9 793 446
1853	4 871 000	1903	10 147 321	1953	9 399 539
1854	5 693 000	1904	9 294 201	1954	9 188 833
1855	6 013 000	1905	8 524 652	1955	8 300 000
1856	6 046 000	1906	7 995 572	1956	8 250 000
1857	6 737 000	1907	7 790 190	1957	7 250 000
1858	6 828 000	1908	7 570 316	1958	6 850 000
1859	6 524 000	1909	7 387 717	1959	6 500 000
1860	6 698 000	1910	7 266 367	1960	6 985 000
1861	6 658 000	1911	7 453 401	1961	7 575 000
1862	7 162 000	1912	7 601 979	1962	6 800 000
1863	7 560 000	1913	8 872 731	1963	5 500 000
1864	7 702 132	1914	8 383 819	1964	5 000 000
1865	8 198 708	1915	8 501 987	1965	5 000 000
1866	8 111 455	1916	8 937 114	1966	5 250 000
1867	7 464 158	1917	9 047 974	1967	5 500 000
1868	7 758 383	1918	11 180 805	1968	5 000 000
1869	7 761 903	1919	13 567 797	1969	4 500 000
1870	7 546 794	1920	13 587 778	1970	3 600 000
1871	7 984 490	1921	13 317 277	1971	3 450 000
1872	8 551 126	1922	11 322 358	1972	3 402 426
1873	10 450 633	1923	10 672 857	1973	2 530 000
1874	10 322 300	1924	11 052 843	1974	1 977 039
1875	10 284 382	1925	11 642 195	1975	1 897 833
1876	10 320 027	1926	13 195 809	1976	1 900 000
1877	9 537 676	1927	14 093 135	1977	1 598 000
1878	8 857 062*	1928	13 527 298	1978	1 564 000
1879	9 971 685	1929	13 573 742	1979	1 454 000
1880	10 724 969	1930	13 531 099	1980	1 275 000
1881	10 959 450	1931	12 837 271	1981	1 043 800
1882	11 572 280	1932	12 801 107	1982	895 900
1883	11 471 162	1933	12 754 312	1983	906 100
1884	12 036 958	1934	13 187 782	1984	697 000
1885	11 649 822	1935	12 252 480	1985	756 000
1886	10 414 902	1936	11 589 891	1986	654 500
1887	6 233 482	1937	11 624 360	1987	715 700
1888	6 443 607	1938	12 111 925		
1889	5 260 952	1939	12 023 708		

TABLE 2
SOUTH FERRIES (NEW FERRY 1897-1922 AND ROCK FERRY 1899-1939)

Year Ending	No.of Passengers	Year Ending	No.of Passengers
1898	225 000§	1919	2 055 548
1899	500 000§	1920	2 623 453
1900	1 270 272	1921	2 622 922
1901	1 560 939	1922	2 375 184
1902	1 432 837	1923	2 616 238
1903	1 981 198	1924	2 744 779
1904	1 778 171	1925	2 917 652
1905	1 860 273	1926	2 793 447
1906	1 883 498	1927	2 809 693
1907	1 891 142	1928	2 462 606
1908	1 995 523	1929	2 113 419
1909	2 009 427	1930	1 663 514
1910	1 972 460	1931	1 196 214
1911	1 969 821	1932	1 226 681
1912	1 988 085	1933	1 132 563
1913	2 300 233	1934	1 124 963
1914	2 460 998	1935	979 184
1915	2 396 383	1936	923 832
1916	2 368 626	1937	889 385
1917	2 186 315	1938	894 459
1918	2 114 056	1939	833 703
		1940	211 745

§ Estimated.

TABLE 3
WOODSIDE GOODS FERRY NO. OF VEHICLES CARRIED

Year Ending	No.of Vehicles	Year Ending	No.of Vehicles	Year Ending	No.of Vehicles	Year Ending	No.of Vehicles
1880	82 105	1896	199 422	1912	392 944	1928	872 589
1881	90 018	1897	221 650*	1913	426 545	1929	924 496
1882	120 953	1898	246 355*	1914	448 478	1930	1 013 105
1883	141 325	1899	269 813*	1915	436 937	1931	1 018 125
1884	161 131	1900	266 105	1916	428 881	1932	1 055 049
1885	154 363	1901	267 859	1917	359 593	1933	1 071 577
1886	152 000	1902	281 712	1918	321 943	1934	1 150 344
1887	147 811	1903	283 830	1919	284 768	1935	478 371
1888	157 633	1904	293 392	1920	392 365	1936	78 455
1889	164 871	1905	297 579	1921	422 883	1937	65 043
1890	185 501	1906	297 373	1922	410 334	1938	61 802
1891	198 952	1907	306 496	1923	502 178	1939	59 929
1892	192 315	1908	318 105	1924	572 302	1940	50 600
1893	189 562	1909	328 856	1925	632 233	1941	40 402
1894	194 149	1910	357 590	1926	698 922	1942	11 201
1895	189 890	1911	384 380	1927	797 928		

* Estimated   Pedal cycles excluded.

Bibliography

Birkenhead Priory and the Mersey Ferry — R. Stewart Brown, State Assurance Co. 1925.
West Coast Steamers, Duckworth and Langmuir 1954.
History of Cheshire, Ormerod 1819.
The Mersey Estuary — J. E. Allison, Liverpool University Press, 1949.
Kelly's (Gore's) and many other Directories as acknowledged in the text.
Whitty's Guide to Liverpool, 1871.
Illustrated London News.
Engineering.
Sea Breezes.
Birkenhead News and Birkenhead and Cheshire Advertiser.
Minute Books and Town Clerk's files of Birkenhead Corporation and predecessors of its ferries undertaking.
Handbooks and publicity matter of Birkenhead Corporation Ferries and Merseyside PTE.
Annual Reports of Merseyside PTE.

Acknowledgements

The author expresses his gratitude to all those who have assisted in any way with the production of this book and, in particular, the outstanding contributions of the following:-
D. N. Thompson, Archivist and other members of the staff of Wirral Borough Libraries.
J. Gordon Read and staff of the former Merseyside County Record Office.
K. W. Swallow, former Director-General of Merseyside PTE and members of his staff.
The Director and Staff of the Williamson Art Gallery and Museum, Birkenhead.
Archivist and Staff of the Liverpool Record Office.
Birkenhead History Society.
J. C. Gillham for valuable editorial services.
J. N. Barlow, H. Campbell, N. N. Forbes, P. L. Hardy, W. Hawkin, J. B. Horne, Martin Jenkins, T. A. Packwood, H. F. Starkey, T. G. Turner, R. L. Wilson, F. Woodland.

Photocredits

Index

1. SHIPS' INDEX

2. PEOPLE INDEX

3. INDEX OF SHIPBUILDERS, SHIPOWNERS & OTHER MARITIME FIRMS.

4. GENERAL INDEX